Brian,

We know how hard you've worked this year and want to thank you for your countless contributions and commitment to our team.

Hope you know how appreciated you are and wish you a joyful and warm holiday season.

With sincere gratitude
Helen & ~~Michelle~~ → (sorry for the scribble!)
Michelle

Zingerman's® BAKEHOUSE

CELEBRATE EVERY DAY

Zingerman's ® BAKEHOUSE

CELEBRATE EVERY DAY

A Year's Worth of Favorite Recipes for Festive Occasions, Big & Small

amy emberling, Lindsay-jean hard,
Lee vedder & corynn coscia

Photographs by E. E. Berger

CHRONICLE BOOKS
SAN FRANCISCO

Library of Congress Cataloging-in-Publication Data available.

ISBN 978-1-7972-1657-7

Manufactured in China.

FSC
www.fsc.org
MIX
Paper | Supporting
responsible forestry
FSC™ C136333

Food styling and prop styling by mollie hayward.
Zingerman's photo assistance by corynn coscia.
Design by lizzie vaughan.
Typesetting by howie severson.

10 9 8 7 6 5 4 3 2 1

Chronicle books and gifts are available at special quantity discounts to
corporations, professional associations, literacy programs, and other
organizations. For details and discount information, please contact our
premiums department at corporatesales@chroniclebooks.com or at
1-800-759-0190.

Chronicle Books LLC
680 Second Street
San Francisco, California 94107
www.chroniclebooks.com

contents

ZINGERMAN'S

ZINGERMAN'S

ZINGERMANS

FOREWORD

People make societies, and societies in turn make us into the people we come to be. Few things aid this two-way exchange better than food. We use food to celebrate and to mourn; to nurture both physically and emotionally; and to give charity as well as to earn "our daily bread."

We use food when we want to strengthen a bond with someone else. Cooking a meal for someone on a fourth or fifth date represents a threshold. Inviting them to your family's Thanksgiving meal is an even more significant one. It also represents the continuing bond between parents and children. Cooking a favorite meal for a kid coming home from college reminds them without words that you will always be in their corner.

I teach a course on the anthropology of food, and the very first time I taught it, I brought my students to visit Amy at Zingerman's Bakehouse. She toured them through the kitchen, and we talked about their decades-old sourdough starter and the criteria they use for selecting ingredients, and then delighted in a selection of Hungarian and other pastries to finish our tour. I also teach a course on the anthropology of time, and so I was interested when Amy told me that she was organizing this cookbook around the theme of the seasons.

As we go through the calendar, we have holidays and meals whose main job is to look backward. Around the time of the spring equinox, Christians and Jewish people celebrate Easter and Passover. In the first, Christians celebrate the death and resurrection of Jesus and share meals together, including ham, spring lamb, and (in my family) the baking of brioche in the shape of the lion and the lamb. During the Passover seder, modern Jewish families memorialize the release of the ancient Jews enslaved in Egypt. The story of the Pesach is retold and participants share bitter herbs, wine, lamb bone, matzo, roast egg, parsley, salt water, and other foods, each representing some aspect of the Passover story.

These meals remind the young and the old alike of where they came from and what binds them together as a people. Food is the perfect vehicle for such remembrances, given the links between taste and smell and memory. In North America, the celebration of Thanksgiving has lost most of its associations with the harvest, now three steps removed from the realities of modern supermarket shoppers. It has become contested for its sanitized depiction of relations between white settlers and First Nations citizens. Yet where Thanksgiving remains most poignant and powerful for many families is in the recipes maintained across the generations.

Each generation has the chance to reinvent their food traditions—do we need to keep the bean casserole? Can't we have something other than turkey?—but it also has the chance to choose favorite foods to form a link between past and present through dishes prepared with reverence and eaten with pleasure.

But not all communal meals are backward-looking. In the African American tradition, eating Hoppin' John (rice, black-eyed peas, onion, and bacon) on New Year's morning promises a prosperous year to come. Some people even add a coin to the cooking pot, making the symbolism manifest. In French-speaking places (including New Orleans), king cake, or "la galette des rois," is served a few days after New Year's, on the holiday of Epiphany. Inside the cake is a tiny figurine of a baby, or sometimes a fava bean, representing the baby Jesus. Whoever gets the figurine in their slice of cake is blessed for the coming year—so much so that they must purchase the next year's king cake!

Whether feasts and celebrations are forward- or backward-looking, they enter the annual rhythms of our lives and become moments of anticipation. Children look forward to their cakes as much as most any other part of their birthday celebrations. Football season means tailgating for many Americans just as Wimbledon means strawberries and cream in England. In Japan, the arrival of fall means that matsutake mushrooms are available. These prized, pungent mushrooms are the subject of poems and high prices, fetching forty dollars per pound or more.

Since 2020, Covid-19 has showed us just how important it is to gather together and share a meal. So often food provides a pretext to reconnect with friends, to mend a strained relationship, or to show gratitude. During the pandemic, we have been severely constrained from following these pathways, from celebrating birthdays, graduations, and holidays over a meal.

This cookbook is a well-timed gift. As we prepare to resume the rhythms that link food, communities, and the seasons, this book will remind us of the many ways that fresh food binds us to one another. I can't wait to dive into the recipes.

—Mike McGovern

Professor of Anthropology, University of Michigan

INTRODUCTION

"We've always gathered around the table together to eat, to sustain, to grow, to share our lives with each other. Now the act of eating together has suddenly become one of the few communal pleasures we are able to enjoy."

—From Zingerman's Community of Businesses Statement of Service for the Covid Crisis, March 24, 2020, written by Mo Frechette, Zingerman's Mail Order Managing Partner

This book was born from our experience during the worldwide Covid-19 pandemic that began for us officially on March 16, 2020, when the state of Michigan mandated the first closing of restaurants in our communities. I imagine that the first shutdown orders included other venues, but my focus, being partners with restaurant owners and serving restaurants, was on food businesses and how the pandemic could change us and even threaten our survival. It was the beginning of our lives being turned, churned, spun, and tossed in many directions.

Our state government asked businesses not to advertise sales or to heavily promote their businesses. The government reasonably didn't want businesses to entice people to come to them unnecessarily or to gather in large crowds searching for deals. This left those of us who spent our time marketing the bakery with time on our hands. We wrote plenty of notifications about our hours, capacity, and safety measures, but we had the energy to do more.

At the same time, many people in our community and around the country were developing a renewed interest in cooking and baking. They had to! They couldn't eat out. This encouraged us to use our time to write the many recipes we had not shared in our book of Bakehouse recipes, *Zingerman's Bakehouse*. First, we created small, focused cookbooklets. One featured soups, another showed some of our breakfast pastries, and we updated our holiday cookie booklet.

While we were writing these cookbooklets, we continued to bake, and our community continued to adjust to the rearranged world. No matter the uncertainty of the pandemic and the inconvenience of shopping—with masks, talking through plexiglass dividers, standing in line because of capacity limits in stores (we had only six guests in at a time for months), customers kept coming to the bakery. People wanted to connect and wanted to celebrate. They continued to have the desire to enjoy food and have the special foods they preferred for small gatherings, personal events, and holidays. Even if people were celebrating alone, they wanted to celebrate and they wanted to have the particular foods that had become traditions for them. Communing with food was still important—perhaps even more important since so little of our normal routines were available to us. We were grateful that they came. We made it our mission to provide as normal and joyful an experience as we could.

The persevering human spirit and desire to celebrate events and carry on traditions inspired us. We decided to write another book, one that was light and joyful— qualities that we have found to be in short supply these past few years. We wanted to write a book that shares recipes to help us celebrate the big and little moments of the year. The original Bakehouse book *Zingerman's Bakehouse* was an introduction to the bakery, our philosophy and approach, and a celebration of our twenty-five years of baking. We published the recipes of many of our most popular products and the foods we believed best represented the kind of bakery we want to be. For this book, caring for our community and providing a joyful experience in our store, in our classes, and in our book became our priority. Here we focus on one theme: the importance of celebrating the large and small special days of our lives with food. The title, *Celebrate Every Day*, speaks to this theme.

CREATING THIS BOOK WAS A COMMUNITY AFFAIR

Zingerman's Bakehouse, our first book, was written by me and Frank Carollo, my partner in the bakery and its founder. Frank retired on December 31, 2020 (as he had planned before the pandemic started; we like to stay on schedule at the bakery). I had no desire to write a new book alone, and, as it turned out, I didn't have to. A group of four of us had already gathered to write the cookbooklets and we thought we could engage with others in the bakery to accomplish our goal. Our normal practice in the bakery is to collaborate in teams and co-create, so that's what we did here. Four of us led the project and worked with our bakers and class instructors to write the book, and a team of Bakehouse staff and home bakers tested all the recipes.

Our idiosyncratic team of four comes with different backgrounds and skill sets. Lindsay-Jean Hard has a passion for sustainability that inspires her in many ways: in her garden, artwork, home, community, and writing—like her own cookbook, *Cooking with Scraps*, a labor of love inspired by her Food52 column of the same name. Lindsay-Jean did the heavy lifting of gathering and organizing the recipes, and then she and I shared in the rewriting of them and the headnotes.

Corynn Coscia is the Bakehouse photographer and marketing manager. After graduating from the University of Michigan, she spent twelve years in Los Angeles working in the entertainment business. She is our person Friday who every team needs and was responsible for organizing the testing of the recipes for the book, giving us her thoughtful feedback, doing a little writing, and editing content.

Lee Vedder is our PhD art history scholar, which every bakery has on staff, right? Lee came to the Bakehouse in 2017 eager to pursue her passion for artisanal baking and to apply her love of history, research, editing, and writing in a new and exciting context. She was the primary bakery copy editor and researcher and writer of some of the historical pieces.

And then there's me. I've been leading our work overall and am the professional baker on the writing team. I had the tough job of tasting the food after each recipe test and then adjusting the recipes to achieve our quality goals. Changing recipes from the large batches we make at the bakery to the home version is more challenging than one might think. The recipes were all tested by a team of over three dozen Bakehouse staff. Each recipe was tested at least twice in the bakery before going to our team of sixteen home bakers.

Creating the book, like baking our food, has been a team project!

Cranberry Orange muffins
$4.49 each

cherry cheese danish
$4.50 each

Lemon Cloud
lighter than air pastry kissed with a touch of our fresh lemon curd
$4.25 each

Prosciutto & Parmesan Croissant
$5.25 each

chocolate croissant
$4.25 each

cinnamon roll
$3.99 each

Currant Scone

DAYS TO CELEBRATE

After thirty years of baking, there are holiday and special days that have become part of our repertoire at the Bakehouse. The assortment reflects our past and current community and our personal lives.

The world, our world, our community, and what we prioritize celebrating is evolving. If we have an appropriate recipe in our repertoire to celebrate with, we included it. We definitely do not have recipes for every holiday that may be celebrated by a group in the United States.

When you look at these pages, you may find that a special day or holiday that is important to you is missing. Just because it's not in the book does not mean that we don't think it's important; we just don't happen to be the best people to supply a recipe to celebrate it . . . at least not yet. We hope to be around for another thirty years and we expect to evolve and learn. Your important holiday may be on our list to bake for, and we welcome your suggestions. Get in touch with us by email or through our website.

THE RECIPES

A critical goal of our book is to supply recipes that make it possible for home bakers to develop baking skills and to be able to create well-prepared baked items on their own. The recipes include the traditional techniques used by artisanal bakers as well as all the "secrets" we've learned over the years through attention and repetition. We are as dedicated to using full-flavored ingredients as we are to technique, and we advise about ingredient choices and recommend sources within the recipes. We also share our newest focus on the flavor and nutritional benefits of using freshly milled whole grains. Sometimes the recipes look long; that's because we want to make sure we've given you thorough instruction. It doesn't mean that they're difficult to make.

Enough jabbering! Let's have some fun. Get your oven ready.

—Amy Emberling
Zingerman's Bakehouse Managing Partner

NO.1

SPRING

SPRING IN ANN ARBOR IS A UNIQUELY WONDERFUL TIME OF YEAR. Sure, a lot of it still might involve a blanket of snow, but we also get early blooms underfoot, the days start to get longer and lighter, and folks begin to shed their winter gear as soon as temperatures rise above freezing. The slowly changing and unpredictable weather helps us transition from the frigid days of winter to the warmer ones ahead.

Springtime unpredictability resonates with me, perhaps because it mirrors my own roundabout path. It took me a startling number of my forty-odd years on this planet to figure out that food was one of the threads that makes me feel most like me; yet looking back, it seems so obvious. Many of my favorite memories are tied to cooking and baking, especially with loved ones.

Now I'm intentionally trying to create special memories in the kitchen with my daughter, Josephine, sometimes even documenting our adventures for our very own "baking show." Spring is an especially fun time to bake together, as it's filled with so many noteworthy days just right for celebrating with homemade treats:

the first day of spring: when it almost certainly does not feel like spring in Michigan, and there's close to a high chance of another snowfall, but we'll take any hopeful sign we can get.

earth day: when we get to be reminded of just how much more we could be doing to take care of our home planet.

mother's day: when, if we're lucky, we get to honor a maternal figure (or multiple!) in our life, or perhaps their memory.

We like to mark these moments with festive foods—a cheery green Key Lime Pie (page 23) to usher in sunnier weather, a flavorful banana bread (page 48) that is kind to Mother Earth, and tender Zinglish Muffins (page 67) for a brunch in mom's honor. As is the case with many of the days we highlight throughout this book, they're special not just when deemed so on a calendar but because each of them invites us to come together—with family, friends, or classmates. Here's to all of the spring baking adventures ahead!

—Lindsay-Jean Hard

KEY LIME PIE

makes one single-crust pie

We're ushering in spring with our own sassy slices of sunshine. Why is Key Lime a spring pie? Isn't citrus a winter crop? Very good questions! And yes, limes are a winter fruit. Well, for some not entirely logical reasons, we decided many years ago to start our spring menu in April with two pies—Coconut Cream and Key Lime. Local fruit for pies is not available in Michigan yet, but we're ready for a change when April rolls around. These cream pies are a nice switch.

This not-too-sweet, not-too-tart Key Lime Pie is a crowd pleaser and quite easy to make.

CRUST

1 cup [120 g] graham cracker crumbs

¼ cup [50 g] granulated sugar

3 Tbsp unsalted butter, melted

FILLING

1¼ cups [390 g] sweetened condensed milk, room temperature

¾ cup [170 g] key lime juice, room temperature

½ cup [115 g] sour cream, room temperature

2 large eggs, room temperature

Whipped cream, for serving (optional)

Spring for us is a season of optimism. The days are getting longer and warmer. The leaves come out on the trees. We shed our winter coats. There are more stands at the farmers' market. We plant our gardens. Along with all of this comes a large menu change at the bakery. We transition from nutty, spicy, and chocolate winter desserts to lighter, fresher flavors. We've chosen two of our most popular spring recipes to share with you. One features rhubarb (see page 24), which is the earliest vegetable available for us to bake with, and this one, for Key Lime Pie, matches the color of early spring leaves.

make the crust

1. Preheat the oven to 300°F [150°C].

2. In a small bowl, stir together the graham cracker crumbs and sugar. Add the melted butter and mix until well combined.

3. Place the graham cracker crumb mixture into a 10 in [23 cm] pie pan. Using your fingertips, press the mixture into the pan so the crust is compact and an even thickness across the bottom and up the sides, to the top of the pan. Place in the refrigerator to chill for 15 minutes.

4. Transfer the pan to a baking sheet and bake for 18 to 22 minutes, or until the crust is nicely browned on the edges. Set aside to cool completely.

make the filling

1. In a medium mixing bowl, whisk together the sweetened condensed milk and key lime juice. Add the sour cream and whisk thoroughly.

2. In a separate small mixing bowl, whisk the eggs. Add the eggs to the key lime filling and whisk until smooth. Pour the filling into the baked and cooled pie shell.

3. Bake the pie for 30 to 35 minutes, until the filling is set and jiggly; it shouldn't take on any color.

4. Cool completely at room temperature, then refrigerate until cold. Serve with whipped cream, if using. The pie will keep in the refrigerator, covered in plastic wrap, for up to 5 days. The pie can also be frozen for up to 2 months. Wrap it well and keep it in a sealed container. Defrost it in the fridge overnight.

RHUBARB CHEESECAKE BARS

makes 16 bars

Rhubarb is one of the first vegetables (yes, it's a vegetable, not a fruit) to pop up in spring gardens in Michigan, and it's a favorite seasonal treat at the Bakehouse. We feature it in its unadulterated glory in our Simply Rhubarb Pie, but we wanted to find another way to highlight its distinctive flavor too.

So we turned it into a not-too-sweet compote and started swirling it into our classic cheesecake, made with farm cheese from our neighbor and sister business, Zingerman's Creamery. (If you have trouble finding farm cheese, simply swap in additional cream cheese.) The slightly tart rhubarb swirl is the perfect foil for our rich, indulgent cheesecake.

This recipe is a little different from the version we make at our bakery. First, we've turned it into bars, because sometimes you just want a couple of bites of cheesecake that you can pick up and eat with your fingers! And, in many bar cookies, the crust is an afterthought—merely a vehicle for the filling. Not so with these. This crust is made with einkorn wheat, the mother of all modern wheat, which lends a nutty flavor to the toasty, buttery crust. And it's a pat-in-the-pan crust, which anyone can handle!

RHUBARB COMPOTE

1 cup [150 g] chopped rhubarb
1 Tbsp honey
1 Tbsp granulated sugar
1 Tbsp water

EINKORN CRUST

½ cup [55 g] einkorn flour
½ cup [70 g] all-purpose flour
¼ cup [50 g] granulated sugar
¾ tsp fine sea salt
5½ Tbsp [80 g] unsalted butter, room temperature

FILLING

8 oz [230 g] cream cheese, room temperature
6 oz [170 g] farm cheese, room temperature (see headnote)
½ cup [100 g] granulated sugar
2 tsp all-purpose flour
2 large eggs, room temperature
1 Tbsp heavy cream
1 tsp vanilla extract
¼ tsp fresh minced mint (optional)

make the rhubarb compote

1. In a small saucepan over medium heat, add the rhubarb, honey, sugar, and water. Stir until the sugar dissolves, then lower the heat to medium-low and simmer until the rhubarb is tender, stirring occasionally, about 5 minutes. The mixture will look fairly thick, like a loose jam; if it looks really liquidy, continue to simmer until the liquid is reduced.

2. Remove the compote from the heat and allow to cool and thicken. The compote can be made ahead of time and refrigerated for up to 5 days.

make the einkorn crust

1. Preheat the oven to 350°F [180°C].

2. Line an 8 in [20 cm] square baking pan with an 8 by 16 in [20 by 40 cm] piece of parchment paper. Push the paper into the corners and up the sides of the pan, forming a sling, and lightly coat with nonstick cooking spray; the overhang will help with removing the bars from the pan.

3. In a small mixing bowl, whisk together the einkorn flour, all-purpose flour, sugar, and salt. Rub the butter into the dry ingredients with your fingertips until a soft, crumbly dough just begins to form and there are no large lumps of butter visible.

4. Transfer the crust mixture to the lined baking pan and press with your fingertips into an even layer over the entire bottom of the pan.

5. Bake the crust for 15 to 18 minutes, until the edges take on some light color.

cont'd

make the filling

1. While the crust is baking, in a large mixing bowl, beat the cream cheese with a wooden spoon until totally smooth, scraping the bowl with a bowl scraper or spatula as needed. If using a stand mixer, use the paddle attachment and beat on medium speed.

2. Add the farm cheese and beat until smooth.

3. In a separate mixing bowl, whisk together the sugar and flour. Add them to the cheese mixture and combine until evenly incorporated. Scrape the bowl well with a bowl scraper or spatula.

4. In the second, now-empty bowl, combine the eggs, heavy cream, vanilla extract, and mint, if using, and gradually add the wet mixture to the cheese mixture and combine, scraping the bowl periodically.

assemble and bake the cheesecake

1. Lower the oven temperature to 325°F [165°C].

2. Pour three-quarters of the filling onto the baked crust. Spoon dollops of the rhubarb compote onto the filling, dollop the remaining filling into the pan, then, using a butter knife, gently swirl the two together.

3. Place the baking pan into a larger pan (like a 9 by 13 in [23 by 33 cm] baking pan) and transfer to the oven. Add boiling water to the larger pan to create a water bath, with the water reaching halfway up the square baking pan.

4. Bake for 40 minutes, or until the surface of the filling is set but still soft.

5. Remove the cheesecake pan from the water bath and allow the cheesecake to cool for 20 minutes at room temperature. To prevent condensation, place the pan of cheesecake in the refrigerator uncovered until completely cool. Once cool, cover the top with plastic wrap and refrigerate until ready to serve.

6. To remove the chilled cheesecake from the pan, use the parchment overhang of the sling and transfer to a cutting board. Cut the chilled cheesecake into sixteen 2 in [5 cm] bars and enjoy. Store cheesecake bars covered in plastic wrap in the refrigerator for up to 5 days or in the freezer for up to 3 months.

PASSOVER

The Jewish holiday calendar is full of rich culinary histories and traditions centered around seasonal harvests and pilgrimage festivals. A weeklong celebration held in early spring, Passover commemorates the Exodus—when Moses led the Israelites out of Egypt, delivering them from slavery to freedom in the Promised Land. The holiday's name comes from the miracle in which God "passed over" the houses of the ancient Israelites in Egypt to spare them from the horrific tenth and final plague, the killing of the firstborn sons by the angel of death.

Themes of the holiday celebration include those of springtime; a Jewish homeland; and a remembrance of Jewish history, social justice, and freedom. Recognition is also paid to those who still experience oppression today. All these themes, as well as a commemoration of the Exodus, are explored during the Passover seder, a festive ritual meal held in Jewish homes at sundown on the first two nights of the holiday. Richly symbolic and carefully choreographed, the Passover seder is one of the most beloved Jewish home rituals.

Foods play a symbolic role during Passover—the most important being unleavened bread, known as matzo. As the story goes, the Israelites fled Egypt so suddenly that they could not wait for their bread to rise and instead baked it quickly in order to take it with them. Today we eat unleavened crackers like matzo as a representation of this bread. Matzo for Passover must be completely prepared, from mixing to baking, in eighteen minutes or less. The thought is that it is not possible for the bread to leaven in this short amount of time. Jews follow strict rules so as not to eat any leavened grains during the entire week. This means generally that foods are made without flours or only from flours or forms of matzo that are blessed for Passover.

At the bakery, we either use matzo or matzo meal in our baking for Passover, or we offer desserts that require no grain at all!

Pignoli Cookies (page 29) are Sicilian cookies that we like serving for Passover, since they're "naturally occurring" grain-free treats, which makes them perfect for the holiday and its unique food rules. Typically made with almond paste and pine nuts, they are often referred to as an almond macaroon. Our version, a favorite of Amy's, is a little different. We added hazelnuts to give them an extra layer of flavor.

Pavlova (page 30) is the iconic dessert of Australia and New Zealand, named after the Russian ballerina Anna Pavlova who performed there in the 1920s. It's a perfect dessert for Passover because it's flour-free. It is light, sweet, and fresh and looks like a fluffy cloud decorated with colorful fruit. Its elegant appearance is reminiscent of the ballerina's classical tutu. It's a light ending to a heavy meal.

Finally, we learned about this Hungarian version of matzo ball soup (page 33) from the famous Jewish Hungarian restaurateur Tibor Rosenstein, who created Rosenstein Restaurant, an iconic Jewish and Hungarian restaurant in Budapest. Tibor came to cooking as a result of a difficult early life. Tibor, his sister, and both grandmothers were the only members of their family to survive World War II. The grandmothers raised the two children in challenging post-war conditions. They decided that Tibor should become a chef because then he would never fear being hungry. We are the lucky recipients of their decision.

This soup is made of goose broth and meat, which is not common in the United States but widely made in Hungary. Roasted goose, goose foie gras, and goose fat are commonly found on menus and in the markets there. They're also featured in many Jewish dishes since the primary goose farmers in Hungary have been Jews. The primary protein enjoyed in Hungary is pork, which was not an area of animal husbandry open to the Jews.

PIGNOLI COOKIES

makes about 36 cookies

These are very simple to make: just toasted hazelnuts and almonds ground with sugar and bound together with some egg white, then covered in pine nuts. For small cookies, they provide a full mouthful of toasted-nut flavor and a touch of sweetness. Pine nuts get star billing in the name since they steal the show as the garnish. These are excellent as treats or sweet endings to any meal.

1 cup [135 g] whole blanched hazelnuts	⅛ tsp fine sea salt
½ cup [70 g] whole blanched almonds	1 tsp honey
	2 egg whites
1 cup plus 1 Tbsp [215 g] granulated sugar	½ cup [70 g] raw pine nuts
1 Tbsp unsalted butter, room temperature	

1. Preheat the oven to 375°F [190°C]. Line two baking sheets with parchment paper. Toast the hazelnuts on a baking sheet for 8 to 10 minutes, or until they become fragrant and lightly browned. Set aside to cool completely.

2. In a food processor, combine the cooled hazelnuts, almonds, and sugar. Process until the nuts are finely ground, but take care to not overdo it, or the nuts will become nut butter.

3. Add the butter, salt, honey, and 1 egg white to the ground nuts and sugar and process until the mixture becomes a thick paste. The dough should be sticky and pliable. If it's not, in a small bowl, beat the remaining egg white with a fork, then add 1 Tbsp to the dough and mix to combine. Reserve the remaining egg white for brushing the cookies later.

4. Using a ⅓ oz scoop (#100), portion out the dough and place each cookie, evenly spaced 1 to 2 in [2.5 to 5 cm] apart, onto the prepared baking sheets. If you don't have a scoop, portion out the dough with a small spoon and, using your hands, form each piece into a ball about the size of a cherry tomato.

5. Lightly press down on the dough balls with the palm of your hand to form them into disks about the diameter of a silver dollar. Using a pastry brush, brush them with the remaining egg white, then press pine nuts onto the tops of the cookies.

6. Bake for 9 to 11 minutes, until the cookies are browning at the edges and golden brown on the bottom. At 9 minutes, the cookies will have a soft center; bake for 11 minutes if you want a crispier cookie.

7. Let the cookies cool on the baking sheets and enjoy. Store in an airtight container for up to a week or in the freezer for up to 3 months. Bring to room temperature before enjoying.

PAVLOVAS

makes 8 individual meringues

We begin by piping a round of vanilla meringue, made from whipped egg whites, sugar, and an acidic element. The recipe simply calls for "vinegar," but any light-colored vinegar will do (apple cider, white wine, etc.)—it's there to help prevent the whipped egg whites from collapsing. The meringue rounds are then baked low and slow until the exteriors are crispy, but the interiors remain marshmallow-like, soft, and smooth.

We like to cover each Pavlova meringue with a thick, wavy layer of freshly whipped, unsweetened cream (a good contrast to the sweet meringue) and then decorate it with a generous amount of colorful fresh fruit.

MERINGUES

4 large egg whites, room temperature

⅛ tsp fine sea salt

1 tsp vanilla extract

1¼ cups [250 g] granulated sugar

2 tsp cornstarch (see Tip)

1 tsp vinegar (see headnote)

TOPPING

1½ cups [345 g] heavy cream

1 Tbsp granulated sugar (optional)

2 tsp vanilla extract

About 3 cups seasonal fresh fruit

TIP!

The rules for Passover baking vary depending on one's Jewish community. For some groups, it is not acceptable to use corn during this period. If that's the case for you, substitute an equal amount of potato starch for the cornstarch; the result will be just as elegant and delicious.

make the meringues

1. Preheat the oven to 300°F [150°C]. Line a baking sheet with parchment paper; set aside.

2. In the bowl of a stand mixer with the whisk attachment, add the egg whites and salt and mix at medium speed until frothy. Add the vanilla extract, increase the speed to high, and whip until soft peaks form. Beat in the sugar, 1 Tbsp at a time, and then whip on high speed for 3 minutes until stiff peaks form and the meringue is shiny.

3. Sprinkle the cornstarch over the whipped meringue, then add the vinegar. Beat on high speed for 10 seconds to combine.

4. On the prepared baking sheet, divide the meringue into eight equal-sized mounds. Using an offset spatula or a spoon, gently spread out each meringue mound into a 3½ in [9 cm] circle that is about 1 in [2.5 cm] thick, making a dip in the center. The meringues do not need to be perfectly shaped or smooth. You may need to use more than one baking sheet.

5. Place the baking sheet in the middle of the oven and lower the temperature to 250°F [120°C]. Bake the meringues for 1 hour, then turn off the heat and leave them in the oven to cool completely for a minimum of 2 hours and as long as overnight.

assemble the pavlovas

1. When ready to serve, in the bowl of a stand mixer fitted with the whisk attachment, add the cream, sugar, if using, and vanilla extract and whip until soft peaks form.

2. Pile the whipped cream on top of each Pavlova meringue and garnish with the fresh fruit. Serve immediately, or within an hour of assembling them. Baked, ungarnished meringues can be stored at room temperature in a cool, dry spot in an airtight container or covered with plastic wrap. Assembled Pavlovas are at their best enjoyed immediately, but can be stored in the refrigerator for up to 1 day; the meringue will soften but will still be worthy of a midnight snack.

TIBOR'S GOOSE AND MATZO BALL SOUP

serves 8 to 10 as a main dish

Give this soup a try! It's quite remarkable. Frozen goose is available online, or you can check your local specialty butcher. It's really worth the effort and will add an extra element of special to your Passover seder. It's most easily prepared over two days. Total preparation time is about 10 hours (with only an hour or so of active work). On day one, roast the goose and prepare the meat for the soup; on day two (about 6 hours), make the stock, matzo balls, and complete the soup with a garnish of fresh parsley.

ROAST GOOSE

One 4 to 4½ lb [1.8 kg to 2.0 kg] package goose quarters

Sea salt and freshly ground black pepper

GOOSE STOCK

Bones from goose quarters

1 [680 g] large celery root, peeled and chopped

3 [340 g] large portobello mushrooms

½ [115 g] large green bell pepper, roughly chopped

1½ [115 g] medium tomatoes, roughly chopped

15 to 20 [115 g] garlic cloves, crushed

1 in [2.5 cm] piece [12 g] fresh ginger, peeled and chopped

5 bay leaves

1 Tbsp peppercorns

1 Tbsp ground nutmeg

8 qt [7.5 L] water

MATZO BALLS

8 oz [225 g] matzo crackers (for Passover), processed in a food processor until some are fine and some are in ¼ in [6 mm] pieces

¾ cup [145 g] goose fat (reserved from roasting the goose quarters)

5 large eggs

⅓ cup [15 g] finely chopped parsley

2½ in [6 cm] piece [30 g] fresh ginger, peeled and minced

1 tsp fine sea salt

1 tsp freshly ground black pepper

day 1: roast the goose quarters

1. Preheat the oven to 375°F [190°C].

2. Generously season the goose quarters with salt and pepper on both sides and place on a wire rack over a rimmed baking sheet.

3. Roast for approximately 70 minutes, or until the internal temperature registers 165°F [75°C] on an instant-read thermometer. Reserve the rendered fat from roasting to use in the matzo balls.

4. After removing the skin off the roasted goose, pick the meat off the bones and chop it into ½ in [12 mm] pieces; discard the skin and reserve the bones.

day 2: make the stock and matzo balls

1. In a large stockpot, add all of the ingredients for the stock. Over medium-high heat, bring the mixture to a boil, then lower the heat to medium-low and simmer for 4 hours, occasionally skimming off any foam that may appear.

2. While the stock is simmering, make the matzo balls. In a large mixing bowl, combine all of the ingredients for the matzo balls, making sure that the eggs and goose fat get fully incorporated into the dry ingredients. Chill the matzo mixture in the refrigerator for 1½ hours until firm.

3. Once firm, use a small scoop or soup spoon to portion out 24 golf ball–size matzo balls. Gently roll the balls in the palms of your hands, then place them back in the refrigerator until the stock is done.

cont'd

4. After simmering for 4 hours, strain the stock through a fine-mesh sieve, then add it back to the stockpot. Over medium-high heat, allow the stock to reduce more, by about 25 percent. You will want 6 qt [5.7 L] of stock to finish the soup.

5. Season the stock to taste, then add the chopped goose meat. Continue cooking for 10 minutes to allow the goose to flavor the stock.

finish the soup

1. Once the stock is reduced and the matzo balls are chilled, bring the soup back to a boil over medium-high heat. Working one at a time, gently add the matzo balls to the simmering soup and cook for 20 minutes, until they increase in size by about 50 percent and become less dense. If you are unsure if they are done, remove one and cut it open to see if it is cooked through to the center.

2. Stock can be refrigerated for up to 5 days or frozen for up to 3 months. Cooked matzo balls can be stored in the refrigerator, separate from the broth, for up to 3 days.

TIP!

If you're serving the soup later, you can remove the cooked matzo balls at this point and store them in a separate container, to preserve their shape. When ready to serve, add the matzo balls back to the soup and gently heat everything back up to the desired serving temperature.

DECORATED SUGAR COOKIES

makes about 12 cookies

This is our go-to sugar cookie recipe for seasonal cookies all year long. We've included our recipe for fondant, a thick, sweet confection made primarily of sugar and used for covering cakes and cookies. Even if you're a fondant skeptic, we encourage you to give it a try; it's not like others that may have left you with a bad taste in your mouth (literally). Since we make our own and don't use any chemicals or preservatives, the flavor is primarily sweet with a touch of vanilla—kind of like the inside of an Oreo cookie. It's relatively simple to make and very user-friendly for decorating, as it takes a long time for it to become unusable. Optional flavorings for your cookie dough include 2 tsp of orange zest or 1 tsp of almond extract.

FONDANT

3 Tbsp plus 2 tsp water, room temperature
1 Tbsp powdered gelatin
5¼ cups [630 g] powdered sugar
¼ plus 1 tsp [90 g] corn syrup
1 Tbsp glycerin (see page 237)
1 tsp clear vanilla extract (see Tip, page 36)
2 Tbsp vegetable shortening
Food coloring, for decorating
¼ cup [35 g] cornstarch, for dusting

SUGAR COOKIE DOUGH

½ cup [110 g] unsalted butter, room temperature
½ cup plus 1 Tbsp [115 g] granulated sugar
1 large egg, room temperature
1 tsp vanilla extract
1⅓ cups [185 g] all-purpose flour, plus more for dusting
½ tsp fine sea salt
⅛ tsp baking soda

make the fondant

1. In a small bowl, combine the water and gelatin. Stir to completely hydrate the gelatin, then set the mixture aside for at least 5 minutes.

2. Melt the gelatin mixture in a microwave for 30 seconds. Alternatively, place the small bowl in a larger bowl filled with hot water and stir until the gelatin melts.

3. In a large mixing bowl, sift in half of the powdered sugar, then add the corn syrup, glycerin, clear vanilla extract, shortening, and melted gelatin and immediately stir with a wooden spoon to combine into a smooth batter. Sift half of the remaining powdered sugar over the mixture and combine until the mixture becomes a shaggy mass. Sift the remaining powdered sugar onto a clean work surface and turn the fondant out of the work bowl.

4. Gently knead the fondant until all of the powdered sugar has been incorporated. The fondant should be smooth and pliable. Do not over-knead the fondant, as it will become very sticky.

5. Double-wrap the fondant with plastic wrap and place it in an airtight container overnight at room temperature before using. It will become more homogeneous overnight.

cont'd

Decorated sugar cookies are perfect for celebrations and holidays that don't have a particular food associated with them. They can easily be customized to the celebratory theme using different cookie cutters and decorating techniques.

We make cheeky conversation hearts for Valentine's Day, beautiful marbled eggs at Easter, and block *M* cookies in the spring and fall for University of Michigan graduation celebrations and football games, respectively. We're hoping they become your go-to too. Get ready to unleash your creativity on cookies!

make the cookies

1. In a large mixing bowl, beat together the butter and granulated sugar until light and creamy. If using a stand mixer, use the paddle attachment and mix on medium speed. Add the egg and vanilla extract and continue creaming until light and fluffy.

2. In a medium mixing bowl, whisk together the flour, salt, and baking soda. Add to the creamed butter mixture and stir until moistened; the dough will be soft.

3. Scrape the dough out onto a piece of plastic wrap and press it into a flat disk about ½ in [12 mm] thick, wrap well, and chill in the refrigerator for 45 minutes. While the dough is chilling, preheat the oven to 375°F [190°C]. Line a baking sheet with parchment paper.

4. Remove the dough from the refrigerator and, while still wrapped, tap it lightly with a rolling pin until it is pliable. Unwrap the dough, place it on a lightly floured work surface, and sprinkle the top of the dough with flour. Roll out the dough to a ¼ in [6 mm] thickness.

5. Using your desired cookie cutters, cut the dough and place onto the prepared baking sheet, 1 in [2.5 cm] apart. Keep similarly sized cookies together on their own baking sheets to help them bake evenly. Scraps of dough can be gently kneaded back together and rolled out again until the dough is used up. To get nice, clean edges, chill the cut cookies prior to baking.

6. Bake the cookies until just browned around the edges and the middle of the cookies have puffed up, 14 to 16 minutes. Let the cookies cool on the baking sheet to room temperature.

decorate the cookies

1. Work with a small amount of fondant at a time and keep the rest tightly wrapped in plastic; it can dry out quickly!

2. To add color, put a drop of food coloring in the center of a portion of fondant and knead it in, adding additional coloring as necessary. (Dust a little cornstarch on your work surface if the fondant is sticking.) Wear gloves for this step if you're worried about staining your hands.

3. Dust the fondant with cornstarch to help you roll it out (like you would use flour when rolling out dough), and brush away any excess. Roll out fondant to a ¼ in [6 mm] thickness. Don't roll it too thin; if you do, the texture of the cookie will be visible through the fondant, which is not desirable.

4. Your fondant is now ready to be cut. If you want to cover the entire cookie, take the same cutter used for the cookies and cut out the fondant. For other shapes or decorations, choose cutters to your taste. Use water (a tiny amount!) to help secure the fondant on top of the cookies or for layering pieces of fondant together. To marble the fondant, combine small fondant pieces of two or more colors and twist and knead them together, then roll out. Fondant can be stored at room temperature, tightly wrapped in plastic wrap inside an airtight container for up to 4 weeks. Cookie dough can be stored in the refrigerator for up to 7 days, or frozen for up to 3 months. Baked cookies, both decorated and undecorated, can be stored at room temperature in an airtight container for up to 7 days, or frozen for up to 3 months.

TIP!

Clear vanilla extract keeps the fondant pure white. It's available in stores that sell cake-decorating materials and online. If you're going to color your fondant, go ahead and use real vanilla extract.

ALMONDINGER COOKIES

makes about 12 cookies

Lindsay-Jean, who enjoys playing with words and is punning all the time, came up with this one. "Almondinger" makes sense as a name because the cookie includes lots of almonds. For Ann Arborites, it has another reference too, making it a hometown cookie. The name is a tribute to Ann Arborite David Allmendinger (1848–1916), who emigrated from Germany at the age of three and became an invaluable contributor to our community. In 1872, he started his own business, the Allmendinger Organ Company. Aside from organ making, Allmendinger's second great interest was landscape gardening. His acre-and-a-half property boasted vegetable gardens, fruit trees, ponds, a croquet lawn, grape arbor, and more—fittingly, in addition to this cookie, he is also honored with an 8-acre park named after him. In researching the life of Mr. Allmendinger, we also discovered that he had been a co-owner of one of the last long-standing, local milling businesses, Michigan Mills. With our own new milling interest and our dedication to supporting the rejuvenation of local milling, we think it's even more fitting to name a cookie after him.

These cookies boast a flavorful blend of coconut (times two, with both coconut oil and toasted coconut) and almonds (times two again, with both almond butter and toasted almonds). And, when made at the Bakehouse, half the flour in this cookie is freshly milled whole-grain Michigan wheat, adding even more flavor.

2½ Tbsp raw whole almonds, plus 12 for garnish, if desired

¼ cup [20 g] unsweetened flaked or shredded coconut, plus ½ cup [40 g] for garnish

⅓ cup [60 g] coconut oil

⅔ cup [130 g] packed dark muscovado sugar

¼ cup [60 g] water

¼ cup [50 g] almond butter

1 tsp vanilla extract

1 cup [110 g] soft white whole-wheat flour (whole-wheat all-purpose flour)

⅓ cup [45 g] all-purpose flour

1 tsp baking powder

⅛ tsp baking soda

¼ tsp fine sea salt

---

1. Preheat the oven to 350°F [180°C]. Line a baking sheet with parchment paper.

2. Toast the 2½ Tbsp of almonds on a baking sheet for 5 to 8 minutes, or until fragrant and golden brown. Set aside to cool completely, then chop with a knife or pulse them in a small food processor until they are half to one-third the size of a whole almond. Do not grind them too small; the large chunks add a nice texture to the cookie.

3. Toast the ¼ cup [20 g] flaked coconut on a baking sheet for 5 to 8 minutes, stirring every 2 minutes, until it's golden brown. Set aside to cool completely.

4. In a small saucepan over medium-low heat, melt the coconut oil, then allow it to cool.

5. In a medium mixing bowl, mix together the cooled coconut oil, sugar, water, almond butter, and vanilla extract with a wooden spoon until the mixture is well combined, smooth, and homogeneous. If using a stand mixer, use the paddle attachment on medium speed.

6. In a small bowl, whisk together the flours, baking powder, baking soda, and salt. Add the flour mixture to the coconut oil mixture and mix by hand, using a wooden spoon, or on low speed if using a stand mixer, until the dough is well combined. Add the almond pieces and toasted coconut to the bowl, mixing just until they are evenly distributed in the dough.

7. Using a small ice cream scoop or a spoon, portion out 12 balls of dough. Press the top of each cookie into the remaining ½ cup [40 g] untoasted coconut, then place on the prepared baking sheet, 2 in [5 cm] apart. Flatten the cookies lightly with the palm of your hand. Gently press a whole almond in the middle of each cookie, if using. Bake until the cookies have browned lightly around their edges, 13 to 15 minutes.

8. Transfer the cookies to a wire rack to cool to room temperature before enjoying. Store in an airtight container at room temperature for up to 5 days or in the freezer for up to 3 months.

THE WORKS GRILLED CHEESE SANDWICH

makes 1 sandwich

You sure don't need a recipe to make a grilled cheese sandwich, but you might want one! This is how we prepare and serve ours on Grilled Cheese Wednesdays at the Bakehouse. The Works has become a customer favorite over the years; it's salty, rich, a little sweet, a little tart, and buttery. What more could you want?

1 tsp spicy brown or Dijon mustard

2 tsp honey

2 Tbsp unsalted butter, room temperature

2 slices of great bread that you love (perhaps Bakehouse White, page 44)

1 heaping cup [90 g] grated exceptional sharp white Cheddar cheese

2 slices of the best tomato that you can find

1. In a small bowl, whisk together the mustard and honey until combined.

2. Butter one side of each slice of bread; this will be the outside of the sandwich.

3. Spread the honey mustard on the inside of one slice of bread. Top the mustard with the grated cheese and then tomato slices. Close the sandwich with the second slice of buttered bread.

4. Heat a skillet over medium heat. Grill the sandwich for 3 minutes on each side or until golden brown and the cheese is melted.

5. Serve warm.

How are holidays and traditions created? Some are obviously connected to the season or to a religion. Grilled Cheese Wednesday is an example of a Bakehouse tradition that came about entirely organically. We decided to try making grilled cheese sandwiches for lunch one day a week and we randomly chose Wednesday.

From the start, the sandwiches were a success (we had humble goals), and we were consistently selling all that we had prepared by 1 p.m. every Wednesday. Nothing fancy about all this, but people put it on their weekly calendar. In warm weather, customers sit outside at the picnic tables. It's a lively and happy scene.

What started in our Bakeshop with minimal expectations has now grown into a weekly tradition. We think, as is the case with many noted days, it's the result of people liking to mark the passage of time—the "time" here being the passage of the workweek. Take this as a nice example of how you can create your own weekly tradition.

Believe it or not, April 12 is National Grilled Cheese Day! We certainly believe that it's a sandwich worthy of its own special day.

TOMATO DE-VINE SOUP

Serves 6 to 8 as a main dish

Grilled Cheese Wednesdays (see page 40) at our Bakeshop wouldn't be complete without creamy Tomato De-Vine soup, and National Grilled Cheese Day wouldn't be either! Enjoy this smooth and mellow version of an American classic— easy to make and loved by many.

Three 28 oz [800 g] cans crushed tomatoes

3 Tbsp granulated sugar

¾ cup [165 g] unsalted butter

¾ cup [110 g] diced yellow onion

1 cup [140 g] all-purpose flour

3½ cups [805 g] whole milk

2 tsp fine sea salt

1½ tsp freshly ground black pepper

1. In a large stockpot over low heat, combine the crushed tomatoes and sugar until hot. Stir frequently to make sure it doesn't burn. Keep an eye on it while you cook the onions.

2. In a separate medium pot over medium heat, add the butter and onions and sauté for 10 to 15 minutes, or until tender and translucent. Add the flour to the onions and stir constantly for 3 to 5 minutes, or until the mixture is a light brown color resembling peanut butter. Increase the heat to medium-high and slowly add the milk to the onion mixture, whisking constantly, to make a very thick béchamel sauce.

3. Remove the stockpot with the tomatoes from the heat, add in the béchamel, salt, and pepper, and purée the soup with an immersion blender until smooth.

4. Return the stockpot of puréed soup to the heat and warm to your desired serving temperature. Refrigerate in an airtight container for up to 1 week.

TIP!

The experience of this soup can be transformed in a number of different ways depending on the tomatoes you choose to use. Go with the grocery store canned tomatoes that you've been enjoying for years and we bet you'll have a comforting, tasty, familiar soup. For something elevated in flavor but still very familiar, we really like the line of canned tomatoes from Bianco DiNapoli. They were created by Chris Bianco, a James Beard Award–winning chef and owner of Pizzeria Bianco, and Rob DiNapoli, a Northern California farmer carrying on the seventy-year farming tradition of his family. If you'd like something with a little different flavor, try using canned fire-roasted tomatoes or maybe even jarred fresh crushed tomatoes from your own garden.

BAKEHOUSE WHITE BREAD

makes 1 loaf

This is our version of the classic French pain de mie. It's an excellent, all-around sandwich bread, rich and flavorful from the inclusion of egg, milk, and butter. It's what grocery store soft bread was based on but is so much better tasting and so much better for us. It has only seven ingredients, all readily recognizable, versus store bread with as many as twenty ingredients, many of which we don't even know how to pronounce.

Our Bakehouse White is a relatively straightforward yeasted bread—what bakers call a straight dough—with the flavor coming from the ingredients more than the process. It will take about 4 hours to make from start to finish with only 30 to 45 minutes of active work.

We love this bread for breakfast toast and for simple American grilled cheese sandwiches. Thinly sliced, it's perfect for a turkey club sandwich. If you prefer the classic square shape of the French version, bake this in a Pullman loaf pan.

¾ cup [170 g] whole milk, room temperature	2½ cups [350 g] all-purpose flour, plus more for dusting
2 Tbsp granulated sugar	1½ tsp fine sea salt
1 large egg, room temperature	¼ cup plus 1 Tbsp [70 g] unsalted butter, room temperature
1 Tbsp plus ½ tsp instant yeast	

I. In a large bowl, add the milk, sugar, egg, and instant yeast. Combine thoroughly with a wooden spoon or whisk. Add half the flour and beat with a spoon until the mixture becomes smooth. Add the remaining flour and salt. Continue to mix until the dough has come together somewhat but is not yet entirely smooth and developed.

2. Mix in the butter, 1 Tbsp at a time, kneading the dough in the bowl until all of the butter is well incorporated. Now the dough is ready to be fully kneaded.

3. Scrape the mixed dough out of the bowl onto a clean, unfloured work surface and knead it for 6 to 8 minutes. Initially, the dough will be wet and sticky but will eventually strengthen and become smooth and elastic. (Do not be tempted to add extra flour to manage the initial stickiness. This will alter the bread's texture in an unintended way.) Place the kneaded dough in a bowl coated with neutral oil or nonstick cooking spray, cover with plastic wrap or a tea towel, and let ferment for 1 hour at room temperature.

4. After 1 hour, uncover the dough and turn it out of the bowl onto a lightly floured work surface. Reshape the dough into a loose round. Allow it to rest, seam side down, covered with plastic wrap or a tea towel for 10 minutes.

5. After 10 minutes, form the dough into its final shape. Lightly press the dough into a rectangle with even thickness, about 8 by 11 in [20 by 28 cm]. Starting at the top short edge, begin folding the dough onto itself, pressing the seam as you go. Continue to roll it until you get to the short end closest to you. Pinch the edge of the loaf, making sure to close the seam tightly.

6. Coat a 9 by 5 in [23 by 13 cm] loaf pan with oil or nonstick cooking spray. Place the loaf in the pan and cover with plastic wrap. Proof in a warm environment, at least 70°F [21°C], for 1 to 1½ hours. (At the bakery, we keep the environment at 82°F [28°C]. If you have a cooler environment, the recipe will still work but the proofing time will be longer.) The bread is ready to bake when the dough passes the touch test: Gently press the pad of a fingertip into the loaf and remove it; the indentation should slowly come back most but not all of the way. The loaf should also crest the lip of the pan.

7. While the dough is proofing, preheat the oven to 375°F [190°C].

8. Bake the loaf for 30 to 35 minutes, or until nicely browned and the internal temperature registers 190°F [90°C] on an instant-read thermometer.

9. Allow the loaf to cool in the pan for 5 minutes, then turn it out onto a wire rack to cool to room temperature before slicing. Store in a bread box or plastic bag at room temperature for up to 5 days or in the freezer, well wrapped in plastic, for up to 3 months.

GREAT IN BREAD

Over the years, customers have requested all sorts of additions to our grilled cheese sandwich—bacon, egg, green chiles, different bread . . . the list goes on. We've resisted their pleas and still keep it simple, focusing on our sourdough bread and cheese with two options: The Classic, with just cheese, or The Works, which adds house-made honey mustard and fresh tomato slices.

At home, though, you can jazz it up, if you feel the need. Our Bakehouse staffers have suggestions of their own to help you achieve grilled cheese perfection:

- Shredded mozzarella on Rustic Italian (see the recipe for the baguette version of this bread on page 130), well-grilled, and, if you want to channel your childhood, served with a dollop of ketchup for dunking

- Good ol' American cheese (yes, the individually packaged slices) on Bakehouse White Bread (page 44)

- The Classic with the addition of sauerkraut or kimchi

- Bacon Pimento Cheese (page 133) on sourdough

- Gouda, a thin slice of ham, and mustard on Rustic Italian (page 130)

- White Cheddar cheese on Parmesan Pepper bread (the recipe for this bread is in our first cookbook, *Zingerman's Bakehouse*)

- Mozzarella cheese, pizza sauce, and zesty pepperoni on Sicilian Sesame Semolina bread (this recipe is also in our first cookbook!) for an at-home re-creation of the Pizza Toasty grilled sandwich you can get at Zingerman's Creamery

- Make the grilled cheese of your choice and give it a little extra something special by sprinkling grated Parmesan cheese or garlic powder on the outside while you're grilling it

4/20 AND THE ANN ARBOR HASH BASH

4/20, or "Weed Day," is the marijuana counterculture holiday observed yearly in the United States and around the world on, you guessed it, April 20. It's an example of a holiday totally disconnected from the seasons or religions or the passage of time, but political events and activism are another source of days people like to celebrate.

Our Magic Brownies—large, wallet-size, and big enough to match the deli-size sandwiches of Zingerman's Delicatessen—have been a part of the Zingerman's experience since the mid-1980s. Their name is a cheeky nod to Ann Arbor's well-known marijuana-friendly culture and activism, which, since 1972, has been celebrated every year in early April with a Hash Bash on the University of Michigan campus.

Fun fact: Our Magic Brownie has been around so long that it's now actually legal in Ann Arbor and the state of Michigan to make and sell truly "magic"— that is, marijuana—brownies! Who woulda thought? And with new and well-established marijuana dispensaries in town getting into the "magic brownie" baking game, we just might have to change the name of ours or risk being charged with false advertising!

BLACK AND WHITE MAGIC BROWNIES

makes one pan of brownies

This is the newest iteration of our Magic Brownie. For years our customers have requested that we make New York–style black and white cookies, which we've resisted. Instead, we created our own spin on the cookie classic in the form of a brownie. We like to say, "It's the Fresh Coast's (Great Lakes's) answer to an East Coast treat."

VANILLA COCONUT MACAROON LAYER

2 large egg whites, room temperature

1 cup [80 g] unsweetened shredded coconut

¾ cup [70 g] desiccated (fine) coconut

¼ cup [20 g] puréed fresh coconut meat (see page 236 for more information)

1 Tbsp heavy cream

¼ tsp vanilla extract

1 Tbsp water

1 tsp corn syrup

½ cup plus 1½ Tbsp [125 g] granulated sugar

⅛ tsp fine sea salt

BLACK MAGIC BROWNIE LAYER

½ cup plus 2 tsp [100 g] unsweetened chocolate, chopped

7 Tbsp [100 g] unsalted butter

¾ cup [105 g] pastry flour (substitute equal parts cake and all-purpose flours)

½ tsp baking powder

2 large eggs

1¼ cups plus 2 Tbsp [270 g] granulated sugar

½ tsp fine sea salt

1 tsp vanilla extract

make the vanilla coconut macaroon layer

I. In a medium mixing bowl, stir together the egg whites, three types of coconut, cream, and vanilla extract.

2. In a small saucepan, bring the water, corn syrup, granulated sugar, and salt to a boil. Remove from the heat and add it to the coconut mixture, stirring with a wooden spoon until well combined. Set aside.

make the black magic brownie layer

I. Preheat the oven to 350°F [180°C]. Coat a 9 by 9 in [23 by 23 cm] baking pan with nonstick cooking spray.

2. In a double boiler or a heatproof bowl set over a saucepan of simmering water, melt the chocolate and butter. Stir to combine and set aside to cool.

3. In a medium mixing bowl, whisk together the pastry flour and baking powder, making sure to eliminate any lumps of flour and distribute the baking powder evenly. Set aside.

4. In a large mixing bowl, whisk together the eggs, sugar, salt, and vanilla extract until well combined and aerated, about 5 minutes. If using a stand mixer, use the whisk attachment on medium speed. Add the melted chocolate mixture and whisk to combine evenly. Stir in the dry ingredients using a rubber spatula. If using a stand mixer, use the paddle attachment and mix on low speed until well combined and there are no lumps of flour.

assemble and bake the brownies

I. Pour the brownie batter into the prepared pan and, using a rubber spatula or a metal offset spatula, carefully spread it to the corners of the pan in an even layer. Using your hands, gently sprinkle the macaroon mixture across the top of the brownie batter in an even layer. Bake for 50 to 55 minutes or until a tester or toothpick inserted in the center is nearly clean and the macaroon topping is a dark golden color. Transfer the pan to a wire rack to cool to room temperature before cutting and serving. Store wrapped in plastic or in an airtight container at room temperature for up to 1 week or in the freezer for up to 3 months.

OH SO A-PEEL-ING BANANA BREAD

makes one loaf

The banana bread is tasty just as is, but it's also ready for imaginative variations. Mix in chunks of your favorite chocolate. Add macadamia nuts. Swirl in some peanut butter. Do all three! We make pecan praline and cover the top before baking! Hmmm, and a little bourbon in the batter might be good if you want to elevate it to an adult treat.

---

1 or 2 [290 g] very ripe organic bananas, peels darkened in spots

¾ cup plus 3 Tbsp [205 g] granulated sugar

2 large eggs, room temperature

½ cup [110 g] unsalted butter, melted

1½ tsp vanilla extract

1½ cups [210 g] all-purpose flour (see Tip for a whole-wheat version)

¾ tsp baking soda

¾ tsp fine sea salt

1 cup plus 2 Tbsp [200 g] semisweet chocolate chunks, optional

---

TIP!

We are enjoying the flavor and nutrition of whole grains at the bakery. If you'd like to include whole wheat in this recipe, we suggest using the following combination of flour in your recipe: ¾ cup plus 2 Tbsp [125 g] whole-wheat flour and ½ cup plus 1½ Tbsp [85 g] all-purpose flour.

Really curious about whole-grain baking? We suggest exploring getting a home mill and grinding your own wheat berries fresh for the recipe.

1. Wash the ripened banana well, tip the ends, remove the very tough spots, and freeze, ideally overnight, but at least for 2 to 3 hours.

2. Defrost the frozen banana in a small bowl in the refrigerator until fully thawed before proceeding with the recipe. Note that as the bananas freeze and defrost, they will turn black. They do not need to be black prior to freezing.

3. Preheat the oven to 350°F [180°C].

4. Place the thawed banana (and the liquid it released) into the bowl of a food processor. Purée until it becomes a smooth paste. You may see tiny dark specks of the peel. This is fine.

5. In a medium mixing bowl, add the puréed banana, sugar, eggs, butter, and vanilla extract, mixing with a wooden spoon until well combined. If using a stand mixer, use the paddle attachment and mix on low speed for 2 minutes.

6. In a separate mixing bowl, whisk together the flour, baking soda, and salt. Add the dry ingredients to the banana mixture in two stages, mixing until the batter is homogeneous. If using a stand mixer, use the paddle attachment on low speed. If you are using chocolate chunks or other additions, fold them in now.

7. Pour the batter into a 9 by 5 in [23 by 13 cm] loaf pan coated with nonstick cooking spray. Bake for 55 to 60 minutes. The banana bread is done when a tester or toothpick inserted into the center comes out clean and the loaf is a nice golden-brown color.

8. Let stand in the pan for 15 minutes, then turn out onto a wire rack to cool before cutting into slices and enjoying. Store in plastic wrap at room temperature for up to 1 week or in the freezer for up to 2 months. Thaw frozen bread at room temperature before enjoying.

Making food at the bakery can generate a surprising amount of waste, both from the preparation of the ingredients for the recipes to the excess of what's not sold at the end of the day. We have always tightly managed how much food we don't sell, and in the last decade we have worked increasingly hard to reduce the waste we generate during our baking. Lindsay-Jean has been our leader in this area. She has a particular passion for not wasting, and even wrote her own book about it, *Cooking with Scraps*. Through her encouragement and ingenuity, we've greatly reduced our waste at the bakery. Thank you, Lindsay-Jean!

This banana bread recipe uses the banana peel and the fruit—yes, a little shocking, but trust us and please give it a try. All you need to do is pop a very ripe, unpeeled banana into the freezer (ideally overnight) and then thaw it before proceeding with the recipe. We promise you that you'll like the result, and so will our Earth because there will be less unnecessary waste.

HOT CROSS BUNS

makes a dozen buns

The Bakehouse's annual spring baking of hot cross buns over Easter weekend has been a holiday staple for years. Our hot cross buns are soft, yeasted rolls enriched with butter, eggs, and oatmeal, which helps them stay moist. We then fancy them up by mixing in flavorful currants, golden raisins, and candied orange and lemon peel. Baked to a golden brown, our buns are then brushed with an apricot glaze and topped with the customary cross in sweet white icing. Folks flock to the Bakehouse for these delectable, once-a-year Easter treats starting on Good Friday through Easter Sunday.

Hot cross buns, brightly colored eggs, and bunny rabbits have long been associated with Easter. Interestingly, these symbols also share some kinship with ancient pagan rituals around the spring equinox, which predate organized Christianity. The Saxons, an early Germanic people who inhabited large parts of what is now modern-day England, Wales, and northern Germany, are known to have celebrated the arrival of spring and the rebirth of nature by baking small cakes or buns marked with crosses to honor the mythical Ēostre, the Saxon goddess of the dawn and personification of spring, fertility, and rebirth.

These cross-marked cakes or buns "sacred" to Ēostre were thought to symbolize the rebirth of the Earth after winter, the four quarters or phases of the moon that make up the lunar cycle, as well as the four seasons and the wheel of life. This tradition of marking buns or bread with a cross, like many other pagan symbols, was most likely incorporated into the celebration of Easter as Christianity spread its influence throughout Europe and the British Isles beginning in the sixth century CE.

Nowhere, perhaps, are hot cross buns more celebrated as an Easter tradition than in Britain. They've been a staple of Good Friday commemorations there since the Middle Ages, when Brother Thomas Rocliffe, a fourteenth-century Catholic monk attached to St. Albans Abbey in England, began baking hot cross buns and distributing them to the poor as Good Friday alms. With our recipe in hand, you can now partake in this Easter tradition by baking up your own delicious hot cross buns.

SOAKER

½ cup [45 g] old-fashioned rolled oats

½ cup [115 g] water, boiling

DOUGH

¼ cup [55 g] unsalted butter, room temperature

½ cup [115 g] whole milk, room temperature

1 large egg, room temperature

2⅓ cups [325 g] all-purpose flour, plus more for dusting

1¼ tsp instant yeast

2 Tbsp granulated sugar

1¼ Tbsp orange zest

¾ tsp fine sea salt

⅓ cup [45 g] currants

2 Tbsp golden raisins

1 Tbsp candied orange peel

1 Tbsp candied lemon peel

EGG WASH

1 large egg

1 large egg yolk

1 Tbsp water

APRICOT GLAZE

2 Tbsp apricot preserves

1 Tbsp water, warm

ICING

1¾ cups [210 g] powdered sugar

1½ to 2 Tbsp water, warm

½ tsp vanilla extract, optional

cont'd

prepare the soaker

1. In a large mixing bowl, mix together the rolled oats and boiling water until well combined. Set aside to cool completely to room temperature.

make the dough

1. In the bowl of a stand mixer fitted with the paddle attachment, add the butter and mix on medium speed to soften. Add in the oat soaker and milk and mix until well blended. Having some chunks of butter is fine.

2. Add the egg and mix to combine. Add the flour, instant yeast, granulated sugar, orange zest, and salt to the mixing bowl. Mix on low speed for 4 minutes. About halfway through mixing, scrape down the sides of the mixing bowl with a spatula and incorporate any dry flour. Increase the speed to medium and mix for 3 minutes. Add the currants, golden raisins, and candied orange and lemon peels to the dough and mix on low speed just until evenly distributed. This will happen quickly, in less than a minute.

3. Place the dough in a bowl lightly coated with neutral oil and cover with plastic wrap. Ferment the dough for 45 minutes at room temperature. After 45 minutes, turn the dough out onto a lightly floured work surface to do a letter fold; this will help develop the structure of the dough. Lightly pat out the dough into a rectangle. Fold two thirds of the dough from bottom to top, then fold the top third to the bottom edge. Fold two thirds of the dough from right to left, then from the left to the right edge.

4. Place the dough back in the lightly oiled bowl and cover with plastic wrap. Ferment the dough a second time for 45 minutes at room temperature. Line a baking sheet with parchment paper.

5. After 45 minutes, turn the dough out onto a lightly floured work surface. Using a bench scraper, divide the dough into 12 equal pieces, each weighing about 2¼ oz [65 g]. Shape the pieces into tight balls and then place each one onto the prepared baking sheet, at least 2 in [5 cm] apart. You may need two baking sheets, depending on what size sheet you have.

6. Cover the shaped dough balls loosely with plastic wrap and proof for 1 hour at room temperature or until the dough passes the touch test: Gently press the pad of a fingertip into one of the buns and remove it; the indentation should slowly come back most, but not all, of the way. The buns will be visibly larger in size.

make the egg wash and bake the buns

1. While the buns are proofing, preheat the oven to 375°F [190°C] at least 20 minutes before baking.

2. In a small bowl, make the egg wash by whisking together the egg, egg yolk, and water until well combined. Right before putting the buns into the oven, using a pastry brush, give each bun an even coat of egg wash. Bake until they are nicely browned and their internal temperature registers 190°F [90°C] on an instant-read thermometer, 15 to 18 minutes.

make the apricot glaze

1. Combine the preserves with the water and stir until blended. If there are large pieces of fruit, strain to remove them.

2. Immediately after removing the baked buns from the oven, brush them with the apricot glaze. Let the buns cool completely to room temperature before applying the cross garnishes in icing.

make and apply the icing

1. Sift the powdered sugar into a medium mixing bowl and add in 1½ Tbsp warm water, whisking slowly, dribbling the remaining water in if necessary, until the icing is at a thick enough consistency for making a cross garnish on top of the bun. (It needs to be on the thicker side, so you may need to adjust with either more water or more powdered sugar.)

2. To apply the cross garnish, fill a pastry bag with the icing. Then cut a ⅛ in [4 mm] hole at the tip of the pastry bag. (If you don't have a pastry bag, a plastic sandwich bag will work too. Fill it with icing, seal it, and form it into a piping shape. Then cut a ⅛ in [4 mm] hole in the point of one corner.) Place the pan of buns in front of you and apply the icing in one continuous line across each row of buns. Rotate the pan of baked buns and apply the icing in one continuous line across each row of buns to complete the cross design.

3. Let the icing dry before serving. Store hot cross buns in an airtight container at room temperature for 2 to 3 days.

RASPBERRY MARSHMALLOW BUNNY TAILS

Adapted from Zingerman's Candy Manufactory
makes 30 marshmallows

Did you know that Easter is second only to Halloween as the top candy-selling holiday in the United States? And a popular marshmallow sweet is probably a frontrunner in those sales. We've got nothing against the well-known, brightly colored variety shaped like small birds, but we'd opt for a pile of homemade marshmallows in our Easter basket any day. Ours are fluffy and flavorful but not overly sweet, and it's easy to change up the flavor too—just swap in a different flavor of preserves. We began making marshmallows at the Bakehouse in the early 2000s, starting with vanilla, then adding chocolate. We then decided on fruity flavors for Easter. The founder of Zingerman's Candy Manufactory, Charlie Frank, led our pastry kitchen for many years and made these tasty gems in that capacity. Then, when he started his own candy business, we relinquished our marshmallow recipe to him as a send-off gift, and the Candy Manufactory has been making them ever since.

3¾ cups plus 1 Tbsp [750 g] granulated sugar	1 Tbsp plus ½ tsp vanilla extract
	2 Tbsp plus 1 tsp corn syrup
1 cup [230 g] water, room temperature	3 [75 g] large egg whites, room temperature
2 Tbsp plus 1 tsp powdered gelatin	½ cup [100 g] raspberry preserves

1. Measure out 2¼ cups [450 g] of the sugar. Take a 13 by 18 in [33 by 46 cm] half baking sheet and generously cover the bottom with the sugar. (You don't need to use the entire amount; some of it will be used to coat the piped bunny tails.)

2. To bloom the gelatin, in a small bowl, combine ⅓ cup [75 g] of the water, the powdered gelatin, and 1 Tbsp of the vanilla extract. Stir to completely hydrate the gelatin, then set the mixture aside for at least 5 minutes.

3. In a medium saucepan, combine the remaining ⅔ cup [155 g] of water, 1½ cups [300 g] of sugar, and the corn syrup. Without stirring, bring the mixture to a boil over medium heat and cook the sugar mixture until it registers 240°F [115°C] on an instant-read thermometer—this is known as the softball stage—then remove from the heat.

4. Meanwhile, once the sugar mixture is close to reaching the softball stage (around 238°F [114°C]), add the egg whites and remaining ½ tsp vanilla extract to the bowl of a stand mixer fitted with the whisk attachment, and whip on high speed until doubled in volume, about 5 to 8 minutes. Take care not to overwhip, or the whites will become lumpy, which will adversely affect the texture of the finished marshmallows.

5. While the egg whites are whipping, heat the gelatin mixture in the microwave for 30 seconds until the gelatin has melted. Alternatively, place the small bowl with the mixture in a larger bowl partially filled with hot water, and stir until the gelatin melts.

6. When the egg whites have doubled in volume, turn the mixer down to medium speed and add the cooked sugar mixture in a slow, steady stream. Aim to pour the sugar syrup down the side of the bowl and avoid getting the sugar mixture on the whip attachment.

cont'd

7. Add the melted gelatin to the egg white mixture, then whip on high speed for 3 minutes, or until the mixture is light, airy, and thick. Fold in the raspberry preserves by hand, using a rubber spatula, until well combined. Take care not to deflate the marshmallows.

8. Transfer the marshmallow mixture into a large piping bag fitted with a star tip; a large tip if you'd like large bunny tails and a small tip if you'd like baby versions. Pipe rosettes in the shape of bunny tails directly onto the sugar-coated baking sheet.

9. Once all the bunny tails are piped, use a spoon to cover them with the remaining sugar, scooping up some from the baking sheet as needed, and allow them to sit uncovered overnight to develop a crisp exterior. (Not all of the sugar will stick to the bunny tails, and the remainder can be reused for another purpose.) Store in an airtight container at room temperature for up to 1 week.

TIP!

If you'd rather skip the piping, these can be made in an 8 in [20 cm] square pan. Prepare the pan by sifting cornstarch to cover the bottom of the pan; then, using a rubber spatula lightly coated with nonstick cooking spray, scrape the marshmallow mixture into the prepared square pan. Sprinkle the remaining cornstarch over the top of the marshmallow mixture and gently press it evenly into the pan. Let the pan of marshmallows sit at room temperature for 1½ to 2 hours before turning them out of the pan and cutting them into sixteen 2 in [5 cm] squares. Toss cut marshmallows in cornstarch to keep them from sticking and store in an airtight container at room temperature for up to 1 week.

FLAVOR VARIATIONS

Coconut: Prepare the baking sheet with a layer of toasted coconut instead of sugar. In place of the raspberry preserves, fold in 1 cup [70 g] of toasted shredded coconut and 2 tsp of coconut flavoring after whipping the egg whites. Top the piped bunny tails with additional toasted coconut.

Peppermint: In place of the raspberry preserves, fold in ½ tsp of peppermint flavoring after whipping the egg whites. Stir to combine well. Add 2 drops of red or green food coloring and fold just to swirl in the color.

Chocolate: Prepare the baking sheet with a layer of sifted natural cocoa powder instead of sugar. In place of the raspberry preserves, sift in ½ cup [40 g] of natural cocoa powder after whipping the egg whites, mixing on low speed just until the cocoa powder is mostly mixed in. Add in ⅓ cup [50 g] semisweet chocolate pieces and fold in by hand with a rubber spatula. Top the piped bunny tails with additional cocoa powder.

Vegetarian: These work just as well with agar-agar powder (not flakes). For step 3: In a medium saucepan, combine ⅔ cup [155 g] of water and 1 Tbsp of agar-agar powder over medium heat, whisking until slightly thickened, about 3 minutes. Then add the remaining 1½ cups plus 1 Tbsp [315 g] of granulated sugar and the corn syrup. Bring the mixture to a boil over medium heat and cook the sugar mixture, whisking occasionally to prevent the agar-agar from solidifying on the bottom of the pan, until it registers 240°F [115°C] on an instant-read thermometer—this is known as the softball stage—then remove from the heat.

KENTUCKY DERBY

RUN FOR THE ROSES PIE

makes 1 single-crust pie

Run for the Roses pie—walnuts, chocolate, and bourbon in a brown sugar custard—is a first cousin to the classic American pecan pie, and some would say they favor the cousin over the original. The filling is particularly special because of the muscovado brown sugar, real butter, vanilla extract, and fresh eggs. Its sweetness is counterbalanced by the full-bodied bourbon, the slight bitterness of the dark chocolate, and the nutty richness of the walnuts. Take all of this tastiness and put it into a buttery crust, and you and your fellow Kentucky Derby watchers won't mind if the horse you bet on loses the race. Top with a scoop of ice cream or a dollop of fresh whipped cream, if desired. This pie would also be welcome at many Thanksgiving celebrations.

Since 1875, the Kentucky Derby, a 1¼ mile [2 km] race of three-year-old Thoroughbred horses, has been held on the first Saturday in May at Churchill Downs in Louisville, Kentucky. It is a party! It is the first of three races collectively known as the Triple Crown, and it tends to draw the largest crowds. It's known for its celebratory feel, well-dressed women wearing spectacular hats, and special beverages and foods like the mint julep and burgoo, a stew of three different meats and vegetables. Thousands of people attend and millions watch and bet on the race all over the world.

It's an event worthy of its own dessert. If you're a fan of pie or the Kentucky Derby (or both!), you're likely familiar with a pie that is named after the famous horse race. So why don't we call our pie Derby pie? A bakery in Kentucky has trademarked that name and gone to great lengths to protect it by filing (and winning) dozens of lawsuits over the years, going after newspapers, websites, and cookbooks, and forcing them to change the name of the recipe in question. Intellectual property! Don't mess with it.

We've respectfully opted to name ours Run for the Roses Pie, a nod to the lush blanket of 554 red roses that is draped over the winning horse. Other inventive names we've seen include Not Derby Pie, Kentucky Race Day Pie (or simply, Race Day Pie), May Day Pie (a reference to when the Kentucky Derby is run), Pegasus Pie (a reference to the Pegasus Parade held at the Kentucky Derby Festival), and Meanspirited Censorship Pie. Regardless of the name, we bet they all taste dee-lish!

PIE DOUGH

1¼ cups plus ½ Tbsp [180 g] all-purpose flour, plus more for dusting

½ tsp fine sea salt

½ cup [110 g] unsalted butter, cold

2½ Tbsp water, cold

PIE FILLING

1 cup [120 g] raw walnut halves

1 cup [320 g] light corn syrup

¼ cup [55 g] unsalted butter

1 cup [200 g] light muscovado sugar, packed

¼ tsp fine sea salt

3 large eggs, room temperature

2 Tbsp bourbon, preferably Kentucky

1 tsp vanilla extract

½ cup [90 g] semisweet chocolate chips

cont'd

make the pie dough

1. In a large mixing bowl, mix together the flour and salt with a fork. Cut the butter into ¼ in [6 mm] cubes and add three-quarters of the cubes to the bowl. Cut the butter into the flour mixture using a pastry blender, two knives, or your hands until the mixture looks like coarse cornmeal. If using your hands, break the pieces of butter up in your fingers and rub the butter and flour together. Pick the mixture up between your hands and rub your palms together as if they're cold; this will break down the butter and rub it all over the flour.

The flour will take on a creamy yellow color during this step. When you pick the mixture up in your hand, it should be possible to squeeze it into a mass that will hold together. When you see the color change and the mixture holds together when squeezed, you know that you've worked the butter in enough. Work quickly so that the butter doesn't become warm. The goal of this step is to cover the flour with fat so that the gluten strands are not able to develop.

2. Add the remaining quarter of the butter and cut it into the mixture as before. These butter pieces should be left pea-size. The chunks of butter will create flakiness in the final pie crust—when they melt during baking, they create steam, which separates layers of the coated flour, making flakes of crust.

3. Create a well in the center of the flour mixture and add the cold water, then use a fork to blend it in. The flour mixture will still be crumbly in the bowl, but it should look moist. If it still looks dry, add up to an additional 1 Tbsp of cold water until the mixture looks moistened but still crumbly. (If the butter has been rubbed into the dough adequately, the amount of water specified should be enough. More water is usually necessary only when the butter has not been adequately distributed. It's not desirable to add more water because it tends to make a tougher crust.)

4. Turn the mixture out onto a clean, unfloured work surface, form it into a mound, and push out sections of dough across the work surface with the heel of your hand. We call this "schmearing." Push each section of dough once, not twice. Make sure to schmear enough so that the dough loses its dry, crumbly appearance. At the end of the schmearing, all of the pie dough will be pushed out flat on the work surface.

5. Fold the dough back onto itself with a bench scraper. Gather it into a ball, pressing it firmly so it holds together, then shape it into a disk and wrap it in plastic wrap. Chill the dough in the refrigerator for at least 1 hour before rolling it out.

roll out the pie dough

1. Remove the chilled dough from the refrigerator. While the dough is still in the plastic wrap, firmly but gently tap on it with a rolling pin until it is flexible. Lightly dust the work surface with flour. Place the unwrapped disk of dough on the work surface and lightly dust the top of the disk with flour.

2. Using a rolling pin, start rolling the dough from the center to the edge, away from you. Do not use too much pressure, or the dough will crack. If this happens, brush away any excess flour near the cracking area and press the dough back together.

3. Stop and give the dough a one-eighth turn. This rotation will prevent the dough from sticking to the work surface and will help you make a perfect circle. Re-flour the work surface and the top of the dough to prevent the dough from sticking. Continue to roll the dough until it's about ⅛ in [4 mm] thick and the circle is about 1 in [2.5 cm] wider than the top diameter of the 9 in [23 cm] pie plate you will be using. Flour is your friend in this process; use it liberally to avoid sticking.

4. When the rolled-out pie dough has reached the correct size, use a pastry brush to brush away any extra flour from the top of the dough. Turn the dough over and brush off any extra flour from the bottom.

5. Gently roll the dough loosely around the rolling pin. Position the edge of the dough over the edge of the pie plate and unroll the dough. Gently ease the dough down into the pie plate, making sure not to stretch the dough. Trim the dough to ½ in [12 mm] from the edge of the pie plate, then roll the excess dough underneath (like rolling a sleeping bag, not just folding it under) to make a thicker edge. Finish the edge with your choice of decorative crimping.

partially blind-bake the pie crust

1. Preheat the oven to 375°F [190°C].

2. Using a fork, dock the pie shell all over the bottom and sides. Place the pie shell in the refrigerator and chill for at least 20 minutes before baking.

3. Remove the chilled pie shell from the refrigerator or freezer and line the chilled crust with parchment paper, pressing it snugly against the bottom and sides.

4. Fill the lined pie shell with dried beans, rice, or pie weights to hold down the parchment paper. (It will take 3 to 4 cups of whatever weights you choose. If using dried beans or rice, they cannot be used for any other purpose, and should be reserved exclusively for use as pie weights.)

5. Bake the pie shell for 25 minutes, or until the edge begins to color. Remove the parchment paper with the weights and bake for an additional 5 minutes. At this point, the crust is considered partially blind-baked. Allow the pie crust to cool slightly while you make the filling.

make the filling and finish the pie

1. Preheat the oven to 350°F [180°C]. Line a baking sheet with parchment paper.

2. Toast the walnuts on a baking sheet for 10 to 12 minutes until they are fragrant and golden brown; set aside to cool. When cooled, chop them into approximately ¼ in [6 mm] pieces.

3. In a medium saucepan over medium heat, melt the corn syrup and butter, heating the mixture until it starts to bubble.

4. In a large mixing bowl, stir together the sugar and salt, breaking up any lumps of sugar with your fingers. Pour the melted butter and corn syrup into the sugar mixture, stirring until well combined and the sugar is dissolved. Let the mixture cool until it is warm but not hot.

5. Add the eggs, bourbon, and vanilla extract to the butter-sugar mixture and stir until homogeneous.

6. Add the chocolate chips and toasted walnut pieces to the mixture and stir until evenly distributed.

7. Pour the filling into the cooled, partially blind-baked pie crust. Place the filled pie on the prepared baking sheet and bake for 50 to 55 minutes, or until the center is set and the filling has a slight jiggle, like a gelatin dessert. If you have any concerns about it not being baked enough, give it another 5 minutes. In this recipe, it's better to err on the side of more baked.

8. The pie is delicious warm or at room temperature. Store pie dough wrapped in disk form or fully formed as a pie shell in the refrigerator for up to 5 days. It can also be frozen, well wrapped, and preferably in an air-tight container, in either form, for up to 3 months. Store the fully baked pie, covered, at room temperature for up to a week; or frozen, well wrapped in plastic, for up to 3 months. Thaw at room temperature before enjoying.

Cake is the go-to American dessert for capping celebratory moments, like birthdays, weddings, and graduations. Graduation parties often call for a cake that can feed a crowd, which is when we opt for a sheet cake like the one following. It's large, easy to make, and easy to serve. We've been making this cake at the bakery for at least a quarter of a century. This means that it's been at literally thousands of Ann Arbor gatherings, making it a safe bet for a diverse crowd on any celebratory occasion.

BUTTERMILK CELEBRATION CAKE

makes a two-layer sheet cake; serves 12 to 24

If "sheet cake" calls to mind lackluster big-box store versions, rest assured that our rendition is something special. Using the highest quality of simple ingredients results in a moist, scrumptious, vanilla buttermilk cake, topped with a silky vanilla Swiss buttercream. If you'd rather ice yours with chocolate Swiss buttercream, simply double the recipe that we use for our OMG Chocolate Cupcakes (page 215). And just in case you want something a little more unusual, we've included a variety of flavor options for the Swiss buttercream (see page 242), all of which pair deliciously with the rich buttermilk cake.

BUTTERMILK CAKE

3 cups plus 2 Tbsp [380 g] cake flour

2½ tsp baking powder

1¾ tsp baking soda

1¾ tsp fine sea salt

1¾ cups [350 g] granulated sugar

1½ cups [330 g] unsalted butter, room temperature

12 [200 g] egg yolks, room temperature

1½ Tbsp vanilla extract

2 cups plus 3 Tbsp [505 g] buttermilk, room temperature

SWISS BUTTERCREAM

9 [315 g] egg whites, room temperature

2¼ cups [450 g] granulated sugar

¾ tsp fine sea salt

3 cups plus 1 Tbsp [675 g] unsalted butter, room temperature

1 tsp vanilla extract

make the buttermilk cake

1. Preheat the oven to 350°F (180°C).

2. Line the bottom of two 9 by 13 in [23 by 33 cm] cake pans with parchment paper and lightly coat the paper and sides of the pans with nonstick cooking spray.

3. In a medium mixing bowl, sift together the flour, baking powder, baking soda, and salt; set aside.

4. In a separate medium mixing bowl, beat the sugar and butter together until light and fluffy, 2 to 3 minutes, scraping down the sides of the bowl as needed. If using a stand mixer, use the paddle attachment and mix at medium speed. Add the egg yolks 2 at a time, beating well after each addition.

5. Once all of the egg yolks are incorporated, add the vanilla extract and beat until well combined.

6. Alternate adding the dry ingredients and the buttermilk to the creamed butter mixture, one-third at a time, mixing well after each addition. Start with one-third of the dry, mix well, then add one-third of the buttermilk, and repeat two more times with the remaining ingredients. If using a stand mixer, use the paddle attachment and mix on low speed. Scrape down the sides of the bowl well throughout. Once all the dry and wet ingredients have been incorporated, beat the batter briefly to make sure it is fully mixed and fluffy.

cont'd

7. Divide the batter evenly between the two prepared cake pans, and bake for 30 to 35 minutes. If your oven bakes unevenly, rotate the pans midway through baking, both from top to bottom and front to back. The cake layers are done when their top surfaces are golden brown and spring back when lightly pressed in the center, their sides pull away from the pan, and a tester or toothpick inserted into the center of each comes out clean.

8. Remove the pans from the oven and allow the cakes to cool in their pans for 10 to 15 minutes. After this initial cooling, transfer the cake layers from their pans to wire racks to cool completely to room temperature before assembling and frosting the cake.

make the swiss buttercream

1. In a medium heatproof mixing bowl, combine the egg whites, sugar, and salt, stirring with a wooden spoon to combine. Place the bowl over a double boiler or saucepan with gently simmering water and heat the mixture, stirring every couple of minutes, until the sugar is completely dissolved and the temperature registers 180°F [82°C] on an instant-read thermometer.

2. Transfer the egg white mixture to the bowl of a stand mixer. Using the whisk attachment, whip on high speed until it has doubled in volume, become thick and shiny, and cooled to room temperature. Check the temperature by touching the underside of the mixing bowl.

3. Once the mixture is at room temperature, set the stand mixer to medium speed and gradually add the soft, room-temperature butter, one small piece at a time, mixing until all of it has been incorporated. The butter should be the same temperature as the egg white mixture to aid successful incorporation.

4. Add the vanilla extract and whip on medium speed to incorporate; then whip on high speed for 1 minute to ensure all the butter is totally combined with the whipped egg whites and sugar mixture.

5. Use immediately or place in an airtight container and chill in the refrigerator for up to 1 week or freeze for up to 3 months. If chilling or freezing, allow the buttercream to come to room temperature and re-whip it before using.

assemble the sheet cake

1. If the cake layers have domed tops, trim them with a serrated knife, positioned horizontally, so they are both flat. Snack on the cake scraps, if desired.

2. Place one cake layer on a cake board or serving tray. Using an offset spatula, spread about one-third of the buttercream over the top of the first cake layer, then place the second layer on top of the buttercream, flipping it over so that the top of the second layer is face down on the buttercream filling. This will give you a nice flat cake top.

3. Thinly coat the entire cake with a thin layer of buttercream, then transfer to the refrigerator or freezer for 10 minutes to set. This is a crumb coat, which, as the name suggests, helps prevent crumbs from getting caught in the buttercream frosting.

4. Finish frosting the cake with the remaining buttercream. Use a spatula or a palette knife to make a decorative design in the frosting, giving the cake a more finished look, or try your hand at decorative piping for an extra-special flourish.

5. Both the cake and the buttercream can be made ahead of time and stored, well wrapped in plastic wrap, in either the refrigerator or freezer to be assembled at a later time. See page 242 for more on getting your buttercream back to room temperature.

6. Store the assembled cake, covered, in a cool spot in your home for up to 2 days or the refrigerator for up to 5 days. It doesn't need to be wrapped tightly, as the frosting will keep the cake moist, but note that it's susceptible to picking up strong odors in the refrigerator, like onions. To freeze an assembled cake, place it in the freezer, uncovered, until frozen solid, about 4 hours; then wrap it tightly in plastic wrap and freeze for up to 3 months.

GOAT CHEESE AND TOMATO GALETTES

makes 8 individual galettes

Galette *is a French word for a free-form pie. It's a rustic but elegant pastry that sounds and looks impressive, especially made as individual servings. Luckily, it's easy to master, making it perfect for special occasions like graduation dinners or open houses. We're filling these with herbed goat cheese and sliced Roma tomatoes, but feel free to fill them as you please! Other small, firm tomatoes, like Campari, would work too. If you can't find ripe and tasty tomatoes, use sundried instead.*

PIE DOUGH

3¾ cups plus 2 Tbsp [525 g] all-purpose flour, plus more for dusting

1½ tsp fine sea salt

1½ cups [330 g] unsalted butter, cold

½ cup [115 g] water, cold

FILLING

1 cup plus 3 Tbsp [270 g] soft goat cheese

1 cup plus 3 Tbsp [270 g] ricotta

2 Tbsp grated Parmesan cheese

¼ cup [15 g] fresh basil, roughly chopped

1 tsp fresh thyme

2 tsp finely chopped fresh rosemary

2 tsp minced garlic

1 tsp fine sea salt

½ tsp freshly ground black pepper

4 Roma tomatoes

EGG WASH

1 large egg

1 egg yolk

1 Tbsp water

make the pie dough

1. In a large mixing bowl, mix together the flour and salt with a fork. Cut the cold butter into ¼ in [6 mm] cubes and add three-quarters of the cubes to the bowl. Cut the butter into the flour mixture using a pastry blender, two knives, or your hands until the mixture looks like coarse cornmeal. If using your hands, break the butter pieces up in your fingers and rub the butter and flour together. Pick the mixture up between your hands and rub your palms together as if they're cold; this will break down the butter and rub it all over the flour.

The flour will take on a creamy yellow color during this step. When you pick the mixture up in your hand, it should be possible to squeeze it into a mass that will hold together. When you see the color change and the mixture holds together when squeezed, you know that you've worked the butter in enough. Work quickly so that the butter doesn't become warm. The goal of this step is to cover the flour with fat so that the gluten strands are not able to develop.

2. Add the remaining quarter of the butter and cut it into the mixture as before. These butter pieces should be left in pea-size chunks to create flakiness in the final pie crust—when they melt during baking, they create steam, which separates layers of the coated flour, making flakes of crust.

3. Create a well in the center of the flour mixture and add the cold water, then use a fork to blend it in. The flour mixture will still be crumbly in the bowl, but it should look moist. If it still looks dry, add up to an additional 1 Tbsp of cold water, until the mixture looks moistened but still crumbly. (If the butter has been rubbed into the dough adequately, the amount of water specified should be enough. More water is usually necessary only when the butter has not been adequately distributed. It's not desirable to add more water, because it tends to make a tougher crust.)

cont'd

4. Turn the mixture out onto a clean, unfloured work surface, form it into a mound, and push out sections of dough across the work surface with the heel of your hand. We call this "schmearing." Push each section of dough once, not twice. Make sure to schmear enough so that the dough loses its dry, crumbly appearance. At the end of the schmearing, all of the pie crust will be pushed out flat on the work surface.

5. Fold the dough back onto itself with a bench scraper. Gather it into a ball, pressing it firmly so it holds together.

6. Cut the dough into eight equal pieces and shape each one into a 4 in [10 cm] disk. Wrap the disks of dough in plastic wrap and chill in the refrigerator for at least 1 hour before rolling them out.

make the filling

1. Preheat the oven to 375°F [190°C].

2. In a medium mixing bowl, combine the goat cheese, ricotta, Parmesan cheese, fresh herbs, garlic, salt, and pepper. Set aside.

3. Cut each tomato into eight ¼ in [6 mm] thick slices or wedges. Set aside.

roll out the pie dough

1. Remove one disk of the chilled dough from the refrigerator. While the dough is still in the plastic wrap, firmly but gently tap on it with a rolling pin until it is flexible but still cold. Lightly dust the work surface with flour. Place the unwrapped disk of dough on the work surface and lightly dust the top with flour.

2. Using a rolling pin, start rolling the dough from the center to the edge, away from you. Do not use too much pressure, or the dough will crack. If this happens, brush away any excess flour near the cracking area and press the dough back together.

3. Stop and give the dough a one-eighth turn. This rotation will prevent the dough from sticking to the work surface and will help you make a perfect circle.

4. Re-flour the work surface and the top of the dough to prevent the dough from sticking. Continue to roll the dough until it's about ⅛ in [4 mm] thick and is about 10 in [25 cm] in diameter. Flour is your friend in this process; use it liberally to avoid sticking.

5. Once the disk of dough has been rolled out to the correct size, use a pastry brush to brush away any extra flour from the top. Turn the dough over and brush off any extra flour from the bottom.

6. Set the dough on parchment on your work surface; this will make it easier to transfer the dough to the baking sheet when you're ready to assemble the galette. Line a baking sheet with parchment paper.

7. Repeat this process with the remaining seven disks of dough.

assemble the galettes

1. For each round of dough, place it on the prepared baking sheet, add a heaping ¼ cup [80 g] of filling in the center of the round, and spread to create a 6 in [15 cm] circle of filling on the dough. Arrange four tomato slices over the filling of each galette.

2. Starting just where the filling ends, fold the edges of the dough over the filling, leaving a 5 to 6 in [12 to 15 cm] circle of filling exposed. Overlap the folds to give it a pleated design. Repeat with the other dough rounds. Be sure to arrange the assembled galettes on the baking sheets with at least 2 in [5 cm] of space between each one.

make the egg wash and bake

1. In a small bowl, whisk together the egg, egg yolk, and water until well combined. Lightly brush the folded/pleated crust edges of each galette with the egg wash.

2. Bake the galettes for 40 to 45 minutes, or until their crusts take on a deep golden color. Do not underbake. Color is flavor in our world.

3. Transfer the galettes to a wire rack to cool to just above room temperature. The galettes can be served warm or at room temperature. Store baked galettes in an airtight container in the refrigerator for up to 3 days. Pie dough can be stored, wrapped in disk form or rolled out, in the refrigerator for up to 5 days. It can also be frozen, well wrapped, and preferably in an airtight container, in either form, for up to 3 months.

MOTHER'S DAY

While celebrations honoring mothers can be traced all the way back to
ancient Greece and Rome, Mother's Day, as we know it today, has more
recent origins, with the first official Mother's Day taking place on May 10,
1908. It was founded by Anna Jarvis—who lost her mother, Ann Reeves
Jarvis, a social activist during the Civil War—as a way to honor mothers
and the sacrifices they make for their children. Jarvis felt strongly that this
celebration should be intimate and personal: a day spent in reverence for
your own mother, not a day to honor all mothers. Ironically, after President
Woodrow Wilson declared Mother's Day a national holiday in 1914 and
merchants nationwide could be seen capitalizing on it, Jarvis became
disillusioned with the very thing she helped create and began putting all
her efforts into shutting it down. However, as we're well aware, Jarvis's
efforts were unsuccessful and Mother's Day celebrations continue to thrive
the world over.

In the United States today, Mother's Day is celebrated on the second Sunday
of May and typically involves showering mothers and mother figures with
cards, gifts, and flowers. Breakfast in bed is a common start to the day,
as is taking Mom out for brunch, which, interestingly, isn't just a special
treat for Mom but a longstanding feminist tradition. Prior to the Civil War,
women weren't permitted to dine out in public during the day; it was seen
as scandalous and inappropriate. The right wasn't secured until the turn
of the century, as part of a broader shift in attitude toward women brought
about by the suffrage movement. The notion of dining out during the day
as a form of women's liberation was reinforced by the gaining popularity of
brunch in America in the 1930s.

An indulgent brunch at home is a great way to show appreciation for
the mothers in our lives. Make it even more special by making a rarely
homemade baked good like our Zinglish Muffins (facing) and turn them
into decadent eggs Benedict. And don't forget dessert! Our light, vanilla-
forward angel food cake is perfect to round out a rich meal. We like ours
with fresh berries and whipped cream.

So pour Mom a mimosa and get baking!

ZINGLISH MUFFINS

makes 10 muffins

You can make these puffy gems several days ahead or start 4 hours before serving time to have the freshest English muffins the mother you're celebrating has probably ever eaten. You'll be amazed at their texture and flavor straight off the griddle.

Be prepared, as this dough is sticky—a sign of high moisture content. Although a little challenging to work with, it's this quality that gives the muffins lots of nooks and crannies and a light, airy texture. Use these muffins, fork-split and toasted to a golden brown, as the foundation for eggs Benedict, or a mouthwatering breakfast sandwich of eggs and sausage or vegetables. If the mother in your life prefers simplicity, try these muffins toasted with a special nut butter.

3 cups plus 1½ Tbsp [435 g] all-purpose flour, plus more for dusting	1¼ tsp instant yeast
	1¼ tsp granulated sugar
1½ cups [345 g] water, room temperature	Cornmeal for dusting
	Clarified butter or ghee for griddling (see Tip, page 68)
1½ tsp fine sea salt	

make the dough

1. In a medium mixing bowl, combine the flour, water, salt, yeast, and sugar and mix with a wooden spoon until the dough forms a shaggy mass. Scrape the dough onto a clean, unfloured work surface and knead for 6 to 8 minutes. This is a very sticky dough, but don't add more flour! Initially, you can knead it in the bowl, if you like; then, as it comes together, move to kneading it on the work surface.

2. Once fully kneaded, place the dough in a medium mixing bowl or container lightly coated in oil or non-stick cooking spray and cover with plastic wrap or a tea towel. Let the dough rise at room temperature until doubled in size, about 1½ hours.

3. Turn out the risen dough onto a lightly floured work surface and divide the dough into ten equal pieces (each one will weigh about 2¾ oz [75 g]). Shape each piece into a small round, as if you were making a dinner roll, and place on a baking sheet dusted with cornmeal several inches apart. Let the rounds rest for 10 minutes.

4. Lightly dust the tops of the dough rounds with flour. Use the palm of your hand or a flat tool, like a spatula, and press each dough round down into a disk 3 in [7.5 cm] in diameter. Dust the tops with cornmeal, enough for a nice garnish at the end of the baking and enough to stop the plastic from sticking in the next step.

5. Cover all the disks loosely with plastic wrap and let them proof for 45 minutes to 1 hour. To assess if the dough is optimally proofed, flour a finger and poke it gently into a dough disk; if the indentation holds its shape, the dough is ready for the next step.

cont'd

griddle the english muffins

1. Traditionally, English muffins are cooked on a griddle or in a skillet. We recommend a large skillet that has a lid. If you are using a cast-iron skillet, preheat it over medium-low heat for 5 to 10 minutes, depending on its thickness. If you are using a skillet other than cast iron, preheat it over medium-low heat for 2 to 4 minutes, depending on its thickness.

2. Rub the skillet with the clarified butter or ghee just like you would prepare a pan to make pancakes. Use your hands or a flat spatula to transfer the dough disks to the skillet, leaving 1 to 2 in [2.5 to 5 cm] between each muffin; cook in batches if you run out of room. Cover the griddle or skillet with a lid to ensure that the muffins cook through and achieve good loft and airiness. Bake the muffins, covered, for 3 to 4 minutes on each side. Check the bottoms of the muffins as they are baking and adjust the heat if necessary. The muffins are fully baked when their internal temperature registers 190°F [88°C] on an instant-read thermometer.

Griddling these muffins is a bit like making pancakes; it takes a bit to get the pan at the perfect temperature and the timing down. Try griddling just a couple to start with to get everything set and then do the remaining ones.

3. Place the muffins on a wire rack to cool. Split the cooled muffins with a fork, toast to your taste, and enjoy! Store in an airtight plastic bag for 3 to 5 days or freeze for up to 3 months.

TIP!

Butter that is clarified can be cooked at higher temperatures without browning or burning because the milk solids and water have been removed. It is great to use when cooking at high temperatures or when griddling something for several minutes and you don't want the item to brown before it is done. Ghee is an Indian version of clarified butter and is readily available in many grocery stores. It's easy to clarify your own butter though. Take a stick of butter (or more) and melt it in a small pot very gently. Remove from the heat. Skim off the residue that will rise to the top of the butterfat. Slowly pour the clear fat into a container, carefully keeping the watery milk solids in the bottom of the pot, which can then be discarded. The clear, clarified butter is now ready for you to use and can be kept at room temperature or in the refrigerator for months.

JAKE'S ANGEL FOOD CAKE

makes one cake; serves 12

Use a real vanilla bean as well as the best vanilla extract you can find to make this cake extra special. Vanilla is the star here, and the light texture is the essential supporting actor.

Why is it called Jake's Cake? Our version is named after Amy's firstborn, Jake, which makes it that much more appropriate for Mother's Day. It's a light and super flexible cake that can be garnished just as your mother would like it.

1 cup [120 g] cake flour	1½ tsp cream of tartar
1½ cups [300 g] granulated sugar	½ tsp fine sea salt
12 egg whites, room temperature	1½ tsp lemon juice
	1 vanilla bean
2 Tbsp water, warm	1 Tbsp vanilla extract

1. Preheat the oven to 350°F [180°C].

2. Using a flour sifter or fine-mesh sieve, sift together the flour and ½ cup [100 g] of the sugar into a mixing bowl; repeat sifting two more times. After the third sifting, pour the flour and sugar mixture back into the sifter and set aside for later.

3. Using a stand mixer with a whisk attachment, place the egg whites in the mixing bowl and beat them on medium speed until light and frothy. Turn the mixer off and add the water, cream of tartar, salt, lemon juice, vanilla bean, and vanilla extract. Start whipping the egg whites on medium speed. Once they have increased their volume by 25 percent, continue whipping and slowly stream in the remaining 1 cup [200 g] of sugar. This process will take 1 to 2 minutes.

4. Once the sugar has been added, turn the mixer to high speed and whip until the sugar is dissolved and the egg whites are firm and glossy. To test this, stop the machine and detach the whisk. Pull the whisk straight up out of the whipped egg whites. They should form peaks and hold their shape (see page 244). This will take 3 to 4 minutes.

5. Remove the bowl from the mixer. Sift one-quarter of the flour mixture over the whipped egg whites and, using the whisk attachment, gently fold by hand until the flour is incorporated. Repeat the process three more times until all of the flour mixture is incorporated into the whipped egg whites. Using a spatula, gently fold the batter in the bowl to incorporate it completely.

6. Gently fill an ungreased 9 in [23 cm] tube pan (angel food cake pan) with the batter and smooth the top with a spatula, pushing the batter up the side of the pan. This helps the cake cling to the side of the pan and reach and maintain better height.

7. Place the cake on the middle rack of the oven and bake for 45 to 50 minutes or until the top is golden and springs back when touched.

8. Invert the cake pan on a wire rack, balancing on its center tube insert (inverting the pan, through its tube, onto the neck of a wine bottle works too) and allow it to cool upside down for 30 to 40 minutes. This will help prevent the cake from collapsing on itself.

9. Once completely cool, take a flexible knife, like a palette knife, and slide it around the edge of the pan and center tube to release the cake. If the pan is a two-piece tube pan, slide the knife under the bottom piece and release the top of the cake. If the pan is one piece, gently shake it to release the cake.

10. Serve with desired garnishes or on its own. Store the cake, well wrapped in plastic wrap or in an airtight container, at room temperature for up to 5 days, or in the freezer for up to 3 months.

NO. 2

SUMMER

SUMMER IS A TIME OF CONNECTION with loved ones as well as the earth. Songbirds trilling at daybreak, mourning doves cooing serenely as the day winds down, and a symphony of crickets and frogs as fireflies dot the dusk air like glitter—these sounds have grounded me in the heart of summer for as long as I can remember.

When I was a kid, these sounds were the backdrop for adventurous times spent at my grandparents' home "up north" in East Jordan, Michigan. I spent many summer weeks exploring their vast property with my big sister, while cicadas and the heat seared the air. We'd spend mornings hunting for Petoskey stones while we stuffed ourselves with wild raspberries, warm from the sun's relentless rays. In the late afternoon, I would help my Japanese grandmother pick dark green spinach leaves from her garden, which she'd dress simply with soy sauce and MSG for dinner that evening. Unbeknownst to me at the time, a deep appreciation for growing, eating, and sharing fresh summer food was beginning to take root.

Today, like my grandma, I find great pleasure in producing my own food. With the soundtrack of the season playing behind me, I tend to my garden, knowing that the true gift of summer lies at the end of my efforts. From the first delicate runner beans to those late-season tomatoes, fresh, flavorful summer produce is more than just the star of the dish. Gathering around a delicious spread of food, much of it fresh from the ground, connects us and fosters a sense of belonging not only to each other but also to the earth. So head out to the garden, your local U-Pick farm, or the farmers' market and collect your ingredients to make something special for your next gathering. Summer cookouts await with big pans of vibrant paella, juicy tomatoes sitting atop burgers hugged by brioche buns baked fresh that morning, and tart cherries nestled in all-butter crusts to finish the meal. Enjoy it all while you can, al fresco, surrounded by friends and family, with the sounds of nature behind you, just as the season intended it.

—*Corynn Coscia*

Memorial Day is unofficially the start of summer. It's a day for honoring the Americans who lost their lives while serving in the military, and the holiday weekend is often observed with parades and family gatherings. At the Bakehouse, it's also the start of blueberry buckle season. A buckle is an American coffee cake that dates back to colonial times—a single-layer cake, baked in a round or square pan, that includes fruit and streusel-style crumb topping. Some recipes, like ours, call for mixing the fruit into the cake batter, while others suggest spreading the fruit between the batter and streusel topping, as a separate layer. The name comes from what happens when the cake is layered in this way: While baking, the fruit and streusel buckle. Although we chose to mix in the fruit, you could try the layering method instead.

Our tender and moist version has a bounty of blueberries, sweet butter, and a touch of orange and cinnamon and is topped with a delectable butter-crumble, "buckled" crust.

BLUEBERRY BUCKLE

makes one cake

This recipe is a classic that we've been making for more than twenty years; it just might become a standard in your repertoire as well. It lends itself to variations, so if you don't have blueberries, substitute a different fruit. See our strawberry version on page 76.

CRUMBLE TOPPING

½ cup plus 1 Tbsp [115 g] brown sugar, packed

½ cup plus 1 Tbsp [80 g] all-purpose flour

½ tsp ground cinnamon

¼ cup [55 g] unsalted butter, room temperature

BATTER

¾ cup plus 1 tsp [155 g] granulated sugar

¼ cup [55 g] unsalted butter, room temperature

½ tsp orange oil, or 1 Tbsp orange zest (see Tip, page 76)

1 large egg, room temperature

½ cup [115 g] whole milk, room temperature

1 tsp vanilla extract

2 cups plus 1 Tbsp [290 g] all-purpose flour

2 tsp baking powder

½ tsp fine sea salt

2 cups [270 g] fresh or frozen blueberries

make the crumble topping

1. Preheat the oven to 350°F [180°C]. Coat a 9 in [23 cm] springform pan or a 9 by 2 in [23 by 5 cm] round cake pan with nonstick cooking spray, and set aside.

2. In a small mixing bowl, add the brown sugar, flour, and cinnamon and stir to combine, taking care to break up any large pieces of brown sugar. Add the butter to the sugar mixture and cut together with a fork, just until the mixture becomes crumbly. Set aside.

make the batter and bake the cake

1. In a medium mixing bowl, add the granulated sugar and butter and beat with a wooden spoon until light and fluffy. If using a stand mixer, use the paddle attachment and mix on medium speed. Add the orange oil and egg and beat until the mixture comes together. Add the milk and vanilla extract and mix to combine. The mixture will look curdled; do not be alarmed.

2. In another medium mixing bowl, whisk together the flour, baking powder, and salt. Add all of the dry ingredients into the bowl with the wet ingredients and mix until smooth. If using a stand mixer, do this on a low speed. Gently mix in the blueberries until just combined. If the blueberries are frozen, they will make the batter very thick. This will still work well; don't defrost the blueberries because they will give off a lot of juice and discolor the batter.

cont'd

3. Pour the batter into the prepared baking pan and smooth the top with an offset spatula. Sprinkle the top of the batter evenly with the crumble mixture. Bake for 55 to 60 minutes, or until a tester or toothpick inserted in the center of the cake comes out clean.

4. Cool the cake in the pan for 5 minutes. This cake can be served from the pan or you can put a plate over the top, flip it over, remove the pan, and then put a serving tray on the now-exposed bottom of the cake and flip again. Serve warm or at room temperature. Store wrapped in plastic, at room temperature, for up to 3 days or in the freezer for up to 3 months.

TIP!

At the Bakehouse, we love intense flavors and are always looking for ways to increase the flavor in our recipes. Sometimes it's not always possible to get the intensity we want with extracts. Fortunately, many years ago we discovered a line of oils and natural flavorings from a company called Boyajian—they are considerably more intense than extracts and are used in small quantities. If you can't find orange oil, substitute 1 Tbsp of orange zest.

STRAWBERRY STRUCKLE

This cake lends itself to many variations. We particularly like this one:

Replace the ground cinnamon in the crumble with 1 tsp of ground ginger. Replace the orange oil and vanilla extract with 1 tsp of vanilla paste. Replace the 2 cups [270 g] of blueberries with 2 cups [270 g] of roasted strawberry pieces (or half roasted strawberries and half strawberry yogurt chips).

To roast strawberries, cut each strawberry in half (or even quarters or sixths if they're large). Arrange the strawberries in a single layer on a rimmed baking sheet lined with parchment paper. Roast at 350°F [180°C] until the juices thicken and the berries are soft and slumpy. Timing will vary depending on how many you roast, but if in doubt, let them go longer. Roasting really concentrates the flavor, and you don't want big wet pieces of strawberries in your struckle. Let them cool and store any extras in an airtight container in the refrigerator for up to a week (try them on yogurt or ice cream!).

The last day of the school year is certainly a day worth marking if you have school-aged children or a teacher in your life. This is the kind of pastry that sends most everyone over the moon with one bite, making them an out-of-this-world special treat to have ready for this much-anticipated day.

COSMIC CAKES

makes 12 sandwich cakes

Cosmic Cakes are our version of whoopie pies, a classic from the great state of Maine. We start with two thin layers of a soft chocolate cake, sandwiched around a filling of vanilla Swiss buttercream, which we then coat with rich, dark chocolate. It's fun to experiment with other flavors though—see page 242 for more options. We're especially partial to the chocolate mint, peanut butter, and banana variations with these.

Making Cosmic Cakes is definitely a project. The cakes and the buttercream can be made ahead of time, leaving their assembly for a later day. If you do not want to tackle tempering chocolate and enrobing the cakes, you can skip that. Just fill the cakes with buttercream, sprinkle them with powdered sugar, and call them whoopie pies instead! If you have friends from Maine, invite them over for the festivities and they'll love you for it.

CHOCOLATE CAKES

1¾ cups [245 g] all-purpose flour

½ cup plus 1 Tbsp [45 g] natural cocoa powder

2 tsp baking powder

2 tsp baking soda

¾ tsp fine sea salt

1 cup plus 3 Tbsp [245 g] granulated sugar

½ cup plus 1 Tbsp [125 g] unsalted butter, room temperature

1½ tsp light corn syrup

2 large eggs, room temperature

½ cup plus 1½ Tbsp [140 g] whole milk, room temperature

SWISS BUTTERCREAM

6 egg whites

1½ cups [300 g] granulated sugar

¼ tsp fine sea salt

2 cups plus 1 Tbsp [455 g] unsalted butter, room temperature

½ tsp vanilla extract

CHOCOLATE COATING

4 cups [680 g] semisweet chocolate, finely chopped (not chips; better to use a bar of high-quality chocolate)

make the chocolate cakes

1. Preheat the oven to 375°F [190°C]. Line two baking sheets with parchment paper.

2. In a medium mixing bowl, using a sifter or fine-mesh sieve, sift together the flour, cocoa powder, baking powder, baking soda, and salt.

3. In a separate medium mixing bowl, cream together the sugar, butter, and corn syrup with a wooden spoon until combined. If using a stand mixer, use the paddle attachment and mix on medium speed. Add the eggs, one at a time, beating well and scraping down the sides of the bowl after each addition.

4. Alternate adding the dry ingredients and the milk to the creamed butter mixture, one-third at a time, mixing well after each addition. Start with one-third of the dry ingredients, mix well, add one-third of the milk, and repeat two more times with the remaining ingredients. Scrape the sides of the bowl well throughout. Once all the dry and wet ingredients have been incorporated, mix the batter thoroughly by hand, using a wooden spoon, or with a standard mixer on medium speed for 1 minute to make it light and fluffy.

cont'd

5. Using a ¾ or 1 oz scoop, portion out the batter into 24 individual cake layers, placing each one, evenly spaced apart, onto the prepared baking sheets. This batter spreads significantly, so give each cake layer lots of room by putting only 6 on each baking sheet. No need to buy a scoop! Use any spoon you have; a tablespoon would work. The point is to have cakes the same size and to yield 24 of them. If you have a scale, make each one about 1½ oz [40 g]. If not using a scoop, spread the batter a little to make it a circle. It will continue to spread to the correct size once it is in the oven.

6. Bake, one sheet at a time, for 12 to 14 minutes, or until the layers look dry, rotating the baking sheets midway through baking from front to back. (Baking more than one sheet at a time may result in flat pancakes that don't rise properly.) Dry-looking cake layers are a good indication that they are done, due to their relative thinness.

7. Allow the cake layers to cool on the baking sheet for 5 minutes before transferring them to a wire rack to cool completely to room temperature. (Optional but sometimes helpful: Place the sheet of baked cake layers in the freezer while making the buttercream filling; this makes them easier to remove from the parchment paper.) The cake layers can be made ahead of time and stored, well wrapped in plastic wrap, in either the refrigerator or freezer to be assembled at a later time.

make the swiss buttercream

1. In a medium heatproof mixing bowl, combine the egg whites, sugar, and salt, stirring with a wooden spoon to combine. Place the bowl over a double boiler or saucepan with gently simmering water and heat the mixture, stirring every couple of minutes, until the sugar is completely dissolved and the temperature registers 180°F [82°C] on an instant-read thermometer.

2. Transfer the egg white mixture to the bowl of a stand mixer. Using the whisk attachment, whip on high speed until it has doubled in volume, become thick and shiny, and has cooled to room temperature.

3. Once the mixture is cool, lower the speed to medium and gradually add the soft, room-temperature butter, one small piece at a time, mixing until all of it has been incorporated. The butter should be the same temperature as the egg white mixture to aid successful incorporation. Add the vanilla extract and whip on medium speed to incorporate, then whip on high speed for 1 minute to ensure all the butter is totally combined with the whipped egg whites and sugar mixture.

4. Use immediately or place in an airtight container and chill in the refrigerator for up to 1 week or freeze for up to 3 months. If chilling or freezing, allow the buttercream to come to room temperature and be sure to re-whip it before using. For tips on how to refresh the buttercream after it is chilled, see page 242.

assemble the cosmic cakes

1. Once the buttercream is ready, line up the cooled cakes on a baking sheet, flat side up; try to match similarly sized cake circles together.

2. Using a scoop or a spoon, portion out 2 to 3¼ oz [60 to 90 g] of buttercream (about ¼ cup) onto the centers of half of the cake circles—the amount depends on your love of buttercream. Then place their corresponding cake circles on top and gently press the sandwich cakes together. Using your finger, wipe the buttercream all around the edges of the cakes, ensuring there are no gaps in the filling.

3. Chill the sandwich cakes in the refrigerator for at least 10 minutes to allow the buttercream to firm up. This prevents it from squishing out the sides when enrobing the cakes in their chocolate coating.

cont'd

temper the chocolate for the coating

1. Line a baking sheet with parchment paper. Place two-thirds of the chopped chocolate in a double boiler or heatproof bowl set over a saucepan of simmering water. Melt the chocolate about three-quarters of the way, then remove it from the heat; at this stage, do not let the chocolate exceed 100°F to 110°F [35°C to 43°C] on an instant-read thermometer. Once off the heat, continue to stir until all the chocolate is melted.

2. Stir in the remaining third of the chopped chocolate, a little at a time, letting it melt before adding more; you may not use all of it. Keep stirring until the melted chocolate is between 85°F and 90°F [30°C and 32°C]. Once it reaches this temperature, do not add any more chopped chocolate. Continue stirring and let it cool to 82°F [28°C].

3. Once the melted chocolate is at 82°F [28°C], place it back over the simmering water. Reheat to 88°F to 92°F [31°C to 33°C] and remove the bowl from the heat.

4. Spread a small spoonful of chocolate on a piece of parchment paper. If it dries quickly with a glossy finish and no streaks, the chocolate is in temper. If it looks dull or streaky, re-temper the chocolate. Heat it to between 85°F and 90°F [30°C and 32°C] and then stir and let it cool to 82°F [28°C]. Reheat to 88°F to 92°F [31°C to 33°C] and remove the bowl from the heat and test again.

5. Once the melted chocolate has been tempered, it must be used before it cools and sets. If it cools to 84°F to 86°F [29°C to 30°C] and is still fairly liquid, it can be reheated to a liquid consistency for dipping; reheat it gently. If it has completely cooled and solidified, it should be re-tempered.

enrobe the cosmic cakes in chocolate coating

1. Working quickly, dip the chilled Cosmic Cakes in the tempered chocolate to coat them, letting any excess chocolate drip off as much as possible. Set the enrobed cakes on the prepared baking sheet.

2. Continue until all the Cosmic Cakes are enrobed, pausing as necessary to reheat the tempered chocolate once it has cooled to 84°F to 86°F [29°C to 30°C]. Be sure to check the temperature of the chocolate as you enrobe, as the chilled Cosmic Cakes will cool the chocolate quickly. Store enrobed Cosmic Cakes in an airtight container in the refrigerator for up to 5 days or in the freezer for up to 2 months. Bring to room temperature before enjoying.

AMAZING BURGER BUNS (FOR AMAZING DADS)

makes 12 buns

Falling right around (or sometimes on) the first official day of summer means Father's Day celebrations often include grilling food.

Depending on where you live, you might call it a cookout or perhaps a barbecue, but either way, if burgers are on the menu, these Amazing Burger Buns should be too. They have a golden color and a rich, soft texture—you'll be amazed by just how much butter you knead into the dough and by how much a delicious brioche bun can elevate a burger.

Making egg-and-butter-rich brioche, in whatever form, for whatever use, is an accomplishment. The father in your life will be impressed and appreciative. It's definitely a dough worth mastering, but it may take some practice. This recipe is best made over two days. On day one, mix, ferment, and fold the brioche dough; on day two, shape the dough into burger buns, proof them, and then bake them.

day 1: make the dough

1. On a cutting board, cut the room-temperature butter into small pieces and set aside. The butter for the dough needs to be pliable but not creamed, melted, or so cold that it is hard and brittle.

2. In a medium mixing bowl, add the water, eggs, sugar, and yeast and stir with a wooden spoon to combine. Add half of the flour and stir well, until the mixture is mostly smooth and has a thick, batter-like consistency. Add the rest of the flour and the salt and stir until the mixture is a thick paste, scraping down the sides of the bowl as needed.

cont'd

DOUGH

1 cup plus 6½ Tbsp [315 g] unsalted butter, room temperature
7½ Tbsp [115 g] water, cold
5 large eggs
5 Tbsp [75 g] granulated sugar
1 Tbsp plus 2 tsp instant yeast
4⅓ cups [615 g] all-purpose flour, plus more for dusting
2½ tsp fine sea salt

EGG WASH

1 large egg
1 egg yolk
1 Tbsp water
5 Tbsp [45 g] untoasted sesame seeds for garnish, optional

Which came first, Mother's Day or Father's Day? Interestingly, the American version of Father's Day was created after Mother's Day. Sonora Scott Dodd was inspired to create Father's Day soon after hearing about the creation of Mother's Day. She admired her father, a Civil War veteran, widower two times over, and single father of fourteen, and she suggested to the Spokane, Washington, Ministerial Alliance that a day to honor fathers should be established. She proposed her own father's birthday of June 5. The Alliance instead chose the third Sunday in June, and the first Father's Day was celebrated on June 19, 1910.

Originally, Father's Day traditions closely resembled those of Mother's Day, with flowers and gift-giving being common practice. Opponents of the day complained that the day attempted to sentimentalize and tame manliness, and eventually traditions shifted toward activities that, at the time, were considered to be especially masculine (fishing, golfing, and building things, for example) and thus the custom of grilling on Father's Day was born. While these days we don't subscribe to postwar gender stereotypes, grilling for Dad on Father's Day is still exceedingly popular.

3. Scrape the dough out of the bowl onto a clean, lightly floured work surface and knead for 8 minutes or until you have a successful windowpane test indicating sufficient gluten development (see page 244 for more information). The dough will be sticky at this stage of the kneading process; to help with the stickiness, use a bench scraper to scrape the dough off your work surface and your hands as you knead. Also, the dough will gain some integrity and smoothness if, after kneading it for 3 to 5 minutes, you let it rest for 2 minutes. Gather it in a ball and let it sit on your work surface. Return to it after a couple of minutes and continue to knead it. Do not add more flour because it will change the texture of the end product.

4. Continue to knead and add the small pieces of pliable butter to the dough in four additions, kneading after each addition until the butter is fully incorporated. It may seem like a bit of a buttery mess. Don't worry—the next steps will help it transform into a more traditional-looking dough.

5. Place the kneaded dough in a bowl lightly coated in neutral oil or nonstick cooking spray, cover with plastic wrap, and ferment it in the refrigerator for 1 hour.

6. After 1 hour, remove the dough from the refrigerator; it will be slightly puffy. Scrape the dough out of the bowl onto a floured work surface, gently form it into an approximate rectangle, and give the dough a letter fold (see the diagram on page 245).

7. Place the folded dough back in the lightly oiled bowl, cover with plastic wrap, and ferment again in the refrigerator for 1 hour.

8. After 1 hour, do another letter fold of the dough. Refrigerate the folded dough in the bowl, covered with plastic wrap, for at least 1 hour before shaping, if you are making the buns that same day. This is a good point in the process to stop and resume on another day. The dough, once fermented and folded, can be held in the refrigerator for up to 3 days before proceeding with the next steps.

day 2: make and bake the buns

1. When you are ready to use your dough, remove it from the refrigerator and divide it into twelve equal pieces, each one weighing about 4 oz [115 g].

2. Line two baking sheets with parchment paper. Gently round each piece into a ball and place them spaced apart on the prepared baking sheets, 6 balls of dough per sheet, then cover them loosely with plastic wrap.

3. Proof the covered dough balls at room temperature for 2 to 2½ hours, or until the dough passes the touch test: Gently press the pad of a fingertip into the dough and remove it; the indentation should slowly come back, most but not all of the way.

4. While the buns are proofing, preheat the oven to 350°F [180°C] at least 20 minutes before baking, and prepare the egg wash.

5. In a small bowl, make the egg wash by whisking the egg and egg yolk together until smooth, then add the water and whisk again. Right before putting them in the oven, brush each bun thoroughly with egg wash and garnish with sesame seeds, if desired.

6. Bake the buns for 18 to 20 minutes, or until golden brown. Check their internal temperature with a digital thermometer; it should be at least 190°F [88°C]. Transfer the buns to a wire rack to cool completely to room temperature before enjoying. Store baked burger buns in an airtight container or bag at room temperature for up to 3 days or in the freezer for up to 3 months. Thaw frozen buns at room temperature. The buns can be eaten at room temperature or warmed before use.

JUNETEENTH

Juneteenth is an important day in our nation's history that was declared a national holiday while we were writing this book. Since 2019, Zingerman's Roadhouse has been marking Juneteenth and exploring African American culinary traditions by hosting a special commemorative dinner together with guest speakers, so we thought it would be fitting to share a couple of the Roadhouse's recipes to serve on the day: Spider Bread (facing) and Black-Eyed Pea and Sweet Potato Salad (page 87).

Juneteenth commemorates the anniversary of June 19, 1865, the day when, at the end of the Civil War, the last enslaved African Americans living in Texas finally received word from the victorious Union Army arriving in Galveston that slavery had been abolished in the Confederate states, thereby freeing them from bondage. While the news of their liberation had come more than two years after president Abraham Lincoln signed the Emancipation Proclamation into law on January 1, 1863, that did not deter them from celebrating their freedom with instantaneous prayer, feasting, song, and dance on the consequential day.

Also known as Freedom Day, Emancipation Day, and Jubilee Day, Juneteenth is a day of remembrance, reflection, and cultural celebration that African Americans have been observing since 1865. Juneteenth festivities across the country vary from region to region, and even family to family. But what unites all the day's barbecues, parties, parades, rodeos, and street fairs celebrating Black independence and culture—and is central to any Juneteenth observance—is the sharing of food, in particular food that pays homage to the culinary traditions of the African diaspora to America that was spurred by the transatlantic slave trade from the sixteenth to the nineteenth centuries.

Every year on June 19, Juneteenth revelers across the country gather to feast on a customary barbecue with all the fixings (for good luck and prosperity)—smoked and grilled sauce-covered meats, greens, black-eyed peas, sweet potatoes, slaws and salads, and cornbread—as well as an assortment of ruby-hued foods and drinks, including red drink, red beans and rice, watermelon, and red velvet cake, all of which symbolize and honor the history and culinary traditions of enslaved African Americans. The color red evokes, on the one hand, the cultural memory of all the suffering and bloodshed endured in this country by enslaved Africans and African Americans throughout the period of slavery and the Civil War. And on a more philosophical note, red acknowledges the culinary traditions and goods—most notably hibiscus—that enslaved Africans brought with them to America. For many of them, especially among the Yoruba and the Kongo people of West and Central Africa, respectively, the color red was of great philosophical and spiritual value, taking on several meanings—sacrifice, transition, and power being the most potent.

SPIDER BREAD

serves 8

Zingerman's Roadhouse's Spider Bread is a unique melding of New England– and Southern-style cornbread, so it might not be a cornbread you're used to. As Zingerman's cofounder Ari Weinzweig explains, it's first cooked in a skillet, preferably cast iron (the name comes from three-legged cast-iron pans called spiders, in which breads like this one were originally made), and it has a swirl of heavy cream baked into the batter that gives it a custardy texture. The Roadhouse's version is especially good because they make it with Anson Mills field-ripened, freshly milled sweet cornmeal from South Carolina. If you plan ahead, you too can order some from Anson Mills. Adapted from Zingerman's Roadhouse.

1 cup [230 g] whole milk	1½ tsp fine sea salt
2 tsp apple cider vinegar	¾ tsp baking powder
2 eggs	¼ tsp baking soda
½ cup [70 g] all-purpose flour	2 Tbsp unsalted butter
½ cup [80 g] coarsely ground cornmeal	1 cup [230 g] heavy whipping cream
¼ cup [50 g] granulated sugar	

1. In a small bowl, whisk together the milk, vinegar, and eggs. In a medium bowl, whisk together the flour, cornmeal, sugar, salt, baking powder, and baking soda. Make a well in the center of the flour mixture, then gradually pour in the milk and egg mixture, stirring until well combined.

2. Warm an ovenproof 10 in [25 cm] skillet over medium-low heat. Add the butter, swirling the skillet as it melts to coat the bottom of the pan. Pour the batter into the skillet and cook for 2 to 3 minutes, or until bubbles begin to form around the edges, then remove from the heat.

3. Starting in the center of the skillet and working toward the outside, slowly pour the heavy cream in a swirl pattern into the batter. Bake on the middle rack of the oven for 20 to 25 minutes, or until the bread is lightly golden around the edges with a soft center. Take care not to overbake, or the bread will lose its custardy texture.

4. Serve warm (in which case it will resemble spoon bread), or cool completely, then cut into wedges for serving. This is best eaten fresh, straight from the oven. If you have some leftover, refrigerate it for up to a couple of days and reheat to enjoy.

VARIATIONS

Although these are not traditional, we couldn't stop ourselves from playing and came up with these two innovations.

Bacon and Sage: Add 4 strips of cooked bacon, roughly chopped, and 10 sage leaves, chopped, to the mixed batter.

Bacon, Cheddar, and Chile: Add 4 strips of cooked bacon, roughly chopped; ⅓ cup [25 g] of shredded Cheddar cheese; and a 4 oz [115 g] can of drained diced green chiles to the mixed batter.

BLACK-EYED PEA AND SWEET POTATO SALAD

serves 6 to 8 as a side dish

Black-eyed peas are a Southern staple, and they're summer-ready in this colorful salad tossed with bitter greens, sweet potatoes, and a sorghum vinaigrette; it also makes for a perfect side dish for a celebratory barbecue. If you're not yet familiar with sorghum syrup, it's made from the stalks of the sorghum plant and is a staple of the middle South. As you might guess from the name, it is sweet, but with a complex flavor profile. Enjoy the rest of the bottle of syrup in a traditional manner—on biscuits for breakfast. The Roadhouse gets sorghum from the great folks at Muddy Pond, deep in the hills of Tennessee, midway between Nashville and Knoxville.

The Roadhouse makes this salad with young mustard greens, but if you have trouble finding them, substitute another tender bitter green, like watercress or arugula. Sturdier greens can work as well, like mature mustard greens or kale; you just might want to shred them instead of roughly chopping. Adapted from Zingerman's Roadhouse.

SALAD

¾ cup [115 g] diced yellow onions

¾ cup [90 g] diced red peppers

1 Tbsp olive oil

1 cup [200 g] uncooked black-eyed peas

4 cups [910 g] water

1 to 2 [210 g] medium sweet potatoes

½ tsp fine sea salt

DRESSING

2 Tbsp apple cider vinegar

1½ Tbsp sorghum syrup

1 tsp Dijon mustard

1½ Tbsp minced shallots

¼ tsp fine sea salt

¼ cup [100 g] olive oil

5 cups [125 g] roughly chopped bitter greens

Freshly ground black pepper

make the salad

1. In a medium pot over medium heat, sauté the onions and peppers in olive oil for 10 to 15 minutes, or until the onions are tender and translucent. Add the black-eyed peas and water. If that's not enough water to cover the peas, add a little more. Simmer, uncovered, for 35 to 45 minutes, or until the black-eyed peas are tender, then remove the pot from the heat and allow to cool. The water may be completely absorbed at this point, but if it is not, drain any remaining water.

2. While the peas are simmering, cook the sweet potatoes. Bring a few inches of water to a boil in a medium pot fitted with a steamer basket. Peel the sweet potatoes, cut them into ½ in [12 mm] chunks, and place them in the steamer. Cover, lower the heat to medium, and steam for 10 to 15 minutes, or until fork-tender. Gently combine the black-eyed peas, sweet potatoes, and salt.

make the dressing and toss the salad

1. In a small bowl, whisk together the vinegar, sorghum, mustard, shallots, and salt, then slowly whisk in the olive oil.

2. In a large bowl, gently mix together the black-eyed peas and sweet potatoes, dressing, and greens. Season to taste with black pepper. Store the salad, undressed, in an airtight container in the refrigerator for up to 3 days. Dress and toss the salad just before serving. Leftovers of dressed salad can still be refrigerated and enjoyed the next day; the greens will just be slightly wilted.

TIP!

For a slightly different texture, try roasting the sweet potatoes. Preheat the oven to 425°F [220°C]. Chop the sweet potatoes into ½ in [12 mm] chunks, then toss them with 1 to 2 Tbsp of olive oil on a rimmed baking sheet. Bake for 30 to 40 minutes, stirring midway through, or until tender and the edges are caramelized.

SUMMER FLING COCONUT AND LIME COFFEE CAKE

makes one large bundt cake

"You put the lime in the coconut ... " and you make a surprise hit coffee cake (not unlike Harry Nilsson's surprise hit song, which is now probably stuck in your head; sorry about that!). Usher in summer breezes with this fresh and zesty coffee cake loaded with coconut and lime. It's just right for breakfast, dessert, a lazy afternoon picnic ... just about anytime, really.

We are often asked who does our recipe development. The answer is sometimes disappointing to people because there's no star product designer. We work together generating ideas, testing recipes, providing feedback, and then tweaking until we get them just right. The idea for this cake started with Sara Green, who worked at the Bakehouse for many years in our pastry kitchen and thought these flavors would be excellent for a summer coffee cake. Thank you, Sara!

FIRST DAY OF SUMMER

By the first official day of summer, Michiganders are already soaking in the season. The balmy temps nudge us outside to turn our faces up to the sun (with sunscreen on, of course) and urge us to make dishes that will send our tastebuds on a tropical vacation. This coffee cake is one of our favorites, just right for being passed between the hands of family, friends, and neighbors at one of the many gatherings that happen during the warm summer months.

½ cup plus 2 Tbsp [60 g] unsweetened shredded coconut

2 cups plus 1 Tbsp [290 g] all-purpose flour, plus more for coating the pan

1¾ cups plus 2 Tbsp [380 g] granulated sugar

1 cup plus 1 Tbsp [235 g] unsalted butter, room temperature

1 cup [240 g] sour cream

⅓ cup [115 g] coconut compound, packed (see page 236 for more information)

2 large eggs

1 tsp vanilla extract

1 tsp lime oil

1 tsp [5 g] fine sea salt

½ tsp baking soda

1. Preheat the oven to 350°F [180°C].

2. Toast the shredded coconut on a baking sheet for 5 to 7 minutes, or until golden brown. Set aside to cool.

3. Thoroughly coat a 10-cup [2.4 L] Bundt pan evenly with nonstick cooking spray, then coat the inside all over with flour. Turn out the pan to dispose of any excess flour. Set aside.

4. In a large mixing bowl, combine the sugar and butter with a wooden spoon until the mixture becomes light and creamy. If using a stand mixer, use the paddle attachment and mix on medium speed. Scrape the sides of the bowl as needed. Add the sour cream and coconut compound to the butter and sugar mixture and mix to combine. Add the eggs, one at a time, mixing thoroughly after each one until the mixture is homogeneous, then add the vanilla extract and lime oil and mix to combine.

5. In a medium mixing bowl, whisk together the flour, salt, and baking soda until well combined.

6. Add all of the dry ingredients to the bowl with the wet ingredients and stir with a wooden spoon until smooth. If using a stand mixer, mix on low speed. Scrape the sides of the bowl as needed. Add the shredded coconut and mix until evenly distributed in the batter.

7. Pour the batter into the prepared Bundt pan, spread evenly with a spatula, and bake for 65 to 70 minutes, or until a tester or toothpick inserted in the center of the cake comes out clean.

8. Cool in the pan for 15 minutes, then turn the cake out onto a rack or a serving platter to cool completely. Store, covered in plastic wrap, at room temperature for up to 2 weeks or in the freezer for up to 3 months.

INDEPENDENCE DAY

Though we tend to think of pie as being a quintessential American dessert, British tradition claims the first cherry pie was served to Queen Elizabeth I in the late sixteenth century. So, adopting tart cherry pie as an Independence Day tribute might make it a subtle nose-thumbing to our separation from Great Britain. It is, at any rate, a tastier act of defiance than Boston Harbor–steeped tea.

CHEERY CHERRY PIE

makes one double-crust pie

Tart cherry pie is a Midwestern staple, and a midsummer harvest of Michigan cherries makes our Cheery Cherry Pie a shoo-in for Fourth of July gatherings. Not to mention, its cheery red filling is naturally patriotic! Instant ClearJel is great for thickening fruit pie fillings without impacting the flavor or color of the filling, but if you can't find it, you can use the same amount of cornstarch instead. The slight downsides of using cornstarch are that it can give the filling a cloudy appearance. Serve slices with a scoop of ice cream or a dollop of fresh whipped cream, if desired.

PIE DOUGH

2½ cups plus 1 Tbsp [360 g] all-purpose flour

1 tsp fine sea salt

1 cup [220 g] unsalted butter, cold

⅓ cup [80 g] water, cold

FILLING

7 cups [910 g] frozen tart cherries, thawed (measure frozen and thaw before using)

¾ cup [150 g] granulated sugar

¼ cup plus ½ Tbsp [45 g] instant ClearJel (see headnote)

1½ tsp lemon juice

EGG WASH

1 large egg

1 egg yolk

1 Tbsp water

1 to 2 Tbsp demerara sugar for garnish (optional)

make the pie dough

1. In a large mixing bowl, mix together the flour and salt with a fork.

2. Cut the cold butter into ¼ in [6 mm] cubes and add three-quarters of the cubes to the bowl. Cut the butter into the flour mixture using a pastry blender, two knives, or your hands. Cut or work the butter into the flour mixture until it looks like coarse cornmeal. If using your hands, break the butter pieces up in your fingers and rub the butter and flour together. Pick the mixture up between your hands and rub your palms together as if they're cold. This will break down the butter and rub it all over the flour.

The flour will take on a creamy yellow color during this step. When you pick the mixture up in your hand, it should be possible to squeeze it into a mass that will hold together. When you see the color change and the mixture holds together when squeezed, you know that you've worked the butter in enough. Work quickly so that the butter doesn't become warm. The goal of this step is to cover the flour with fat so that the gluten strands are not able to develop.

3. Add the remaining quarter of the butter and cut it into the mixture as before. These butter pieces should be left in pea-size chunks to create flakiness in the final pie crust—when they melt during baking, they create steam, which separates layers of the coated flour, making flakes of crust.

cont'd

4. Create a well in the center of the flour mixture and add the cold water, using a fork, to blend it in. The flour mixture will still be crumbly in the bowl, but it should look moist. If it still looks dry, add up to an additional 1 Tbsp of cold water until the mixture looks moistened but still crumbly.

If the butter has been rubbed into the dough adequately, the amount of water specified should be enough. More water is usually necessary only when the butter has not been adequately distributed. It's not desirable to add more water, because it tends to make a tougher crust.

5. Turn the mixture out onto a clean, unfloured work surface, form into a mound, and push out sections of dough across the work surface with the heel of your hand. We call this "schmearing." Push each section of dough once, not twice. Make sure to schmear enough so that the dough loses its dry, crumbly appearance. At the end of the schmearing, all of the pie crust will be pushed out flat on the work surface.

6. Fold the dough back onto itself with a bench scraper. Gather it into a ball, pressing it firmly so it holds together.

7. Cut it into two equal pieces, shape each one into a disk about 1 in [2.5 cm] thick, and wrap with plastic wrap. Chill the dough in the refrigerator for at least 1 hour before rolling it out.

make the filling

1. Place a colander over a medium mixing bowl and strain the thawed cherries, reserving the juice. Check for pits. You can lightly press on the cherries to help release more juices. Use 1 cup [230 g] of juice for the filling; discard any extra. If you don't have enough, add water to get to the right amount. Keep the cherries in the colander over the bowl to let any remaining juice drain while you proceed to the next step.

2. In a medium saucepan over medium heat, combine the sugar, ClearJel, and strained cherry juice together and stir to dissolve. Bring the mixture to a boil, stirring constantly. Boil for 1 minute. The mixture should be thickened and, if using ClearJel, will have a clear and shiny appearance (see headnote). Remove the saucepan from the heat.

3. Add the lemon juice and thawed cherries to the thickened cherry juice mixture and stir to combine. Cool to room temperature before using. The filling can be prepared ahead of time and kept covered and refrigerated for up to 5 days.

roll out the bottom crust

1. Preheat the oven to 400°F [200°C]. Remove one piece of the chilled dough from the refrigerator. While the dough is still in the plastic wrap, firmly but gently tap on it with a rolling pin until it is flexible but still cold. Lightly flour the work surface. Place the unwrapped disk of dough on the work surface and lightly dust the top of the disk with flour.

2. Using a rolling pin, start rolling the dough from the center to the edge, away from you. Do not use too much pressure, or the dough will crack. If this happens, brush away any excess flour near the cracking area and press the dough back together.

3. Stop and give the dough a one-eighth turn. This rotation will prevent the dough from sticking to the work surface and will help make a perfect circle.

4. Reflour the work surface and the top of the dough to prevent the dough from sticking. Continue to roll the dough until it's about ⅛ in [4 mm] thick and the circle is about 1 in [2.5 cm] wider than the top diameter of the 9 in [23 cm] pie plate you will be using. Flour is your friend in this process. Use it liberally to avoid sticking.

5. When the crust has reached the correct size, use a pastry brush to brush away any extra flour from the top of the pie dough. Turn the dough over and brush off any extra flour from the bottom. One way to do this is to roll the dough up on your rolling pin and then unwind it with the bottom surface now facing up.

assemble and bake the pie

1. Gently roll the dough loosely around the rolling pin. Position the edge of the dough over the edge of the pie plate and unroll the dough. Gently ease the dough down into the pie plate, making sure not to stretch the dough. Pour the cooled cherry filling into the pie.

2. Make the egg wash by whisking together the egg, egg yolk, and water until well combined. Lightly brush the top outer edge of the pie dough (bottom crust) with the egg wash.

3. Using the second piece of pie dough, roll out the top crust, using the same method as before, until it's ⅛ in [4 mm] thick and slightly larger than the top diameter of the pie plate so that it will comfortably cover your filling. Roll up the top crust loosely around your rolling pin and, starting at one side of the pie, gently unroll the crust over the filling. Trim the crusts, leaving 1 in [2.5 cm] of excess to form the border.

4. Fold the excess dough from the bottom crust over the top crust and seal by lightly pressing both layers together with your fingers against the top of the pie plate. Finish the edge with your choice of decorative crimping.

5. Brush the entire top of the pie with egg wash and cut four 2 in [5 cm] vents in the top of the crust at even intervals to allow the steam to escape as the pie bakes. There will be egg wash leftover. Sprinkle the top crust with demerara sugar, if desired.

6. Place the filled pie on a baking sheet lined with parchment paper and bake for 45 to 55 minutes. The pie juices should be bubbling in the center and the crust will take on a deep golden color. Do not under-bake; color is flavor in our world.

7. Let the pie cool to room temperature before serving (this will allow the juices to thicken). Pie dough can be stored, wrapped in disk form or fully rolled out, in the refrigerator for up to 5 days. It can also be frozen, well wrapped and preferably in an airtight container, in either form, for up to 3 months. Store the finished pie, covered, at room temperature for up to 5 days. This pie can also be frozen for up to 3 months.

FRESH FRUIT TART

makes one tart; Serves 8

In the summer, we like to use berries and stone fruits, but don't limit this recipe to one season; in the winter, use it to highlight citrus fruits. Stick with one type of fruit, or use a mix! We tend to slice anything strawberry-size or larger. This fruit tart is best eaten the same day as it's assembled, but if you like to work ahead, the crust and pastry cream can be made well in advance of assembling and serving the full tart.

make the pâte sucrée tart crust

1. In a medium mixing bowl, cream the butter, sugar, and salt together with a wooden spoon until the mixture is light and fluffy. If using a stand mixer, use the paddle attachment on medium speed for 2 to 3 minutes. Scrape down the sides of the bowl if necessary. Add the egg yolk and orange zest, if using, and continue mixing until the yolk is incorporated. Add all of the pastry flour to the bowl and mix only until the dough forms a ball. Knead with your hands a few times to ensure the ingredients are well incorporated into the dough.

2. Lightly coat the bottom and sides of the tart pan with nonstick cooking spray.

3. There are several methods you can use to put the dough into the tart pan. For each method, start by placing the tart pan on a baking sheet. This will make it much easier to handle when it is hot.

4. We like to crumble the dough around the tart pan, and, using our fingertips, press the dough on the bottom and up the sides of the pan to an even thickness, approximately ¼ in [6 mm]. If you'd rather roll it, form the dough into a disk, wrap it in plastic wrap, and refrigerate for at least 1 hour before rolling out. For detailed instructions on rolling out dough and placing it in the pan, see Roll Out the Bottom Crust in Cheery Cherry Pie (see page 92) or Roll Out the Pie Dough in Chocolate Chess Pie (see page 168).

cont'd

PÂTE SUCRÉE TART CRUST

½ cup [110 g] unsalted butter, room temperature

¼ cup [50 g] granulated sugar

⅛ tsp fine sea salt

1 egg yolk, room temperature

1 Tbsp fresh orange zest (optional)

1½ cups plus 1 Tbsp [220 g] pastry flour

PASTRY CREAM

1 cup [230 g] whole milk

¼ cup [35 g] cornstarch

5 egg yolks

1 cup [230 g] heavy cream

½ cup plus 1 Tbsp [115 g] granulated sugar

½ tsp vanilla bean paste (or one vanilla pod)

⅛ tsp fine sea salt

¼ cup [55 g] unsalted butter

1 tsp vanilla extract

APRICOT GLAZE

¼ cup [85 g] apricot preserves

2 Tbsp water

4 to 5 cups (weight will vary) fresh fruit, sliced if large

FARMERS' MARKET DAY

Michigan is an incredibly agriculturally diverse state, and our farmers' markets are overflowing with produce in the summertime. If you're anything like us, it's easy to find yourself wanting one of everything and buying more than you know what to do with. When that happens with fruit, we like to make a fruit tart to show off our bounty.

blind bake the tart crust

1. Preheat the oven to 350°F [180°C].

2. Using a fork, dock the crust all over the bottom and sides (see page 242). Line the crust with parchment paper, pressing it snugly against the bottom and sides. Fill with dried beans, rice, or pie weights, all the way up the edges to hold down the parchment paper and to support the dough on the sides so that it doesn't slip down during baking. It will take 3 to 4 cups of whatever weights you choose. (If using dried beans or rice, they cannot be used for any other purpose, and should be reserved exclusively for use as pie weights.)

3. Store pâte sucrée tart dough, wrapped in plastic wrap, in disk form or fully formed as a tart shell in the refrigerator for up to 5 days or in the freezer, well wrapped and preferably in an airtight container, for up to 3 months.

4. Bake the crust for 15 to 18 minutes, or until the edges of the crust are beginning to look dry, like they are no longer raw but are not coloring yet. Remove the parchment paper with the weights, then continue to bake the crust until well browned, another 18 to 20 minutes.

5. Remove from the oven and allow to cool completely before assembling the tart.

make the pastry cream

1. In a medium saucepan off heat, whisk together the milk and cornstarch until the cornstarch has dissolved. Still off heat, add the egg yolks and whisk until the egg yolks have been completely mixed in, then add the heavy cream, sugar, vanilla bean paste, and salt. If using a vanilla pod, split the pod in half lengthwise and, with the back of a paring knife, scrape out the seeds and add them to the cream.

2. Place the saucepan over medium heat and cook the mixture, stirring constantly with a whisk, and bring to a light boil. Continue to cook for 1 minute, stirring constantly.

3. Remove the pastry cream from the heat and pour it into a medium mixing bowl. Beat the pastry cream with a clean whisk until it cools slightly and becomes smooth and shiny. If using a stand mixer, use the whisk attachment and whip on medium speed for 4 minutes until it cools slightly. Add the butter and vanilla extract and whisk until smooth.

4. Place plastic wrap directly onto the surface of the pastry cream to prevent a skin from forming. Refrigerate and cool until at least room temperature, or for up to 5 days.

make the apricot glaze

1. Combine the preserves and water in a medium saucepan over medium heat and simmer until it has reduced and thickened to a jammy consistency. You can check the thickness by dipping a room-temperature metal spoon in the glaze; it should coat the spoon and not flow too quickly. Set aside to cool slightly while you assemble the tart.

assemble the tart

1. Spread the pastry cream into the tart shell, filling it about three-quarters full, and level it with an offset spatula.

2. Starting at the outside edge, decorate the tart with the fresh fruit, either randomly or in concentric overlapping circles. Try to cover all of the pastry cream with fruit so that no pastry cream is showing through.

3. After arranging the fruit, gently brush a light coat of warm apricot glaze on the fruit, rewarming it first if necessary. Try not to get any glaze on the tart shell. The idea is to make the fruit look shiny. If not serving the tart immediately, refrigerate. Take the chilled tart out about 30 minutes before serving to allow the fruit and pastry cream filling to come to room temperature, when the tart will be at its best. The tart can be covered and refrigerated for 2 days.

CARROT CAKE CUPCAKES WITH CREAM CHEESE FROSTING

makes 12 cupcakes

Since acquiring our stone mills, we've been making this carrot cake recipe with our freshly milled whole-grain flour. We've adjusted this recipe to work easily for you at home. You could be brave, buy a home mill, and use 100 percent whole-wheat flour though. We also use whole organic carrots that are washed and left unpeeled. And just in case you were wondering, carrot skin is not only just as edible as any other part of the carrot, but it's also full of flavor, nutrition, and fiber, so why throw it out?

Some easy and pretty decoration options include using fresh flowers, edible flowers, or elements from the cake, like a whole toasted walnut half and cinnamon or nutmeg scrapings. Be bold and decorate them with raw carrot curls! Or, go to page 35 and make our fondant and then create fondant decorations of your choice.

make the cupcakes

1. Preheat the oven to 350°F [180°C].

2. Toast the walnuts on a baking sheet for 10 to 12 minutes, or until fragrant and lightly colored; start checking them after 8 minutes. Allow the nuts to cool completely to room temperature, give them a rough chop, and set aside.

3. Line the cups of a standard 12-cup muffin pan with cupcake liners. If you prefer not to use liners, coat the cups and top of the pan with nonstick cooking spray. Set the prepared pan aside.

cont'd

CUPCAKES

⅓ cup [40 g] raw walnuts

1 cup [200 g] brown sugar, packed

¾ cup plus 1 Tbsp [180 g] unsalted butter, room temperature

2 large eggs

1 tsp vanilla extract

⅔ cup [90 g] all-purpose flour

½ cup plus 1 Tbsp [80 g] all-purpose whole-wheat flour

1 tsp ground cinnamon

½ tsp ground nutmeg

½ tsp baking powder

½ tsp baking soda

¼ tsp fine sea salt

2 cups [195 g] grated carrots

CREAM CHEESE FROSTING

½ cup plus 2 Tbsp [150 g] cream cheese, room temperature

⅔ cup [150 g] unsalted butter, room temperature

1½ tsp lemon juice, room temperature

1 tsp vanilla extract

3 cups [300 g] powdered sugar

WEDDINGS AND ANNIVERSARIES

In 2000, we established our Cake Studio at the Bakehouse and began specializing in custom-decorated celebration cakes. We wanted to bake celebratory desserts for the important life events of our community—weddings, anniversaries, birthdays, graduations, and showers, to name just a few—and being able to create custom-decorated cakes for every occasion has gone a long way toward fulfilling this mission.

One of the most fun aspects of our work in the Cake Studio is getting to participate in changing flavor and decorating trends for weddings and anniversaries, cupcakes being one of them. Some years during wedding season, it seems like that's all we make, either in lieu of a large, tiered, custom cake or as festive party favors. They are just so cute, not to mention easy to present, serve, and eat!

4. In a large mixing bowl, cream together the brown sugar and butter with a wooden spoon until light and fluffy. If using a stand mixer, use the paddle attachment and mix on medium speed. Add the eggs to the creamed butter mixture, one at a time, beating to incorporate each egg completely before adding the next one. Add the vanilla extract. The mixture will look separated, but this is okay!

5. In a separate medium mixing bowl, whisk together the flours, the cinnamon, nutmeg, baking powder, baking soda, and salt. Add the dry ingredients to the wet ingredients and mix until thoroughly combined. If using a stand mixer, use the paddle attachment and mix on low speed. Add the carrots and toasted walnuts and mix gently until they are evenly distributed and the batter is homogeneous. Divide the batter among the 12 muffin cups, filling each one two-thirds full. Portion out any remaining batter among the 12 cups.

6. Bake for 20 to 22 minutes. The cupcakes are done when they spring back when lightly pressed in the center and an inserted tester or toothpick comes out clean. Cool for 5 minutes in the pan, then transfer the cupcakes to a wire rack to cool completely to room temperature before frosting them.

make the cream cheese frosting

1. In a medium mixing bowl, beat the cream cheese with a wooden spoon until there are no lumps remaining. If using a stand mixer, use the paddle attachment and beat on medium speed. Add the butter and beat until smooth. Add the lemon juice and vanilla extract and stir to combine.

2. Using a sifter or fine-mesh sieve, sift the powdered sugar into the bowl and then mix the frosting until completely smooth. Take care not to mix for too long, as the frosting may become soupy and unable to hold its shape on the cupcakes. If this happens, chill the frosting in the refrigerator until it firms up to a usable consistency.

3. Pipe or spread the frosting on the cooled cupcakes. Decorate as you wish. Store frosted cupcakes in an airtight container in the refrigerator for up to 5 days. Allow them to come to room temperature before enjoying.

WHOLE-WHEAT FUNKY CHUNKY COOKIES

makes about 24 cookies

Once we began milling our own whole-grain flours, we found a surefire way to make our Funky Chunky Cookies even better. Our secret? We replaced traditional all-purpose flour with a freshly milled whole-wheat flour. We're bowled over by how much moister and more flavorful the cookies are now with their rich, chewy texture. They also keep for longer because the bran left in whole-wheat flour holds moisture and makes the cookies more nutritious (not that it really matters because this is a treat, after all!). If you have trouble tracking down these two different freshly milled whole-wheat flours, feel free to use a 100 percent whole-wheat flour of your choice for both.

Some of us were a tad skeptical about making this switch, thinking that whole-grain cookies, and sweets in general, are often heavy and dry. Not so! If you have a home mill, grind your own whole-grain flour. If you don't, we highly recommend it. Milling your own flour is as easy as grinding coffee beans, and the improved flavor and texture is well worth it. We're on a mission to make home mills as common as food processors.

1 cup [120 g] raw walnuts	1 tsp vanilla extract
1 cup [200 g] brown sugar, packed	1½ cups [210 g] whole-wheat flour
½ cup plus 1 Tbsp [125 g] unsalted butter, room temperature	½ tsp baking soda
	½ tsp fine sea salt
1 large egg, room temperature	1½ cups [240 g] semisweet chocolate chunks
1 egg yolk, room temperature	

1. Preheat the oven to 350°F [180°C]. Line a baking sheet with parchment paper.

2. Toast the walnuts on a separate baking sheet for 8 to 10 minutes, or until fragrant and golden brown.

3. In a medium mixing bowl, cream together the sugar and butter until well combined. If using a stand mixer, use the paddle attachment and mix on medium speed.

4. In a small bowl, mix the egg, yolk, and vanilla extract together. Slowly stream the egg mixture into the butter mixture, mixing until light and creamy. Scrape the sides of the bowl as needed.

5. In a separate medium mixing bowl, whisk together the flour, baking soda, and salt until well combined. Add the flour mixture to the creamed mixture and mix by hand, using a wooden spoon, or with a stand mixer at low speed, until the dough is well combined. Add the walnuts and chocolate chunks and mix just until they are evenly distributed in the cookie dough.

6. Using a small ice cream scoop or a spoon, portion out 24 cookies and place them on the prepared baking sheet 2 in [5 cm] apart so that they have room to spread while they bake.

7. Flatten the balls lightly with the palm of your hand. Bake for 10 to 12 minutes or until the cookies have browned lightly around their edges. For soft cookies, remove them from the oven when the centers of the cookies are still soft. For crisp cookies, bake them until the center of the cookies are just set.

8. Transfer the cookies to a wire rack to cool. Enjoy them warm or at room temperature. Store the cookies in an airtight container at room temperature for up to 5 days or freeze them for up to 3 months. Thaw frozen cookies at room temperature before enjoying.

NATIONAL CHOCOLATE CHIP COOKIE DAY

We are forever trying to make our recipes better. Chocolate chip cookies, arguably the most beloved American cookie, is a tough one to improve upon or find a distinctive version of among the many great recipes already available. But that hasn't stopped us from trying, and we think this one is a winner. Give it a try on August 4, which is National Chocolate Chip Cookie Day, or any day you're looking for an old spin on a new favorite.

Marking the unofficial end to summer, Labor Day weekend is the perfect time to celebrate with a fruit cobbler. Ours is named with a nod to the colors of University of Michigan and another end-of-summer milestone, when the city explodes with students returning to campus.

MAIZE AND BLUE COBBLER

makes one cobbler

A nod to the University of Michigan's school colors, maize and blue, this cobbler is made with fresh Michigan peaches and blueberries, and a biscuit topping made with freshly milled Michigan soft white whole-wheat flour. While peaches are still in season here in Michigan in early September, we know they might not be in other areas, so frozen peaches and blueberries can also be used in this recipe in place of the fresh fruit—or you can substitute local fruit that is in season. Serve topped with a scoop of ice cream or a dollop of fresh whipped cream, if desired.

FRUIT FILLING

¾ cup [175 g] water, room temperature

¼ cup [50 g] brown sugar, packed

3 Tbsp granulated sugar

1½ Tbsp cornstarch

1½ Tbsp lemon juice

3 cups [375 g] sliced peaches

¾ cup [105 g] blueberries

BISCUITS

1 cup plus 2 Tbsp [160 g] soft white whole-wheat flour (whole-wheat all-purpose flour)

1 Tbsp plus 1 tsp granulated sugar

2 tsp baking powder

½ tsp fine sea salt

¼ cup [55 g] unsalted butter, cold

6 Tbsp (90 g) whole milk, cold

6 Tbsp (90 g) heavy cream, cold

TOPPING

½ cup [55 g] toasted pecans (optional)

3 Tbsp demerara sugar (optional)

make the filling

1. Preheat the oven to 400°F [200°C]. Lightly coat a 9 in [23 cm] baking pan or dish with nonstick cooking spray.

2. In a large mixing bowl, combine the water, sugars, cornstarch, and lemon juice. Mix well to combine, then add the peaches and toss well to coat. This mixture will be thin. Transfer to the prepared baking pan and sprinkle the blueberries evenly over the top of the peach mixture.

3. Bake for 20 to 25 minutes or until the very edges of the mixture are bubbling. This bubbling is what activates and thickens the cornstarch.

make the biscuits

1. While the filling bakes, in a medium mixing bowl, whisk together the flour, sugar, baking powder, and salt. Cut the cold butter into ¼ in [6 mm] cubes and add it to the bowl, tossing to coat.

2. Begin breaking down the butter chunks by either cutting with a pastry blender or squeezing them between your thumbs and fingers and rubbing into the flour. Most of the butter should be in large, flat shards about the size of a dime. This mixture will have a floury appearance.

3. Create a well in the center of the dry ingredients and add the cold milk and heavy cream. Using a fork, blend in the wet ingredients; the dough will seem quite wet, the texture of a drop biscuit.

cont'd

finish the cobbler

1. Sprinkle the toasted pecans, if using, over the warm fruit mixture. Using a spoon or a portioner, drop golf ball–size pieces of the biscuit dough onto the filling and flatten the dough pieces into disks gently with your fingers until they are ¼ to ½ in [6 to 12 mm] thick. Don't worry about covering the entire surface of the fruit with the biscuit dough; just aim to cover most of it. These disks of dough across the top of the fruit mixture create your "cobbles."

2. Sprinkle demerara sugar, if using, on top of the biscuit topping to add flavor and texture.

3. Bake for 20 to 25 minutes, or until the biscuit topping is golden brown and the fruit mixture is bubbling on the sides of the pan. Don't be afraid to let the biscuit topping get more deeply brown; this will add a nice toasty flavor to the entire dessert.

4. Serve warm or at room temperature. Cobbler is best enjoyed the same day that it's baked but can be stored, covered with plastic wrap, at room temperature for up to 2 days or in the refrigerator for up to 5 days. Reheat the cobbler before serving.

RASPBERRY PATTI POCKETS

makes 8 pastries

We start with our flakiest, all-butter pie dough, fill it with raspberry preserves, bake until golden brown, and garnish with a drizzle of raspberry glaze. Of course, if raspberry isn't your jam, swap in your preserves of choice. It's a simple recipe, so use delicious butter and preserves to make them shine. Whatever you choose, these little hand pies are sure to satisfy.

DOUGH

1 cup [140 g] cake flour

1 cup [140 g] all-purpose flour, plus more for dusting

2 tsp granulated sugar

¾ tsp fine sea salt

1 cup [220 g] unsalted butter, cold

¼ Tbsp [60 g] water, cold

FILLING

½ cup [160 g] raspberry preserves

EGG WASH

1 large egg

1 egg yolk

1 Tbsp water

GLAZE

½ cup [60 g] powdered sugar

2 Tbsp raspberry preserves

1 Tbsp water, warm

For an extra-special send-off on the first day of school, try our take on a certain well-known hand-held packaged breakfast pastry. Treat the kids to them as a sweet surprise, or turn them into a family baking project and make them a day or two ahead of time. The dough can be made days ahead and refrigerated or frozen. Completely assembled, unbaked pockets can be made a couple of days ahead as well, and completely baked pockets can be warmed up the morning of school. This is a flexible recipe that will add fun on that first day back.

make the pie dough

1. In a medium bowl, whisk together the flours, granulated sugar, and salt. Cut the cold butter into ¼ in [6 mm] cubes and add it to the bowl. Working quickly, with a pastry blender, cut the butter into the flour until the mixture looks like coarse cornmeal with pea-size pieces of butter. If you do not have a pastry blender, you can use two butter knives or your hands. If using your hands, break the pieces of butter up in your fingers and rub the butter and flour together. Pick the mixture up between your hands and rub your palms together as if they're cold. This will break down the butter and rub it all over the flour.

The color of the flour will become a creamy yellow. A good way to tell if you've broken the butter down adequately is to compare the color of your flour to that from the bag. It should look notably more yellow. If you do not rub the butter in enough at this stage it will seem dry in the next stage and you'll be tempted to add in more water. Added water is what makes the dough tough so take your time in this step and work the butter in.

2. Create a well in the center of the flour mixture and add the cold water. Mix with a fork until a dough forms. Be patient; it may take a couple of minutes for the dough to come together. You can use your hands and actually knead the dough to get it to come together. Adding more water will make the dough tough so it's best to avoid it. The dough should have streaks of butter and no dusty flour.

3. Place the ball of dough onto a large piece of plastic wrap and flatten it into a rectangle about ½ in [12 mm] thick. Wrap the dough in the plastic wrap and chill in the refrigerator for 30 minutes to 1 hour before rolling it out. The dough can be kept refrigerated for a week at this point or frozen for up to several months if you'd like.

cont'd

roll out and cut the pie dough

1. Remove the dough from the refrigerator. While the dough is still wrapped in plastic, firmly but gently tap on it with a rolling pin until it is flexible but still cold. Lightly dust the work surface with flour. Place the unwrapped rectangle of dough on the surface and lightly dust the top of the dough with flour.

2. Using a rolling pin, start rolling the dough away from you. Stop and give the dough a quarter turn every so often to prevent the dough from sticking to the work surface and to help you maintain the rectangular shape. Flour is your friend in this process; use it liberally to avoid sticking.

3. Re-flour the work surface and the top of the dough as needed to prevent the dough from sticking. Continue to roll and rotate the dough until it's about ⅛ in [3 mm] thick and a rectangle that is 12 by 16 in [30 by 41 cm].

4. When the dough has reached the correct size, use a pastry brush to remove any extra flour from the top of the dough. Turn the dough over and brush off any extra flour from the bottom. Cut your dough into sixteen rectangles, each 3 by 4 in [7.5 by 10 cm]. (You will have leftover dough scraps that can be baked with cinnamon and sugar or around slices of apples.)

assemble the pastries

1. Preheat the oven to 400°F [200°C]. Line a baking sheet with parchment paper.

2. In the middle of each bottom piece of dough, spoon 1 Tbsp of preserves. Use your finger or a pastry brush to lightly wet the edges of the bottom piece with a small amount of water. Place a top piece of dough over the filling and press around the edges to seal the two pieces of dough together. Press the edges with a fork to make sure the layers stick together, and also to give the edges a decorated look. Place the pastry on the prepared baking sheet and repeat with the remaining dough rectangles.

3. In a small bowl, make the egg wash by whisking together the egg, egg yolk, and water until well combined. Using a pastry brush, generously apply egg wash to each pastry. Remove any pooling egg wash, however, to avoid having scrambled eggs on your pastry. Poke the tops of the pastries with a fork to provide steam vents. If your pockets are very soft, refrigerate them for at least 30 minutes to get them to firm up; they will hold their shape better when baking if they are chilled. At this point, you can also hold them for a day or two in the fridge and bake them close to the time you'd like to serve them.

4. Bake for 25 to 30 minutes, or until golden brown. Let cool on the baking sheet.

make the glaze

1. While the pastries are in the oven, in a medium bowl, combine the powdered sugar, preserves, and water. Whisk well until completely combined and clumps are minimized; the glaze should be thick enough to hold its shape in lines on top of the pastries. If you need to make the glaze more liquidy, add more warm water, a little at a time. If you need to make the glaze firmer, add more powdered sugar.

2. Drizzle the glaze on top of each pastry and let cool until the glaze sets up. Store baked pastries in an airtight container at room temperature for up to 4 days or in the freezer raw or baked for up to 3 months. Our baked Patti Pockets reheat beautifully, and when you're ready to bake raw frozen pastries, increase the baking time by 3 to 5 minutes.

LOCAL SPOONFUL CREAMY BAKED OATMEAL

makes one pan of oatmeal

This isn't humble oatmeal; it's an elevated version fit for the first day of school. It is nourishing and delicious, getting everyone ready for the big day.

With a little bit of advance planning, you can enjoy creamy, custardy oatmeal without ever standing over a hot stove, constantly stirring a pot. Most of the work is done the night before; in the morning, the oatmeal bakes while everyone gets ready for the day. It also microwaves incredibly well so it can be made on the weekend and reheated on school mornings.

Why do we call this Local Spoonful? Because it's a bowlful of Michigan! We use Michigan dairy, maple syrup, and oats—and top it with Michigan dried cherries too. We also like to finish each serving off with a handful of toasted walnuts and a splash of cream ... and maybe a little extra maple syrup. Live in Wisconsin, Maryland, or New Mexico? Create a version that makes it your own local spoonful. Whatever you do, try it cold the next day with a little milk and fresh berries.

3 large eggs	1 tsp vanilla extract
1½ cups [340 g] whole milk	1½ tsp ground cinnamon
1½ cups [340 g] heavy cream	1 tsp fine sea salt
⅓ cup [105 g] maple syrup	2 cups [200 g] rolled oats

1. The night before, in a medium mixing bowl, lightly beat the eggs with a whisk, then add in the milk, cream, maple syrup, vanilla extract, cinnamon, and salt, whisking until well combined. Add the oats to the custard mixture, mixing until well combined.

2. Pour the mixture into an ungreased 8 by 8 in [20 by 20 cm] baking pan, cover with plastic wrap, and refrigerate overnight.

3. The next morning, preheat the oven to 350°F [180°C].

4. Stir the oatmeal (the mixture tends to settle during its overnight rest). Cover the baking pan with aluminum foil and vent with two or three small holes. Place the baking pan into a larger pan (like a 9 by 13 in [23 by 33 cm] baking pan) and add just-boiled water to create a water bath, with the water reaching halfway up the inner baking pan.

5. Bake the oatmeal in its water bath for 45 to 50 minutes, or until set—it should bounce lightly or jiggle a bit, but not look watery or loose in the middle.

6. Remove the pan of baked oatmeal from the water bath and cool, covered, for 5 to 10 minutes before cutting to serve. Store, covered, in the refrigerator for up to 4 days.

CHICKEN AND CHORIZO PAELLA

serves 8 to 10 using an 18 in [46 cm] paella pan

Serve this at your paella party with a large green salad, and you'll have satisfied celebrants. Beer and wine are recommended too! Adapted from Zingerman's Delicatessen.

6 to 8 cups [1.4 L to 1.9 L] unsalted chicken stock	1 cup [115 g] Spanish spicy chorizo, ¼ in [6 mm] slices
1 Tbsp saffron	2½ cups [300 g] diced yellow onion
1 Tbsp fine sea salt, plus more for seasoning	1¼ cups [325 g] diced tomatoes
Freshly ground black pepper	1½ Tbsp minced garlic cloves (about 5 cloves)
12 [700 g to 1 kg] chicken thighs, boneless, skin-on	3 cups [540 g] paella rice, Bomba or Calasparra
Olive oil or a neutral vegetable oil	1½ cups [175 g] green beans, cut into 1 in [2.5 cm] pieces
1 cup [115 g] Spanish sweet chorizo, ¼ in [6 mm] slices	One 8 oz [230 g] jar roasted piquillo peppers, cut into strips

1. Pour the chicken stock into a medium stockpot. Add the saffron and salt and, over medium-high heat, bring the stock to a simmer, then lower the heat to low to keep warm.

2. Set your gas grill to high heat. Salt and pepper the chicken thighs on both sides.

3. Place the paella pan on the grill and add enough olive oil to nicely cover the bottom, about ⅓ cup [43 g]. When the oil is nice and hot, add the chicken thighs, skin side down, to brown, 5 to 7 minutes. (If the pan doesn't seem hot enough, turn up the heat.) When the skin sides are done, turn them over and brown the other side for an additional 5 to 7 minutes. Once the chicken thighs are browned on both sides (they won't be cooked through), transfer them to a plate, cover with foil, and set aside.

4. Add both chorizos to the pan and sauté until lightly brown, 2 to 3 minutes. Add the onion, tomatoes, and garlic and cook until the onions are translucent, 5 to 7 minutes.

5. Turn the temperature of the grill to 400°F [205 °C] or medium-high. Add the rice to the pan and toss with the cooked vegetables. Cook, stirring occasionally, for 3 to 5 minutes. It may be necessary to add some oil to the pan at this point. Spread the rice and vegetable mixture evenly over the bottom of the pan.

6. Add 5 cups [1.2 L] of the chicken stock and close the lid of the grill. Cook for 10 minutes, until the rice is still al dente. Do not stir the rice while cooking; the goal is to create a crispy bottom, the socarrat, and stirring would ruin that possibility.

7. While the rice is cooking, steam the green beans separately: Set a steamer basket in a medium or large saucepan filled with 1 to 2 in [2.5 to 5 cm] of water and add the beans. Bring to a boil over high heat, then lower the heat to medium, cover, and steam the beans until crisp-tender, 3 to 5 minutes. (Doing this extra step allows you to make sure that the green beans are the perfect texture and bright green color when the dish is served. If you want to use your judgment, you can skip this step and add the beans raw to the paella with enough time to cook them before serving.)

8. After the initial 10 minutes of rice cooking, add the browned chicken thighs to the paella pan, nestling them in the rice. Add more stock if it's been fully absorbed by the rice, close the lid of the grill, and cook for another 10 minutes.

9. Spread the green beans and roasted pepper strips evenly over the rice, close the lid, and cook for 10 more minutes. Check the rice for doneness; the grains should remain separate and be very slightly al dente, and the stock should be absorbed. If the rice isn't quite done, continue to cook with the grill lid closed, adding more stock if the rice is dry.

10. Once the rice is done, if you want to make sure you have a crispy bottom, open the grill lid, turn up the heat, and cook for 30 seconds or so until you hear the rice crackling.

11. Remove the pan from the grill and let rest for 10 to 15 minutes before serving. To store, see page 113.

PAELLA PARTY

Every year, Zingerman's Deli holds several big paella parties. It's a tradition that's more than a quarter century old and a great scene to experience. On party day, the Deli's outdoor patio is dotted with industrial-size grills covered in paella-filled pans and guests enjoying each other's company in a festive atmosphere with great food.

Paella, we believe, is one of the quintessential party dishes for a crowd. We suggest serving it anytime the weather permits an outdoor party. It will take the cook about 45 minutes to prepare, so there's lots for guests to watch and it's nice for the paella master to have company.

For many of us, a paella party is a once-a-year endeavor, so we do it up right, buying the best ingredients we can find—they definitely make a difference. The best rice for paella is Spanish short- to medium-grain rice; look for Bomba, also known as Valencia rice, and Calasparra, both of which are capable of absorbing large quantities of flavorful stock. Other essential ingredients include fine saffron (indulge in the fragrant real deal), sweet onions, Spanish chorizo, chicken thighs, good olive oil, and a rich, high-quality chicken stock, which will add an additional depth of flavor to round out the entire dish.

Then comes the cooking. For a paella of this size, you need an 18 in [46 cm] heavy-duty paella pan and an outdoor grill large enough to hold it. If grilling isn't your thing, we've also included a recipe for the stovetop. Whichever way you choose to make the dish, the critical element of the cooking method is all about the rice. It is cooked slowly, and the prize is the socarrat—the caramelized layer of rice at the bottom of the pan. To develop the socarrat, the rice is never stirred once the liquid is added. Follow our directions and you'll have a good chance of developing it. If you aren't successful, don't worry; the paella will still taste delicious.

STOVETOP CHICKEN AND CHORIZO PAELLA

Adapted from Zingerman's Delicatessen

Serves 4 to 6 using a 12 in [30.5 cm] paella pan

3 cups [680 g] unsalted chicken stock	⅓ cup [40 g] Spanish spicy chorizo, ¼ in [6 mm] slices
1½ tsp saffron	1 cup [140 g] diced yellow onion
1½ tsp fine sea salt, plus more for seasoning	¾ cup [195 g] diced tomatoes
Freshly ground black pepper	2 garlic cloves, minced
6 [350 to 500 g] chicken thighs, boneless, skin-on	1 cup [180 g] paella rice, Bomba or Calasparra
Olive oil or a neutral vegetable oil for cooking	¾ cup [90 g] green beans, cut into 1 in [2.5 cm] pieces
⅓ cup [40 g] Spanish sweet chorizo, ¼ in [6 mm] slices	4 oz [115 g] jar roasted piquillo peppers, cut in strips

1. Pour the chicken stock into a medium stockpot. Add the saffron and salt, bring the stock to a simmer over medium-high heat, then lower the heat to low to keep warm.

2. Salt and pepper the chicken thighs on both sides. Place the paella pan on the largest stove burner over medium-high heat. Add enough cooking oil to nicely cover the bottom, about ¼ cup [34 g]. When the oil is nice and hot, add the chicken thighs, skin side down, to brown, 5 to 7 minutes. When the skin sides are done, turn them over and brown the other side for an additional 5 to 7 minutes. Once the chicken thighs are browned on both sides (they won't be cooked through), transfer them to a plate, cover with foil, and set aside.

3. Add both chorizos to the pan and sauté until lightly browned, 2 to 3 minutes. Add the onion, tomatoes, and garlic and cook until the onions are translucent, 5 to 7 minutes. Add the rice to the pan and toss with the cooked vegetables. Cook, stirring occasionally, for 3 to 5 minutes. It may be necessary to add some oil to the pan at this point. Spread the rice and vegetable mixture evenly over the bottom of the pan.

4. Add 3 cups [680 g] of chicken stock and simmer for 10 minutes until the rice is still al dente. You may need to turn down the heat. Do not stir the rice while cooking; the goal is to create a crispy bottom, the socarrat, and stirring would ruin that possibility (see page 111).

5. While the rice is cooking, steam the green beans separately. Set a steamer basket in a medium to large saucepan filled with 1 to 2 in [2.5 to 5 cm] of water and add the beans. Bring to a boil over high heat, then lower the heat to medium, cover, and steam the beans until they are crisp-tender, 3 to 5 minutes.

6. After the initial 10 minutes of rice cooking, add the browned chicken thighs to the paella pan, nestling them in the rice. Add more stock if it's been fully absorbed by the rice, and cook for another 10 minutes.

7. Spread the green beans and roasted pepper strips evenly over the rice and cook for 10 more minutes. Check the rice for doneness; the grains should remain separate and be very slightly al dente, and the stock should be absorbed. If the rice isn't quite done, continue cooking, adding more stock if the rice is dry.

8. Once the rice is done, if you want to make sure you have a crispy bottom, turn up the heat and cook for 30 seconds or so until you hear the rice crackling.

9. Remove the pan from the stove and let the paella rest for 10 to 15 minutes before serving. Paella leftovers, no matter the method of preparation, are delicious. Transfer them to a container, cover, and enjoy them for 2 to 3 days, if they last that long.

SPANISH MUSICIAN'S TART

makes one tart

Musician's tart is one of the mythical desserts we made at the bakery for only a season or two, which old-time employees and long-standing customers bring up with loving memories. Also Spanish in origin, we think it's perfect for a festive "special" occasion, like a paella party. Its name stems from a centuries-old custom in Catalonia, an autonomous region in northeastern Spain, where itinerant musicians wandering the countryside would often receive payment for their musical entertainment with dried fruits and nuts, nourishing food that would keep well on their travels. This Catalan custom came to be known as the "musician's dessert," which is still served to this day, having been updated by turning the musician's "pay" into a rich and satisfying tart.

If you don't have a 10 in [25 cm] tart pan, you can improvise with a smaller one or with individual-size pans.

PÂTE SUCRÉE TART CRUST

1 recipe Pâte Sucreé Tart Crust (page 94), made with 1 Tbsp orange zest added to the dough

FILLING

6 Tbsp [55 g] raw whole almonds

6 Tbsp [55 g] raw whole cashews

½ cup [55 g] raw pine nuts

1 cup [115 g] dried pears, cut in half

⅔ cup [150 g] dates, pitted and cut in half

3 Tbsp brown sugar, packed

½ tsp sea salt

6 Tbsp [90 g] pear juice (can substitute water)

1½ Tbsp water

CARAMEL TOPPING

5 Tbsp [75 g] unsalted butter, room temperature

⅓ cup plus 1 Tbsp [80 g] brown sugar

3 Tbsp corn syrup

1½ Tbsp heavy cream

½ tsp sea salt

make the pâte sucrée tart crust

1. Follow the instructions on page 94 to make and blind bake the pâte sucrée tart crust in a 10 in [25 cm] tart pan.

make the tart filling

1. Preheat the oven to 350°F [180°C]. Toast the almonds and cashews on a baking sheet for 10 to 12 minutes, or until they are fragrant and the cashews are golden in color; set aside to cool. Toast the pine nuts separately on a baking sheet for 5 minutes or until golden in color. Keep an eye on the pine nuts, as they can burn quickly.

2. In a medium saucepan over medium-low heat, bring the pears, dates, brown sugar, salt, pear juice, and water to a simmer. Lower the heat to low and continue to simmer for 20 to 30 minutes. The goal is to cook the dried fruit until it is soft and to reduce the liquid so that the tart filling is the thickness of jam. Cool until warm but not hot.

3. Using a food processor or an immersion blender, purée the warm pear and date filling to a smooth, spreadable paste.

make the caramel topping

1. In a small saucepan over medium heat, melt the butter. Add the brown sugar, corn syrup, heavy cream, and salt to the saucepan and cook until the mixture begins to boil, stirring to keep it homogeneous. Remove from the heat and set aside.

cont'd

assemble and bake the tart

1. Preheat the oven to 325°F [165°C].

2. With your blind-baked tart crust still in the pan for added support, spread the fruit purée evenly over the bottom of the crust. If using a different size pan, fill the tart two-thirds of the way up the sides of the shell. Scatter the nuts over the fruit purée, making sure that the three types of nuts are evenly distributed.

3. After giving the caramel a good stir in the pan, slowly pour it evenly over the nuts, covering them.

4. Bake for 15 to 20 minutes or until there is some bubbling along the top edge of the tart. Set aside to cool at room temperature; refrigerating the tart can help firm up the caramel.

5. Once cooled, cut, serve, and enjoy! Store the tart covered at room temperature or in the refrigerator for up to 5 days, or well wrapped in plastic in the freezer for up to 3 months.

OURS IS SEPTEMBER 13! The Bakehouse's birthday, in late summer, is a perfect time to start the transition into fall flavors and fruit. Our Caramel Apple Cake captures all of the flavors of a caramel apple with spiced apple butter cake, apple butter filling, and salted caramel Swiss buttercream. Choosing the flavor of one's birthday cake was certainly a big deal for us as children. Seeing the requests come into the bakery for adult birthday cakes makes us think that it's not something most of us outgrow. There are many cake and icing recipes in this book for you to choose from for the birthday cake on your menu, but Caramel Apple is the cake we like to celebrate ours with.

CARAMEL APPLE CAKE

makes one two-layer cake

We make our salted caramel buttercream with dulce de leche, a staple sweet spread, like a milk jam, used in South America in baking and as a condiment on things like bread and ice cream. It literally means "sweet of milk" and is made by slowly heating milk, sugar, and vanilla. The mixture thickens and the sugars caramelize, turning it the color of butterscotch. Our favorite brand is La Salamandra from Argentina. They make it only with milk from their grass-fed herds, sugar, and vanilla—no additives or preservatives.

APPLE BUTTER CAKE LAYERS

1¾ cups [245 g] all-purpose flour

2 tsp baking soda

1¼ tsp ground cinnamon

¾ tsp fine sea salt

½ tsp ground nutmeg

1 cup [200 g] brown sugar, packed

½ cup plus 2 Tbsp [140 g] unsalted butter, room temperature

2 large eggs, room temperature

1 tsp vanilla extract

1¼ cups [345 g] apple butter

¼ cup [60 g] whole milk

SALTED CARAMEL SWISS BUTTERCREAM

¾ cup [150 g] granulated sugar

3 egg whites

¾ tsp fine sea salt

1 cup [220 g] unsalted butter, room temperature

¼ tsp vanilla extract

⅓ cup plus 2 Tbsp [140 g] dulce de leche

FILLING

⅓ cup [85 g] apple butter

make the apple butter cake layers

1. Preheat the oven to 350°F [180°C]. Line two 8 in [20 cm] round cake pans with parchment paper and lightly coat them with nonstick cooking spray. If you don't have parchment paper, butter the bottom and sides of each pan lightly and then flour it, knocking out any extra flour once the pan is fully coated.

2. In a medium mixing bowl, sift together the flour, baking soda, cinnamon, salt, and nutmeg.

3. In a large mixing bowl, beat the brown sugar and butter together with a wooden spoon until light and fluffy, 2 to 3 minutes, scraping down the sides of the bowl as needed. If using a stand mixer, use the paddle attachment and mix at medium speed. Add the eggs one at a time, mixing well after each addition. Once the eggs are incorporated, add the vanilla extract and mix until well combined.

4. In a small bowl, combine the apple butter and whole milk. Alternate adding the dry ingredients and the apple butter mixture to the creamed butter mixture, one-third at a time, mixing well after each addition. Start with one-third of the dry ingredients, mix well, and then add one-third of the apple butter mixture, and repeat two more times with the remaining ingredients. Scrape down the sides of the bowl well throughout. Divide the batter between the prepared pans and smooth the tops with a spatula.

cont'd

5. Bake the cake layers for 30 to 35 minutes, or until a tester or toothpick inserted in the center of each comes out clean. Allow the cake layers to cool in their pans for 10 to 15 minutes. After this initial cooling, transfer the cake layers onto wire racks to cool completely to room temperature before assembling and frosting the cake.

make the salted caramel swiss buttercream

1. In a medium heatproof mixing bowl, combine the sugar, egg whites, and salt, stirring with a wooden spoon to combine. Place the bowl over a double boiler or saucepan with gently simmering water and heat the mixture, stirring every couple of minutes, until the sugar is completely dissolved and the temperature registers 180°F [82°C] on an instant-read thermometer.

2. Transfer the egg white mixture to the bowl of a stand mixer. Using the whisk attachment, whip on high speed until it has doubled in volume, become thick and shiny, and cooled to room temperature.

3. Once the mixture is cool, set the speed to medium and gradually add the butter, 1 small piece at a time, mixing until all of it has been incorporated. The butter should be the same temperature as the egg white mixture to aid successful incorporation.

4. Add the vanilla extract and whip on medium speed to incorporate, then whip on high speed for 1 minute to ensure all the butter is totally combined with the whipped egg whites and sugar mixture.

5. Add the dulce de leche and mix until well combined, then adjust the salt to taste.

6. Use immediately or place in an airtight container and chill in the refrigerator for up to 1 week or freeze for up to 3 months. For tips on how to refresh the buttercream after it is chilled, see page 242.

assemble the cake

1. If the cake layers have domed tops, trim them with a serrated knife, positioned horizontally, to make them flat. (Snack on the cake scraps, if desired.)

2. Place one cake layer on a cake board or serving tray. Using an offset spatula, spread the apple butter filling over the top of the first cake layer, then place the second layer on top of the apple butter, flipping it over so that the top of the second layer is face down on the filling. This will give you a nice, flat surface to frost.

3. Thinly coat the entire cake with buttercream and transfer to the refrigerator or freezer for 10 minutes to set. This is a crumb coat, which, as the name suggests, helps prevent crumbs from getting caught in the buttercream frosting. It does not need to be neat or perfect. Usually, you can see the cake through the buttercream after this coat.

4. Finish frosting the cake with the remaining buttercream. Use your spatula or a palette knife to make a decorative design in the frosting, giving the cake a more finished look.

5. Both the cake layers and the buttercream can be made ahead of time and stored, well wrapped in plastic wrap, in either the refrigerator or freezer to be assembled at a later time.

6. Store the assembled cake in a cool place for up to 2 days and in the refrigerator for up to 5 days. It doesn't need to be wrapped tightly; the frosting will keep the cake moist, but note that it's susceptible to picking up strong odors in the refrigerator, like onions, so you may want to cover it in plastic or store it in an airtight container. To freeze an assembled cake, place it in the freezer, uncovered, until frozen solid, about 4 hours; then, wrap it tightly in plastic wrap and freeze for up to 3 months.

NO.3

FALL

FALL HAS BEEN MY FAVORITE SEASON FOR AS LONG AS I CAN REMEMBER. Growing up in Michigan with close family and living most of my adult years on the East Coast among dear friends and colleagues, I've had the great fortune to experience and celebrate the captivating sights, sounds, smells, and tastes of the fall season in both spectacular and comforting fashion. From the cool, crisp days of autumn in September and October, outdoors in nature, on through the chilly and cozier days of November, spent inside and ushering in the holiday season with Thanksgiving, fall is a veritable feast for the senses: Basking in the feel of cooler temperatures and crisp air after a long, hot, stifling summer. Partaking in the bounty of the season's harvests—apples, pears, squash, greens, corn—at local farmers' markets, U-Pick orchards, and apple cider mills. Reveling in the kaleidoscope of spectacular color as the summer-green foliage bursts into fall's signature brilliant hues of crimson, gold, orange, and russet. The sound of crunching leaves underfoot when hitting the trail on glorious fall hiking expeditions in the mountains or the forests along a lakeshore or river. The smell of woodsmoke emanating from campfires after a day of hiking and festive bonfires ushering in the harvest season. And then there are the smells and tastes of the abundance of fall harvest foods: warm spices, comforting soups, and celebratory feasts prepared together with family and friends in a warm and bustling home kitchen. I love it all! And the new lease on life and energy I feel, and the heightened desire to connect with nature and with my friends and family, near and far, when fall rolls around, just seems to grow with every passing year.

The fall recipes and celebration days we've included in this book capture the essence of the season's most beloved culinary traditions and time-honored occasions that bring friends, family, and community together for a special meal, commemoration, or simply to indulge in a favorite fall treat.

—Lee Vedder

ROSY RED APPLE PIE

makes one double-crust pie

Amy's family often eats leftover fruit pie for breakfast—she calls it "Burgess Breakfast" after her mother-in-law's maiden name. If you haven't yet tried fruit pie for breakfast, we suggest that you adopt Amy's family tradition as your own. We love using a combination of butter and lard for apple pie crusts, but feel free to substitute all butter if you'd rather. For decades American bakers used lard frequently when making sweet things; it was the most accessible and affordable fat available. It fell out of fashion when shortening became more common. Both lard and butter give valuable texture and flavor qualities to the crust. By combining them, we get the best of both of them. Shortening is the easiest of the fats to work with but it has the least flavor, so we skip it.

PIE DOUGH

2½ cups plus 1 Tbsp [360 g] all-purpose flour (see page 236 for flour options)

2 tsp fine sea salt

2 tsp granulated sugar

½ cup [110 g] unsalted butter, cold

½ cup [110 g] leaf lard, cold (optional, substitute with butter)

⅓ cup [80 g] water, cold

FILLING

5 or 6 [900 g] Ida Red apples

1 Tbsp lemon juice

½ cup [100 g] granulated sugar

3 Tbsp cornstarch

1 tsp ground cinnamon

¼ tsp sea salt

¼ cup [55 g] unsalted butter, room temperature

EGG WASH

1 large egg

1 egg yolk

1 Tbsp water

make the pie dough

1. In a large mixing bowl, mix together the flour, salt, and sugar with a fork.

2. Cut the cold butter into ¼ in [6 mm] cubes and add to the bowl. Cut the butter into the flour mixture, using a pastry blender, two knives, or your hands. Cut or work the butter into the flour until the mixture looks like coarse cornmeal. If using your hands, break the pieces of butter up in your fingers and rub the butter and flour together. Pick the mixture up between your hands and rub your palms together as if they're cold. This will break down the butter and rub it all over the flour.

The flour will take on a creamy yellow color during this step. When you pick the mixture up in your hand, it should be possible to squeeze it into a mass that will hold together. When you see the color change and the mixture holds together when squeezed, you know that you've worked the butter in enough. Work quickly so that the butter doesn't become warm. The goal of this step is to cover the flour with fat so that the gluten strands are not able to develop.

3. Cut the lard into ¼ in [6 mm] cubes and cut it into the flour mixture as before with the butter. The lard pieces should be left in pea-size chunks to create flakiness in the final pie crust—when they melt during baking, they create steam, which separates layers of the coated flour, making flakes of crust.

4. Create a well in the center of the flour mixture and add the cold water, using a fork to blend it in. The flour mixture will still be crumbly in the bowl, but it should look moist. If it still looks dry, add an additional 1 to 2 Tbsp [15 to 30 g] of cold water, until the mixture looks moistened but still crumbly.

cont'd

FIRST DAY OF FALL

A colorful display of changing leaves, cozy hoodies, and crisp, cool evenings—all reliable signs that the season is changing, but nothing signals the arrival of autumn quite like apple season. It's Michigan's largest fruit crop!

We get our apples from Nemeth's Farm, a family-owned and operated orchard less than 30 minutes from the bakery. We love the apples, our relationship with the Nemeth family, and even the beautiful wooden crates the apples are delivered in. To make this classic apple pie, we tuck a mound of those local Ida Red apples tossed in cinnamon sugar inside a flaky double crust. We leave the gorgeous rosy red apple peels on for flavor, color, nutrition, and food waste reduction—it's a win-win when less prep work results in a better pie! If you don't have Ida Red apples, try Northern Spy, Pink Lady, Honeycrisp, or a blend of apple varieties.

And our Sugar Crisp Muffins (page 129) make us think of crisp autumn days, hot apple cider, and the start of the school year (but we wouldn't turn one down at other times of the year, either).

If the butter has been rubbed into the dough adequately in step 2, the amount of water specified should be enough. More water is usually necessary only when the butter has not been adequately distributed. It's not desirable to add more water, because it tends to make a tougher crust.

5. Turn the mixture out onto a clean, unfloured work surface, form into a mound, and push out sections of dough across the work surface with the heel of your hand. We call this "schmearing." Push each section of dough once, not twice. Make sure to schmear enough so that the dough loses its dry, crumbly appearance. At the end of the schmearing, all of the pie crust will be pushed out flat on the work surface.

6. Fold the dough back onto itself with a bench scraper. Gather it into a ball, pressing it firmly so it holds together. Cut the dough into two equal pieces, shape each one into a disk, and wrap with plastic wrap. Chill the dough in the refrigerator for at least 1 hour before rolling it out.

make the filling

1. Preheat oven to 400°F [200°C]. Line a baking sheet with parchment paper.

2. Core and slice each apple into eight pieces; you should have about 7 cups' worth of apple slices. In a large bowl, toss the apple slices with the lemon juice and set aside.

3. In a small bowl, stir together the sugar, cornstarch, cinnamon, and salt and set aside.

roll out the bottom crust

1. Remove one piece of the chilled dough from the refrigerator. While the dough is still in the plastic wrap, firmly but gently tap on it with a rolling pin until it is flexible but still cold. Lightly flour the work surface. Place the unwrapped disk of dough on the work surface and lightly dust the top of the disk with flour.

2. Using a rolling pin, start rolling the dough from the center to the edge, away from you. Do not use too much pressure, or the dough will crack. If this happens, brush away any excess flour near the cracking area and press the dough back together.

3. Stop and give the dough a one-eighth turn. This rotation will prevent the dough from sticking to the work surface and will help make a perfect circle.

4. Reflour the work surface and the top of the dough to prevent the dough from sticking. Continue to roll the dough until it's about ⅛ in [4 mm] thick and the circle is about 1 in [2.5 cm] wider than the top diameter of the 9 in [23 cm] pie plate you will be using. Flour is your friend in this process. Use it liberally to avoid sticking.

5. When the rolled-out pie dough has reached the correct size, use a pastry brush to brush away any extra flour from the top of the dough. Turn the dough over and brush off any extra flour from the bottom. One way to do this is to roll the dough up on your rolling pin and then unwind it with the bottom surface now facing up.

6. Using a rolling pin, gently roll up the pie dough loosely around the pin. Position the edge of the dough over the edge of the pie plate and unroll the dough. Gently ease the dough down into the pie plate, making sure not to stretch the dough.

fill the pie

1. Toss the apples with the sugar mixture until the dry ingredients are moistened.

2. Line the apple slices into the pie shell to fill in any gaps, building the apple mound up. Press the apples down slightly (they will be mounded very high). Pour any of the sugar mixture that is left in the bowl over the apples. Evenly distribute small pieces of the butter on top.

top the pie

1. Make the egg wash by whisking together the egg, egg yolk, and water until well combined. Lightly brush the edge of the pie dough with the egg wash.

2. Using the second piece of pie dough, roll out the top crust, using the same method as before, until it's ⅛ in [4 mm] thick and slightly larger than the top diameter of the pie plate, so that it will comfortably cover your filling. Roll up the top crust loosely around your rolling pin and, starting at one side of the pie, gently unroll the top crust over the filling. Trim the crusts, leaving 1 in [2.5 cm] of excess to form the border.

3. Fold the excess dough from the top crust under the lip of the bottom crust and seal by lightly pressing both layers together with your fingers against the top of the pie plate. Finish the edge with your choice of decorative crimping—pinch the dough with your fingers, mark with a spoon or a fork; the choice is yours. Brush the entire top of the pie with egg wash and cut four 2 in [5 cm] vents in the top of the crust at even intervals to allow the steam to escape as the pie bakes. Pie dough can be stored, wrapped in disk form or fully rolled out, in the refrigerator for up to 5 days. It can also be frozen, well wrapped and preferably in an airtight container, in either form, for up to 3 months.

4. Place the filled pie on the prepared baking sheet and bake for 70 to 80 minutes. The pie juices should be bubbling in the center and the crust will take on a deep golden color. Do not underbake; color is flavor in our world.

5. Let the pie cool to room temperature before serving (this will allow the juices to thicken). Store the baked pie, covered, at room temperature for up to 3 days. This baked pie can also be frozen for up to 3 months.

SUGAR CRISP MUFFINS

makes 12 muffins

What happens when a buttermilk nutmeg muffin and a cinnamon sugar doughnut fall in love? Sugar Crisp Muffins are born. If you love old-fashioned cake donuts but don't want to get into frying first thing in the morning (or perhaps anytime), try these muffins instead. They're definitely a treat! To make your muffins just like ours, skip the muffin liners when baking, and dip the whole muffin, not just the top, in melted butter followed by the cinnamon sugar. We know! Indulgent and delicious.

MUFFINS

2 cups [280 g] all-purpose flour

2 tsp baking powder

¾ tsp fine sea salt

½ tsp baking soda

½ tsp ground nutmeg

⅔ cup [125 g] granulated sugar

⅔ cup [145 g] unsalted butter, room temperature

2 large eggs, room temperature

1½ tsp vanilla extract

⅓ cup [80 g] whole milk, room temperature

2½ Tbsp buttermilk, room temperature

CINNAMON SUGAR TOPPING

6 Tbsp [75 g] granulated sugar

1½ Tbsp ground cinnamon

½ cup [110 g] unsalted butter, melted

make the muffins

1. Preheat the oven to 350°F [180°C]. Line the cups of a standard 12-cup muffin pan with muffin liners or, if you prefer, lightly coat the cups with butter or nonstick cooking spray and set aside.

2. In a medium mixing bowl, whisk together the flour, baking powder, salt, baking soda, and nutmeg.

3. In another medium mixing bowl, cream together the sugar and butter with a wooden spoon until the color lightens. If using a stand mixer, use the paddle attachment and beat on medium speed. Add the eggs to the creamed mixture, mixing until combined, followed by the vanilla extract.

4. In a small bowl, whisk together the milk and buttermilk.

5. Alternate adding the dry ingredients and the milk mixture to the creamed butter, one-third at a time, mixing well after each addition. Start with one-third dry, mix well, then add one-third of the milk mixture, and repeat two more times with the remaining ingredients. Mix on low speed, if using a stand mixer.

6. Spoon equal amounts of muffin batter into the prepared muffin pan. Bake for 18 to 20 minutes or until golden brown and the center of each muffin springs back when touched. Let cool completely in the pan.

make the cinnamon sugar topping

1. Meanwhile, whisk together the sugar and cinnamon for the topping. Dip the tops of the cooled muffins in melted butter and then in the cinnamon sugar.

2. These are best eaten the day they are made, but can be stored at room temperature in an airtight container and enjoyed the next day. For longer storage, freeze muffins prior to dipping in butter and cinnamon sugar in an airtight container for up to 3 months, and complete the final step once they have thawed.

RUSTIC ITALIAN BAGUETTES

makes 4 baguettes

This recipe requires some planning ahead to make, but the bread itself is delightfully uncomplicated. It's a classic Italian white bread with a mild crumb and a thin crust made with a handful of ingredients, including organic wheat flour, water, sea salt, a little yeast, and—the one thing you won't find listed in the recipe—a fair amount of time. The flavor is almost creamy with just a touch of natural sweetness. We find it continues to be one of our most popular breads because of its broad appeal and versatility. We recommend slicing up these Rustic Italian Baguettes and serving them with tasty Bacon Pimento Cheese (page 133).

POOLISH

¾ cup plus 1 Tbsp [115 g] all-purpose flour

½ cup [115 g] water, room temperature

⅛ tsp instant yeast

BAGUETTES

2¼ cups [520 g] water, room temperature

½ tsp instant yeast

6½ cups [910 g] all-purpose flour, plus more for dusting

1 Tbsp plus ½ tsp fine sea salt

½ cup [115 g] water, for steaming

make the poolish

1. In a medium mixing bowl, combine the flour, water, and yeast and stir together until combined.

2. Cover the bowl with plastic wrap and ferment at room temperature for 8 hours. This will make 1 cup [230 g], all of which will be used in making the baguettes. The poolish can be used at this point or refrigerated and used the next day.

make the baguettes

1. In a large mixing bowl, stir together the water, poolish, and yeast with a wooden spoon. Add half the flour and continue mixing with a wooden spoon until well combined; the mixture will resemble thick pancake batter. Add the salt and remaining flour and keep mixing until the dough becomes shaggy and starts to just barely form a ball.

2. Scrape the dough out of the bowl onto a clean, unfloured work surface. Knead the dough for 6 to 8 minutes, or until you have a successful windowpane test indicating sufficient gluten development (see page 244 for more information).

3. Coat the now-empty mixing bowl with nonstick cooking spray, then place the dough back in the bowl, cover with plastic wrap, and ferment for 3½ hours.

4. Preheat the oven, with a cast-iron or ovenproof skillet placed on the bottom rack, to 450°F [230°C] at least 1 hour prior to baking.

5. Turn out the fermented dough onto a floured work surface. Divide it into four equal pieces and form each one into an oval. Place the ovals of dough seam side up on a lightly floured work surface and cover with plastic wrap coated with nonstick cooking spray. Let them rest for 30 minutes.

cont'd

On any given Saturday in the fall, more than 100,000 fans of University of Michigan football gather for a home game at "The Big House"—the largest football stadium in the United States—and enjoy a pregame tailgate. Hours before the game, local golf courses, parking lots, and neighborhood backyards are packed with Wolverine fans and maize-and-blue regalia. Revelers toss footballs, play cornhole, gently rib those who dare to wear the colors of opposing teams, and, of course, eat and drink.

Here are some ideas that we love to serve at a tailgate, but would be just as enjoyable while watching a game at home.

6. Uncover the ovals of rested dough, lightly dust the tops with flour, and turn them over. To shape them into their final baguette shapes, take one oval and gently pat it into a roughly 8 in [20 cm] square with the palm of your hand. Now roll this into a cylinder, starting with the edge farthest from you. Roll it toward yourself one-third of the way, gently pressing the folded edge into the dough. Repeat twice; the last fold will meet the bottom edge. Seal the edges by pressing down with the base of your hand. Then roll it to approximately 15 in [38 cm] long, starting from the center, applying even pressure, and slightly tapering the ends. Repeat with the remaining ovals of dough.

7. Place the shaped baguettes in a well-floured linen (called a couche, see page 239) seam side up and separated by pleats; then cover them with more of the linen. Alternatively, you can use well-floured parchment paper in the same manner. Make sure to be liberal with the flour in this step (there should be enough that the baked baguette has a coating of toasted flour, as in the photo above). Let the baguettes proof in their couche for 45 minutes to 1 hour at room temperature, or until each passes the touch test: Gently press the pad of a fingertip into the dough of each and remove it; the indentation should slowly come back, most, but not all, of the way.

8. When ready to bake, transfer the baguettes, seam side down, to a piece of parchment paper. Use a razor blade (lame, see page 239) or a very sharp knife to score each baguette with six or seven cuts. Place the cut baguettes and parchment paper on a baking sheet and transfer it to the oven. Add the water to the hot skillet on the bottom of the oven and immediately close the door. Bake for 8 minutes, open the oven door to release the steam, and then continue to bake for 17 to 20 minutes more, or until the baguettes are golden brown and the internal temperature registers 190°F [88°C] on an instant-read thermometer.

9. Place the baguettes on a cooling rack and cool completely before serving. Store at room temperature for 2 to 3 days or freeze, well wrapped, for up to 3 months.

BACON PIMENTO CHEESE

serves 8 as an appetizer

We love eating pimento cheese as a dip with slices of Rustic Italian Baguettes (page 130) or our traditional Bavarian Soft Pretzels (page 147). It's a crowd-pleasing snack at tailgates in Ann Arbor before we all go to the Big House for football games. Feel free to skip the bacon if you'd like to make classic pimento cheese.

"While everyone in the South knows this stuff at a level of intimacy my family would have reserved for chopped liver, it's still relatively unheard of up here in the North. Small slices of toast spread with pimento cheese and topped with a bit of crisp bacon and a leaf or two of celery make a superb appetizer. Pimento cheese sandwiches with bacon and tomato are terrific too. I like them grilled, but they're actually very good toasted as well." —Ari Weinzweig Recipe originally published in Zingerman's Guide to Better Bacon: Stories of Pork Bellies, Hush Puppies, Rock 'n' Roll Music and Bacon Fat Mayonnaise by Ari Weinzweig.

1. In a small frying pan over medium heat, add the bacon. After it colors on one side, flip it and cook until nicely browned on the second side. You want the bacon to be quite crispy; this will make for better texture in the end. Remove the bacon from the pan and let it cool on paper towels to soak up any extra grease. Once cool, chop into ¼ in [6 mm] pieces.

2. In a large mixing bowl, fold together the bacon, Cheddar, mayonnaise, red peppers, and olive oil until well combined. Add the black pepper, cayenne, and salt. Mix well and enjoy. Store in an airtight container, refrigerated, for up to 1 week.

---

3 strips of bacon

3 cups [220 g] coarsely grated sharp Cheddar cheese (we use the two-year-old raw milk Cheddar from Grafton Village)

1 cup [230 g] mayonnaise

¼ cup [35 g] diced roasted red peppers

¾ tsp olive oil

¼ tsp freshly ground black pepper

¼ tsp (or to taste) cayenne pepper

Pinch of coarse sea salt

MICHIGAN DOUBLE CHOCOLATE COOKIES

makes about 24 cookies

These cookies are a perfect treat for a gathering, whether it's a tailgate, a neighborhood block party, or a work event. They are easy to make, easy to serve, easy to eat, and well liked by all!

They have a wonderfully tender texture and lots of chocolate flavor—chocolate dough and chocolate chunks, hence the double *in the name. Make them extra special by choosing unique or particularly high-quality chocolate to use as the chunks. Feel free to use two flavors of chunks if that seems fun to you. Love nuts? Toast any kind you like and mix them in. We'd reduce the amount of chocolate chunks a touch to make this possible.*

What's "Michigan" about these cookies? Our whole-wheat flour is Michigan hard red spring wheat that we mill ourselves for optimal flavor.

1 cup plus 1 Tbsp [190 g] semisweet chocolate, for melting

1 cup plus 2 Tbsp [255 g] unsalted butter, room temperature

½ cup plus 2 tsp [115 g] granulated sugar

½ cup plus 1 Tbsp [115 g] brown sugar, packed

1 large egg, room temperature

2 tsp vanilla extract

2⅓ cups [325 g] whole-wheat flour

5 Tbsp [25 g] unsweetened cocoa powder

1½ tsp baking soda

½ tsp fine sea salt

2 cups [360 g] semisweet chocolate chunks

1. Preheat the oven to 350°F [180°C]. Line a baking sheet with parchment paper.

2. In a double boiler or metal bowl set over a saucepan of simmering water, melt the semisweet chocolate, stirring frequently. Set aside to cool slightly.

3. In a large mixing bowl, cream together the butter and sugars with a wooden spoon until well combined. If using a stand mixer, use the paddle attachment and mix at medium speed. Scrape down the sides of the bowl and mix until homogeneous. Add the melted chocolate to the creamed mixture and mix until there are no streaks of chocolate. Scrape down the sides of the bowl with a spatula and get underneath the mixture to make sure the chocolate is evenly incorporated. Add the egg and vanilla extract and mix thoroughly.

4. In a separate bowl, using a sifter or fine-mesh sieve, sift together the flour, cocoa, baking soda, and salt, then whisk until well blended. Add the dry ingredients to the creamed mixture and stir until well combined. Add the chocolate chunks and mix just until they are evenly distributed in the cookie dough.

5. Using a small ice cream scoop or a spoon, scoop the cookie dough onto the prepared baking sheet lined with parchment paper, spacing them 2 in [5 cm] apart.

6. Bake the cookies until the edges have just set, 13 to 15 minutes. For soft cookies, remove them from the oven when their centers are still slightly wet in appearance. (We prefer these cookies to be on the lightly baked end of the spectrum, as it shows off their tender texture best in this form.)

7. Place the cookies on a wire rack to cool to room temperature. Store cooled cookies in an airtight container at room temperature for up to 7 days or freeze for up to 3 months.

The Jewish New Year can fall anywhere from early September to early October. It marks the beginning of a ten-day period of prayer, ending with Yom Kippur, and is a time of self-reflection and hope for a sweet new year. Many of the foods most associated with the holiday refer to sweetness, like honey, or abundance, like pomegranates. Challahs are also made in specific shapes—turbans—to denote the cyclical nature of life. It's clear it's Rosh Hashanah when you walk into the bakery and we are happily making Halvah Swirl Cheesecake (facing), Not-Just-Chocolate Babka (page 139), and Bumble Honey Rye Cake (page 143) for the festivities.

Jewish cuisine is hard to define because it is so broad and varied. There are Jewish communities all over the world from Ethiopia to India to Morocco to Singapore, and, of course, in Israel, throughout Europe, and in the United States. The foods in each community often reflect the culinary traditions of the members, the local ingredients available to them, and the cuisine of their non-Jewish neighbors. The two most known culinary traditions are Ashkenazi (central and eastern European) and Sephardic (North African, Turkish, and Middle Eastern). The Halvah Swirl Cheesecake is our effort to have some fun by mixing the two traditions together. The cheesecake is definitely Ashkenazi in origin, while the tahini and halvah are Sephardic. Together they make for a big, flavorful, joyous, and indulgent dessert, perfect for your Rosh Hashanah celebration.

Babka (meaning "little grandmother") is the Jewish version of Eastern and Central European yeasted coffee cakes. Its origin is uncertain and most likely complicated. Some believe these cakes are the relative of a Ukrainian fertility cake; others believe it is the Russified version of panettone; while some surmise that it is the creation of Jewish bakers, taking scraps of the Sabbath challah and adding preserves or dried fruit to them for a little treat. Regardless, it has been a standard in American Jewish bakeries since the nineteenth century, and in recent years, it has made a resurgence with the newest generation of Jewish bakers and foodies.

Finally, Bumble Honey Rye Cake (page 143) is always on our menu for Rosh Hashanah, which is often celebrated with honey, a sweet symbol of the joy of life and optimism for what's to come. Sometimes apples are dipped in honey and sometimes honey is used as an ingredient in the dishes served to celebrate.

HALVAH SWIRL CHEESECAKE

makes one small cheesecake

Our newest addition to the holiday menu is a super decadent cheesecake: Two fillings—vanilla tahini and chocolate—are swirled into a rich dark chocolate crust. To make it even more indulgent, we include chunks of halvah, a flaky, melt-on-your-tongue sesame confection of Middle Eastern origin.

CHOCOLATE CRUST

1¼ cups plus 1 Tbsp [200 g] chocolate brownies or crisp chocolate cookies

2 Tbsp unsalted butter

1 Tbsp semisweet chocolate (55 to 65% cacao)

VANILLA TAHINI CHEESECAKE FILLING

½ cup plus 1 Tbsp [135 g] cream cheese, room temperature

½ cup plus 1 Tbsp [135 g] farm cheese, room temperature (or substitute the same amount of cream cheese)

½ cup [100 g] granulated sugar

2 tsp all-purpose flour

1 large egg, room temperature

1 egg yolk, room temperature

1 Tbsp heavy cream

2 tsp vanilla extract

½ cup [100 g] tahini

CHOCOLATE CHEESECAKE FILLING

3½ Tbsp cream cheese, room temperature

3½ Tbsp farm cheese, room temperature (or substitute the same amount of cream cheese)

¼ cup [50 g] granulated sugar

2 large egg yolks, room temperature

¼ tsp vanilla extract

¼ cup [45 g] semisweet chocolate (55 to 65% cacao)

3 Tbsp heavy cream

½ cup plus 2 Tbsp [95 g] halvah, cut into chunks

make the chocolate crust

1. Preheat the oven to 300°F [150°C].

2. If using brownies, cut them into cubes and toast them on a baking sheet in an even layer until dry, about 45 minutes. Let cool, then place in a food processor and grind into fine crumbs. If using crisp chocolate cookies, no oven drying is necessary; just grind them in a food processor into fine crumbs.

3. In a small, heavy saucepan over low heat, melt the butter and chocolate together. Transfer to a medium mixing bowl and stir together with the crumbs until fully combined.

4. Lightly coat the sides and bottom of a 6 in [15 cm] springform pan with nonstick cooking spray or soft butter. Press the crumb mixture into the pan so that the crust is compact and an even thickness across the bottom and goes 1 in [2.5 cm] up the sides of the pan.

5. Carefully wrap the outside of the springform pan with aluminum foil and place it in a larger pan with 3 in [8 cm] sides. This will be the water bath in which it bakes, and the foil prevents water from leaking into the cheesecake.

make the vanilla tahini cheesecake filling

1. In a large mixing bowl, use a wooden spoon to beat the cream cheese until totally smooth, scraping down the sides of the bowl as needed. If using a stand mixer, use the paddle attachment and beat on medium speed.

2. If using farm cheese, smooth the curds by processing it in a food processor first. Add the farm cheese to the bowl and beat the two cheeses together until smooth.

3. In a separate mixing bowl, whisk together the sugar and flour. Add them to the cheese mixture and combine until evenly incorporated. Scrape down the sides of the bowl well.

cont'd

4. In a small bowl, mix the egg, egg yolk, cream, and vanilla extract together, then gradually add it to the cheese batter, mixing and scraping the bowl periodically. Add the tahini and mix in completely. Scrape the bowl well and set aside.

make the chocolate cheesecake filling

1. In a medium mixing bowl, use a wooden spoon to beat the cream cheese until totally smooth, scraping down the sides of the bowl as needed. If using a stand mixer, use the paddle attachment and beat on medium speed.

2. If using farm cheese, smooth the curds by processing it in a food processor first. Add the farm cheese to the bowl and beat the two cheeses together until smooth. Add the sugar and mix until thoroughly combined.

3. In a small bowl, mix the egg yolks and vanilla extract together and gradually add it to the cheese batter, mixing and scraping the bowl periodically.

4. In a saucepan over low heat, or in the microwave in a microwave-safe bowl, warm the chocolate and heavy cream together until the chocolate is melted. Be careful not to burn the chocolate. Stir until the mixture is homogeneous. Add the chocolate and cream mixture to the cheese batter and mix in completely. Scrape the bowl well.

assemble and bake the cheesecake

1. Place chunks of halvah evenly over the bottom crust, then pour the chocolate filling into the crust, followed by the vanilla tahini filling on top. If the fillings look nicely marbled, then the cheesecake is ready to be baked. If the fillings do not look nicely marbled, use a spoon and very lightly swirl the batters together.

2. Carefully transfer the prepared cheesecake to the oven and fill the water bath pan slowly with boiling water until it reaches halfway up the outside of the springform pan.

3. Bake for 1½ to 2 hours, or until the top surface is set and the cheesecake moves like gelatin when jiggled, not like waves. The cheesecake is completely baked when a tester or toothpick inserted in the center comes out moist but is not coated in batter and the internal temperature registers 175°F [80°C] on an instant-read thermometer.

4. Turn the oven off and allow the cheesecake to rest for 20 minutes in the oven, still in the water bath. Remove the pan from the oven and run a warm, dry, offset spatula around the edge of the cheesecake; this will help prevent cracks as the cheesecake cools. Cool for 20 minutes at room temperature, then transfer to the refrigerator, uncovered, to cool completely; this will help prevent condensation. Once cool, cover the top with plastic wrap.

5. When the cheesecake is fully cooled, it may be carefully removed from the springform pan. To remove the cheesecake from the pan, first remove the sides of the springform pan. Next, use a knife or offset spatula to loosen the cheesecake from the bottom of the pan. Using a wide spatula, transfer the cheesecake to a serving plate or platter.

6. Serve chilled and keep refrigerated. This cheesecake freezes very well if you'd like to make it ahead of time. Store in the refrigerator, well wrapped in plastic, for up to 5 days or in the freezer for up to 3 months.

NOT-JUST-CHOCOLATE BABKA

makes one loaf

We love our version of babka, and it's not just chocolate, as the name implies! Rather, it's a multi-flavored layering of chocolate, cinnamon, orange, and raisins. They come together in a complex and satisfying way, well worth all of the steps in getting there. And with the classic babka twist for shaping, it's pretty too, making it a perfect sweet to usher in a sweet new year on Rosh Hashanah. Making our babka requires some effort; you might say it's a project. We suggest making it over a couple of days. All of the components, except for the dough, can be made two or more days ahead, which we think is a smart way to spread out the effort. It's best, though, to wait and make the dough within 24 hours of baking. Although we wrote the recipe for one babka, it's not a crazy idea to make two at once. Doubling the recipe won't make it onerous to manage, and since it freezes well after baking, you can enjoy one right away and have the other waiting for another occasion.

DOUGH

1 Tbsp plus 1½ tsp water, room temperature

1 Tbsp plus ½ tsp granulated sugar

½ tsp instant yeast

2 large eggs, room temperature

1 cup plus 2 Tbsp [160 g] all-purpose flour, plus more for dusting

¾ tsp fine sea salt

⅓ cup plus ½ Tbsp [80 g] unsalted butter, room temperature, cubed

RAISINS

⅓ cup plus ½ Tbsp [70 g] granulated sugar

2 Tbsp plus 1 tsp water

1 Tbsp orange zest

¼ cup [35 g] flame raisins

¼ cup [35 g] golden raisins

CHOCOLATE GANACHE

¼ cup [45 g] semisweet chocolate

¼ cup [45 g] heavy cream

STREUSEL TOPPING

7 Tbsp [70 g] chocolate brownies or crisp chocolate cookies

1 Tbsp all-purpose flour

2 tsp granulated sugar

1 Tbsp unsalted butter, cold, cut into ¼ in [6 mm] pieces

⅛ tsp vanilla extract

CINNAMON SUGAR

3 Tbsp granulated sugar

1 Tbsp ground cinnamon

make the dough

1. Using a stand mixer with the paddle attachment, place the water, sugar, yeast, and eggs into the mixing bowl. Mix on medium speed until thoroughly combined, less than 1 minute. Add half the flour and mix for 30 seconds until a lumpy batter forms. Scrape down the sides of the bowl, then add the remaining flour and the salt and mix the dough on the lowest speed until no flour remains at the bottom of the bowl, 1 minute. To develop the dough structure, increase the speed to medium-low and mix for 2½ minutes.

2. With the mixer running on medium-low, add one piece of butter at a time. Do not add another piece until the previous one has been fully incorporated; this will take approximately 5 minutes. Scrape down the sides of the bowl as needed. The dough is done when all of the butter has been incorporated.

3. Place the dough in a large container coated with a neutral oil or nonstick cooking spray, cover with plastic wrap, and place in the refrigerator to ferment for 30 minutes.

4. Remove the fermented dough from the refrigerator and turn it out onto a lightly floured work surface. Gently form it into an approximate rectangle, and give the dough a letter fold (see the diagram on page 245). Fold the dough away from you about two-thirds of the way, then all the way toward you, as if you were folding a letter in thirds to put inside of an envelope. Then repeat this process from right to left and left to right, making a sideways envelope. Put the dough back into the oiled container and refrigerate, covered, for another 30 minutes.

5. Do another letter fold following the previous steps, then put the dough back into the oiled container. Refrigerate the twice-folded dough, covered, for a minimum of 1 hour or up to 24 hours.

cont'd

prepare the raisins

1. In a small saucepan over medium heat, bring the sugar, water, and orange zest to a simmer until the sugar is dissolved. In a medium mixing bowl, pour the sugar mixture over the raisins and let them sit in the syrup at room temperature for at least 1 hour or up to 24 hours. Be sure to drain the raisins prior to using them in the babka.

make the chocolate ganache

1. Place the chocolate pieces in a small mixing bowl. In a saucepan over medium heat, bring the heavy cream to a boil. Pour the hot cream over the chocolate, stirring until smooth, then set aside to cool.

prepare the streusel topping

1. If using brownies, preheat the oven to 300°F [150°C]. Cut the brownies into cubes and toast them on a baking sheet in an even layer until dry, about 45 minutes. Set aside to cool. Place the cooled brownies in a food processor and grind into fine crumbs. If using crisp chocolate cookies, no oven drying is necessary; just grind them in a food processor into fine crumbs.

2. In a small mixing bowl, combine the crumbs, flour, and sugar. Add the butter pieces and the vanilla extract to the bowl and work them into the dry ingredients by hand or with a pastry blender until the mixture resembles crumbs of varying sizes. Refrigerate or freeze until ready to use.

make the cinnamon sugar

1. In a small mixing bowl, whisk together the sugar and cinnamon.

assemble and shape the babka

1. Coat a 9 by 5 in [23 by 12 cm] or 8½ by 4 ½ in [21.5 by 11 cm] loaf pan with nonstick cooking spray or butter.

2. On a lightly floured work surface, roll out the chilled dough into a 9 by 12 in [23 by 30.5 cm] rectangle. Position the dough in a landscape orientation so the 12 in [30 cm] side is facing you. Brush away any excess flour.

3. Spread the soft chocolate ganache over the dough, leaving a ½ in [12 mm] border at the top edge. Sprinkle the streusel topping, then the cinnamon sugar, and then the drained raisins evenly over the chocolate ganache.

4. Starting with the long edge closest to you, roll the dough into a tight cylinder away from you, keeping the roll even all the way across and avoiding the "snake that ate a bowling ball" look.

5. Once rolled, pinch the long seam of the cylinder together and then seal the dough firmly on both open ends of the roll.

6. Using a bench scraper, split the rolled cylinder evenly down the middle lengthwise, cutting all the way through, to expose the layers of dough and chocolate; it will be messy! Twist the two pieces together, as if braiding them, trying to keep the sides with exposed filling facing up as much as possible.

7. Place the babka twist into the loaf pan, pushing down the ends of the dough, then pick up all the filling that may have fallen out and sprinkle it on top of the babka.

8. Cover lightly with plastic wrap and let the babka proof at room temperature until the dough is level with the lip of the pan, 2 to 2½ hours.

bake the babka

1. Preheat the oven to 350°F [180°C].

2. Place the babka on the middle rack of the oven and bake for 35 to 40 minutes, or until deep golden brown and the internal temperature of the babka registers 165°F [74°C] on an instant-read thermometer. Be aware that it can be hard to get an accurate temperature reading on this bread due to all the delicious fillings!

3. Allow the babka to cool in the pan for 5 minutes before turning it out onto a wire rack to cool to room temperature. Slice and serve once the babka is at room temperature. Store in a plastic bag at room temperature for 3 to 5 days or in the freezer, well wrapped in plastic, for up to 2 months.

BUMBLE HONEY RYE CAKE

makes one small bundt cake

Our honey cake has an ingredient list evocative of the cake's Ashkenazi Eastern European roots: buckwheat honey, rye flour, and black tea, all common ingredients to the region. Fortunately for us, we are able to get Michigan rye and buckwheat honey, thus making this a local cake as well as a traditional one. It's easy to make, is deeply flavorful, and can be eaten at any time of the day. If you're serving it as dessert, try it warm with ice cream or whipped cream.

Now we're whispering because this feels a little inappropriate . . . This cake is also good for a Christian holiday that happens in December every year and is an exceptional understudy for gingerbread on a cold winter night.

½ cup [40 g] sliced almonds

1½ cups [170 g] whole-grain rye flour

¾ tsp baking soda

¼ tsp fine sea salt

½ tsp ground cinnamon

¼ tsp ground cloves

¼ tsp ground ginger

¼ tsp ground nutmeg

1 large egg, room temperature

½ cup [100 g] granulated sugar

¼ cup [50 g] vegetable oil

½ cup [170 g] buckwheat honey

½ cup [115 g] brewed standard black tea, cooled to room temperature

1 Tbsp fresh orange zest

½ Tbsp fresh lemon zest

⅓ cup [60 g] golden raisins

1. Preheat the oven to 350°F [180°C].

2. Toast the almonds on a baking sheet for 8 to 12 minutes, or until fragrant and golden brown. Set aside to cool completely.

3. In a medium bowl, whisk together the rye flour, baking soda, salt, and spices.

4. In a large bowl, whisk together the egg and sugar, then stir in the oil, honey, and black tea. Slowly whisk the dry ingredients into the wet ingredients, mixing until smooth. Add the orange and lemon zests, raisins, and all but 1 Tbsp of the almonds to the batter, stirring with a wooden spoon until just combined.

5. Generously coat a 6-cup [1.4 L] Bundt pan with nonstick cooking spray. (Don't have one? See another pan option in the Tip.) Evenly sprinkle the reserved 1 Tbsp of almonds over the bottom of the Bundt pan. Pour the batter into the prepared pan and bake for 35 to 40 minutes, or until a tester or toothpick inserted into the center comes out clean and the surface bounces back to the touch.

6. Let the cake cool in the pan for 10 minutes, then turn it out onto a wire rack to cool completely. Store the cake, covered, at room temperature for up to 3 days or in the freezer, well wrapped in plastic, for up to 3 months.

TIP!

If you don't have a 6-cup Bundt pan, this cake can also be baked in an 8½ by 4½ in [21.5 by 11 cm] loaf pan. Rather than sprinkling the reserved almonds into the bottom of the pan, use them to top the batter after you've poured it into the pan. Bake for 50 to 55 minutes, or until a tester or toothpick inserted into the center comes out clean and the surface bounces back when gently poked. Let the cake cool in the pan for 10 minutes, then turn it out of the pan onto a wire rack to cool completely.

Food is a part of holiday rituals both festive and solemn. Yom Kippur is the Jewish holiday often referred to as the Day of Atonement. It is a somber day of the year distinguished by prayer and fasting. Breaking the fast is often done with a small meal of bagels, bialys, cream cheese, and smoked fish.

The bialy (pronounced *bee-AH-lee*), described by some as a delicious cross between an onion bagel and an English muffin, hails from the city of Bialystok, in what is now northeastern Poland. There, prior to the twentieth century, these hearth-baked, onion-and-poppy-seed-stuffed rolls were crafted primarily by Jewish bakers and enjoyed at every meal.

Upon immigrating to the United States, scores of Jewish bakers from the Bialystok region, with their bialy recipes in hand, settled in New York City on Manhattan's Lower East Side, where they proceeded to build a robust bialy-baking industry. By the 1930s, the bialy was so central to immigrant Lower East Side Jewish life that bialy bakers had seen fit to create their own union, the Bialy Bakers Association, separate from the Bagel Bakers Association.

Today, bialys are an endangered species. But here at the Bakehouse, this bialy tradition lives on. Zingerman's cofounder, Ari Weinzweig, tells the story:

We've been making bialys at the Bakehouse almost since we opened. One of the first things that drew us to wanting to work with our bread mentor, Michael London, back in 1992, was that we discovered that he had the bialy recipe from Kossar's, the classic spot on the Lower East Side to get bialys. I was really excited that we got to learn from someone who'd learned the recipe at the (American) source.

BIALYS

makes 12 bialys

Bialys are chewy, flat, disk-shaped rolls with indented centers filled with slow-roasted onions and poppy seeds. They were once readily available in American urban centers with Jewish communities, but now they've become difficult to find. By sharing our recipe, we hope to revive their popularity. They're delicious on their own or with many of the same fixings and accompaniments you'd eat with a bagel. Enjoy!

ONION FILLING	DOUGH
4½ cups [650 g] diced yellow onions	2⅓ cups [540 g] water, room temperature
2 Tbsp [25 g] vegetable oil	6 cups plus 1½ Tbsp [855 g] all-purpose flour, plus more for dusting
1 Tbsp [10 g] poppy seeds	
½ Tbsp [10 g] fine sea salt	1½ tsp instant yeast
	1 Tbsp [20 g] fine sea salt

make the onion filling

1. Preheat the oven to 375°F [200°C]. Line a large baking sheet and three half baking sheets (13 by 18 in [33 by 46 cm]) with parchment paper.

2. In a large bowl, toss the onions with the oil, poppy seeds, and salt.

3. Spread the onions on the large baking sheet and roast in the oven for about 60 minutes. The thinner the layer of onions, the quicker they will cook. Stir them after each 15-minute increment, and remove from the oven when they are well caramelized. Cool to room temperature.

make the dough

1. In a large mixing bowl, add the water, half of the flour, and the yeast and mix with a wooden spoon until it looks like a thick pancake batter. Add the remaining flour and the salt. Mix until all of the flour is incorporated and the dough is beginning to come together.

2. Turn the dough out of the bowl onto a clean, unfloured work surface and knead for 5 minutes until the dough becomes cohesive and smooth and has some

elasticity. Resist the temptation to add extra flour at this point; it is not necessary, even if the dough feels sticky while kneading.

3. Place the kneaded dough in a large mixing bowl or container lightly coated with oil or nonstick cooking spray, and cover it with plastic wrap or a tea towel. Ferment the dough for 2 hours in a warm location.

shape, fill, proof, and bake the bialys

1. Turn the fermented dough out onto a clean, unfloured work surface. Divide it into twelve equal pieces, gently round each piece, and set them seam side down on a now well-floured work surface. Lightly dust the tops with flour and cover with plastic wrap. Let rest for 30 minutes.

2. Take each piece of rested dough and, using your fingers, press the center down while gently stretching it into a 4 in [10 cm] disk with raised edges. The thin center impression should be about 2 in [5 cm] in diameter. Place four bialys on each half-sheet baking sheet, evenly spaced apart.

3. Place 1 Tbsp [20 to 30 g] of onion filling in the center of each bialy. Cover the bialys with plastic wrap or a tea towel and proof them for about 1 hour. This proofing time will vary depending on the temperature of the dough and the environment. The dough, once sufficiently proofed, should look puffy and if you poke it with your finger, an indentation should remain visible.

4. Preheat the oven to 475°F [240°C].

5. Press the centers of all the bialys down again before baking; if you don't, the centers will puff up rather than remain indented. Bake for 12 to 14 minutes, until just golden with some darker spots.

6. Remove from the oven and enjoy them while slightly warm, or cooled to room temperature. Store bialys at room temperature in a plastic bag or an airtight container for up to 3 days, or in the freezer for up to 3 months. Thaw frozen bialys at room temperature before enjoying.

BAVARIAN SOFT PRETZELS

makes 12 pretzels

Our traditional German-style, Bavarian soft pretzels, dipped in mustard or spread with tasty Bacon Pimento Cheese (page 133), are an irresistible addition to Oktoberfest festivities. We make ours the old-fashioned way with a bit of lard and a lye dip to get the distinctive pretzel flavor, color, and texture: soft inside and chewy outside. Substitute butter for lard if you'd like to make them vegetarian and skip the lye bath if you're making these with kids (see Tip, page 149).

6 cups plus 2 Tbsp [860 g] all-purpose flour	1 Tbsp [20 g] barley malt (substitute honey)
2 cups [455 g] water, room temperature	1 Tbsp [20 g] fine sea salt
2 Tbsp [30 g] lard, room temperature	¼ cup [60 g] food-grade lye
2 Tbsp [20 g] instant yeast	2 to 4 Tbsp coarse kosher salt or pretzel salt, for garnish

OKTOBERFEST

Oktoberfest is a beer-centered festival originating in Munich, Bavaria, Germany, that lasts about sixteen days from mid-September until the first Sunday in October. It originated in 1810 and is still hugely popular, attended by millions of people annually. Its popularity has grown so strong that revelers across the world who can't make the trip to Munich often find a way to celebrate in their hometowns. Here in the United States, communities may throw their own festivities, usually in the form of street fairs. Restaurants and bars often feature German-style beers and traditional German food during this timeframe. Want to throw your own Oktoberfest party? We've included two of our favorite recipes that are perfect to celebrate with: Bavarian Soft Pretzels and 5 O'Clock Cheddar Ale Soup (page 150). These will make excellent additions to your full menu.

1. In a large mixing bowl, add half of the flour, the water, lard, yeast, and barley malt and stir with a wooden spoon to make a thick batter. Add the salt and remaining flour and mix until the dough forms a shaggy mass.

2. Turn the dough out of the bowl onto a clean, unfloured work surface and knead for 8 to 10 minutes; it will be a very stiff dough. Make sure all the dry ingredients are incorporated.

3. Once the dough has been kneaded, test it with the windowpane test (see page 244) and immediately portion it out into twelve equal pieces, each weighing 4 oz [115 g]. Pre-shape each piece into a 6 to 8 in [15 to 20 cm] log and cover with plastic wrap. Let the pieces rest on the work surface for 5 minutes.

4. Shape each piece of rested dough into a twist. To do so, roll each piece into a rope that is 24 in [61 cm] in length, keeping the middle section (the "belly") slightly fatter and tapering the tips. Leaving the dough on the table, create a U shape with the belly section closest to you and the tips facing away. Cross the two ends. Cross the ends again, creating a twist. Fold the tips down and press them into the "belly" (see the diagram on page 245). Repeat with the remaining dough.

5. Ferment the shaped pieces for 30 minutes, uncovered at room temperature. This will allow a skin to form over the pretzels so they keep their shape when you dip them in the lye just before baking. (At this point, the pretzels can be refrigerated, uncovered, for up to 1 hour.)

6. While the pretzels are fermenting, preheat the oven to 400°F [200°C].

7. Prepare the lye dipping solution by mixing the lye into 5 cups [1.2 L] of room-temperature water. This is a 5% lye solution. Be careful and wear gloves; it is corrosive. Whisk the water gently while adding the lye to it. Do not add water to the lye.

cont'd

8. Consider how many pretzels you can bake at one time in your oven before doing this next step. Only dip the number you can bake immediately. Dip each pretzel into the lye solution, allowing some of the moisture to drip off, then let the pretzels drain either on a wire cooling rack or by shaking them well.

9. Coat an aluminum pizza screen or a baking sheet lined with parchment paper with nonstick cooking spray. Place the pretzels on the screen or sheet, and with a lame (see page 239) or a sharp knife, score each of their thick bellies with a straight horizontal cut, then sprinkle them with coarse salt. (The belly is the part at the bottom of the pretzel that is not twisted.) After scoring the pretzels, remove the gloves and wash your hands and arms.

10. Bake the pretzels for 13 to 15 minutes, or until deep brown. Let cool on the screen or baking sheet until they are cool enough to touch. Store soft pretzels in a paper bag at room temperature for up to 2 days, or in the freezer, in an airtight container, for up to 1 month. We do not recommend freezing the raw dough. Thaw frozen pretzels at room temperature before enjoying.

TIP!

As an alternative to dipping your pretzels into a lye bath, you can use a solution of baking soda and water: Simply mix ½ cup [120 g] of baking soda into 5 cups [1.2 L] of room-temperature water and proceed with the recipe. This is a safer solution that approximates the results of lye.

5 O'CLOCK CHEDDAR ALE SOUP

serves 6 to 8 as a main dish

This soup is another perfect way to include beer in your Oktoberfest festivities. You may enjoy it so much that it becomes a standard in your soup repertoire. At the bakery, we make it year-round—it's been a Thursday choice in our shop for at least a decade. It's been so long that none of us can remember exactly when we started to make it. Its distinctive flavor comes from sharp Cheddar cheese, sherry vinegar, Marash pepper, and a well-chosen amber ale. You'll need one bottle of ale and part of another for the recipe—feel free to enjoy the rest of the second bottle yourself as you cook! Pair it with our Bavarian Soft Pretzels (page 147) for dunking.

VEGETABLE STOCK

2 large [185 g] carrots	
1 medium [160 g] yellow onion	
2 large [140 g] celery stalks	
2 or 3 fresh parsley sprigs	
1 or 2 fresh thyme sprigs	
1 bay leaf	
2 whole black peppercorns	
7 cups [1.7 L] water	

SOUP

½ cup [110 g] unsalted butter	1 cup [140 g] diced yellow onion
1¼ cup [150 g] diced celery	1 cup [140 g] diced carrot
	3 [25 g] garlic cloves, minced
	Fine sea salt
	14 oz [400 g] amber ale
	1 cup [140 g] all-purpose flour
	4¾ cups [1.1 L] whole milk
	8 cups [640 g] grated sharp Cheddar cheese
	3 tsp Marash pepper flakes
	1 tsp ground white pepper
	3 tsp sherry vinegar

make the vegetable stock

1. Cut the carrots, onion, and celery into large pieces. In a medium stockpot, add the vegetables, parsley, thyme, bay leaf, peppercorns, and water. Bring the stock to a boil over medium-high heat, then lower the heat to medium-low and simmer gently, partially covered, for 1 hour.

2. Strain the simmered stock through a fine-mesh sieve, discard the solids, and reserve 4 cups [910 g] for the soup. Any extra stock can be refrigerated or frozen for later use; if you come up a little short, add water to make up the difference.

make the soup

1. In a large stockpot over medium heat, melt the butter, then add the celery, onion, carrot, garlic, and a generous sprinkle of salt and sauté until the vegetables are tender and the onions are translucent, 10 to 15 minutes. Take care not to brown them. Add the ale, lower the heat to medium-low, and simmer for 5 minutes.

2. In a medium stockpot, bring the vegetable stock to a simmer. If it cooks down below 4 cups [910 g], add more water.

3. Add the flour to the vegetable mixture, stir, and cook over medium heat until the mixture thickens and starts to stick to the pot. Gradually pour in the milk, stirring as you do, and bring the soup to a simmer. Add the hot vegetable stock to the soup.

4. Remove the soup pot from the heat and purée with an immersion blender. Return the pot to low to medium heat and slowly add the Cheddar, stirring constantly to avoid scorching. Turn off the heat and stir in the Marash pepper, white pepper, and vinegar.

5. Season with additional salt if needed and serve. Store in an airtight container in the refrigerator for up to 5 days.

HALLOWEEN

Here in Michigan, kids grow up accustomed to layering winter coats either under or over their Halloween costumes (or stubbornly refusing once they're old enough to, and suffering the chilly consequences). So, a belly-warming soup is just the thing for pre- or post-trick-or-treating to take the edge off of a crisp evening. Our butternut squash soup is a fall favorite among regular customers at the Bakehouse—and it might become a family favorite of yours too.

Come fall, guests and staff alike also get excited for the return of pumpkin goodies to our Bakeshop—pumpkin muffins, pumpkin cheesecake, pumpkin pie, and our Pumpkin Cupcakes with Cream Cheese Frosting (page 154).

KICKIN' BUTTERNUT SOUP

Serves 6 to 8 as a main dish

As you might deduce from the name, we make this soup with butternut squash, but feel free to switch up the squash and call yours Kickin' Kabocha or Kickin' Pumpkin! If you like, you can call it Kickin' Pumpkin no matter what type of squash you use—there's no botanical distinction that makes a pumpkin a pumpkin. In fact, that can of pumpkin purée lurking in the back of your pantry? It's likely made with other types of winter squash, like butternut!

Our soup's kick comes from a combination of chipotles in adobo sauce, fresh cilantro, and smoked cumin. We love the flavor that smoked cumin lends to this soup, but if you can't find it, regular ground cumin will be just fine. It's not necessary, but if you'd like to make your own vegetable stock for this soup, we share our recipe as a part of the 5 O'Clock Cheddar Ale Soup (page 150).

2 medium [1.8 kg] hard-skinned squash, like butternut or sugar pie pumpkins

½ cup plus 1 Tbsp [125 g] unsalted butter

1½ cups [200 g] diced yellow onion

1½ cups [200 g] diced celery

1½ cups [200 g] diced carrots

1 Tbsp fine sea salt

1 tsp freshly ground black pepper

5 cups [1.2 L] vegetable stock

Scant ¼ cup [50 g] chipotle peppers in adobo sauce (see Tip)

1½ tsp ground smoked cumin

1⅔ cups [380 g] heavy cream

1 bunch [75 g] fresh cilantro, leaves finely chopped

TIP!

Use an ice cube tray to freeze the remaining chipotles with adobo sauce—we stick one chile and a little sauce in each cup and then transfer to a labeled airtight container or freezer bag once frozen.

1. Preheat the oven to 375°F [190°C]. Line a baking sheet with parchment paper.

2. Cut the squash or pumpkin in half lengthwise, leaving the skin on, and scoop out the stringy interior and seeds, which you can discard or save for another use.

3. Place the squash halves on the prepared baking sheet, skin side up, and roast in the oven until fork-tender, 45 minutes to 1 hour. Allow the cooked squash to cool until comfortable enough to handle.

4. While the squash is cooling, in a large stockpot, melt the butter over medium heat, add the onion, celery, carrots, salt, and black pepper, and sauté until soft, 10 to 15 minutes.

5. Scoop out the roasted squash flesh and add it to the stockpot, discarding the skins. Add the vegetable stock until the vegetables are just covered in liquid. Any additional stock can be reserved for another use. Bring the soup to a boil over medium-high heat. Cover, lower the heat to medium-low, and let simmer for 10 minutes.

6. Remove the pot from the heat, add the chipotle peppers with adobo sauce and smoked cumin, and purée the soup with an immersion blender until smooth.

7. Add the heavy cream and cilantro and stir well to combine. Season to taste with additional salt and black pepper.

8. Return the pot to the stove and warm the soup over medium-low heat to your desired serving temperature. Store the soup in the refrigerator for up to 5 days. Soups with cream don't freeze well, but if you'd like to plan ahead, make the soup through puréeing; it can be frozen in an airtight container for up to 3 months. Add the heavy cream and cilantro when ready to serve.

PUMPKIN CUPCAKES WITH CREAM CHEESE FROSTING

makes 12 cupcakes

Made with seasonal spices and iced with cream cheese frosting, these pumpkin cupcakes are perfect for Halloween parties and appeal to both adults and kids alike. We like to garnish each of these with an adorably tiny fondant pumpkin. To do the same on yours, see our fondant recipe on page 35.

PUMPKIN CUPCAKES

1 cup [140 g] all-purpose flour

1 tsp fine sea salt

½ tsp baking soda

1¼ tsp ground cinnamon

½ tsp ground nutmeg

½ tsp ground ginger

½ tsp ground cloves

½ tsp ground allspice

½ cup plus 1 Tbsp [115 g] granulated sugar

½ cup plus 1 Tbsp [115 g] brown sugar, packed

¼ cup [55 g] unsalted butter, room temperature

1 large egg, room temperature

½ cup [115 g] pumpkin purée

¼ cup [60 g] whole milk

CREAM CHEESE FROSTING

½ cup plus 2 Tbsp [150 g] cream cheese, room temperature

⅔ cup [150 g] unsalted butter, room temperature

1½ tsp lemon juice, room temperature

1 tsp vanilla extract

3 cups [300 g] sifted powdered sugar

make the pumpkin cupcakes

1. Preheat the oven to 325°F [165°C]. Line the cups of a standard 12-cup muffin pan with cupcake liners. If you prefer not to use liners, coat the cups with nonstick cooking spray. Set aside.

2. In a medium mixing bowl, whisk together the flour, salt, baking soda, and spices. Set aside.

3. In the bowl of a stand mixer fitted with the paddle attachment, cream the sugars and butter on medium speed until light and well blended. Scrape down the sides of the bowl as needed. Add the egg, beating to incorporate completely. Then add the pumpkin purée and milk, mixing until just combined. Take care not to add too much air to the mixture.

4. With the mixer on low speed, slowly add the dry ingredients, mixing until well combined.

5. Divide the batter among 12 muffin cups. Bake the cupcakes for 25 to 27 minutes. The cupcakes are done when they spring back when lightly pressed in the center and an inserted tester or toothpick comes out clean.

6. Let the cupcakes cool in the pan for 5 minutes, then transfer them to a wire rack to cool completely to room temperature.

make the cream cheese frosting and assemble

1. In a medium mixing bowl, lightly beat the cream cheese until there are no lumps remaining. Add the butter and beat until smooth. Add the lemon juice and vanilla extract and stir to combine. Add the powdered sugar and stir until completely smooth.

2. To frost the cooled cupcakes, dollop frosting (eyeball a couple of tablespoons) on top of each cupcake with an offset spatula or butter knife, then spread to smooth the frosting and cover the cupcake.

3. Alternatively, place the frosting into a large piping bag fitted with a ½ in [12 mm] circle tip. Depending on the size of your piping bag, you may only want to use half of the frosting at a time. Pipe a swirl of frosting on top of the cupcake. These cupcakes, once assembled, keep well in the refrigerator, in an airtight container, for up to 1 week. Let them come to room temperature before serving.

Being kind to our guests, each other, and our community is a value we take super seriously at Zingerman's. We also try to connect the world in a positive way through the education and sharing of traditional, full-flavored foods. For these reasons, World Kindness Day, a day intended to highlight community and focus on the positive power of kindness, is one we enjoy promoting.

MOROCCAN HARIRA SOUP

serves 6 to 8 as a main dish

We think that Moroccan Harira Soup (the national soup of Morocco) is a perfect fit for World Kindness Day. There's nothing quite as comforting as a warm bowl of soup, and the combination of green lentils, chickpeas, spices, and vegetables makes this one a nourishing meal in a bowl. It also just so happens to be gluten-free and vegan, so it's easier to share with folks who might have dietary restrictions.

Feel free to dial up the amount of harissa if you'd like a little more of a kick, or put a little bowl of harissa on the table so that everyone can adjust the heat level to their liking. Enjoy it with our Za'atar Flatbreads (page 158).

3 Tbsp olive oil	1 tsp ground cumin
4 cups [560 g] diced carrot	½ tsp ground turmeric
2 cups [280 g] diced yellow onion	1 bunch [75 g] finely chopped fresh parsley
1 cup [120 g] diced celery	1 bunch [75 g] finely chopped fresh cilantro
Fine sea salt and freshly ground black pepper	1 cup [180 g] dried chickpeas, soaked overnight
10 cups [2.3 L] vegetable stock (see page 150)	1 cup [200 g] green lentils
One 14.5 oz [415 g] can crushed tomatoes	¼ cup [60 g] lemon juice
1 Tbsp harissa paste	

1. In a large stockpot, heat the oil over medium heat until shimmering, then add the carrot, onion, celery, and a generous sprinkle of salt and pepper. Sauté the vegetables until just slightly tender, about 10 minutes.

2. Add the stock, crushed tomatoes, harissa, cumin, turmeric, and three-quarters of the chopped herbs, reserving one-quarter for garnish. Bring to a boil over medium-high heat, then lower the heat to medium-low and simmer, uncovered, for 25 minutes.

3. Drain the soaked chickpeas, then add them to the pot and simmer, uncovered, until almost tender, about 20 minutes. Add the lentils and simmer, uncovered, until tender, another 15 to 20 minutes. By this point, the liquid in the stockpot will have reduced a fair amount—that's to be expected. Add the lemon juice and simmer for another 5 minutes.

4. Taste the lentils and chickpeas; they should be tender but not mushy. If they are not yet tender, continue to simmer. If much of the water has been absorbed, you may want to add a little, ½ to 1 cup [115 to 230 ml] to aid in further cooking. Continue to simmer until the chickpeas and lentils are the right texture and the soup has a thick consistency. Taste and season with additional salt and pepper, as needed.

5. Serve the soup garnished with the reserved chopped parsley and cilantro. Store leftover soup in an airtight container in the refrigerator for up to 1 week or in the freezer for up to 3 months.

ZA'ATAR FLATBREADS

makes 4 flatbreads

These flatbreads, topped with za'atar, a Middle Eastern spice mix, pair nicely with our Moroccan Harira Soup (page 157); depending on how many folks you're sharing the soup with, you might want to make a double batch of flatbreads to ensure a sense of full hospitality and so you're guaranteed to be able to enjoy one the next day with a fried egg on top. This could be beneficial beyond just a tasty start to your day; in the Middle East, some parents encourage their children to eat za'atar for breakfast, telling them it will make them smarter!

We can't promise any mental benefits from eating this bread, but we can promise that za'atar is a delicious addition to your spice collection. This Middle Eastern spice mix is bright, nutty, and earthy. The blend varies from region to region but generally includes toasted sesame seeds and sumac along with a combination of dried oregano, marjoram, and/or thyme. Sometimes you'll also find za'atar with additional ingredients like salt, dried orange zest, and dried za'atar (an herb also known as hyssop).

DOUGH

1½ cups [210 g] all-purpose flour, plus more for dusting
½ cup [115 g] water
1 Tbsp olive oil
1 tsp fine sea salt
¾ tsp instant yeast

ZA'ATAR TOPPING

1 Tbsp za'atar
3 Tbsp olive oil
¼ to ½ tsp fine sea salt (optional)

make the dough

1. In a medium mixing bowl, combine the flour, water, olive oil, salt, and yeast and mix with a wooden spoon until the dough forms a shaggy mass. Scrape the dough onto a clean, unfloured work surface and knead for 5 minutes, or until the dough is smooth, evenly hydrated, and has some elasticity.

2. Using a bench scraper or chef's knife, divide the dough into four equal pieces. Shape each piece into a ball and place on a clean, unfloured work surface. Cover the dough pieces with plastic wrap or a tea towel and let rest for 45 minutes.

3. Put a baking stone in the oven and preheat the oven to 500°F [260°C].

make the za'atar topping

1. Check to see whether or not your za'atar contains salt; if it does contain salt, do not add any to your topping mixture. In a small bowl, combine the za'atar, olive oil, and salt, if using, and stir to make a slurry.

shape and bake the flatbreads

1. Lightly flour the work surface. Using a rolling pin, roll each rested ball into a 6 in [15 cm] circle.

2. Cover the dough circles lightly with plastic wrap and allow to proof for 20 minutes. The dough is ready when you poke it gently with your finger and the indentation remains visible.

3. Choose the tool you'll use to transfer the flatbreads to the stone. The best option is a baking peel, but an inverted baking tray will also work. Gently move one or two dough circles (the number you think you can successfully transfer at the same time onto the stone in the oven) to the peel. Garnish each one with one-quarter of the za'atar topping and place on the baking stone in the oven.

4. Bake for 8 to 10 minutes, until lightly browned on the bottoms and around the edges. You can check the bottom by lifting a flatbread with a small spatula.

5. Repeat the baking process with the remaining flatbreads. Enjoy while warm. Store in an airtight container at room temperature for several days. These reheat well in an oven at 300°F [150°C] for 5 to 7 minutes.

NUTTY BUTTERBALL COOKIES

makes about 60 little cookies

For a sweet kindness, try our Nutty Butterball Cookies. Beloved the world over, butterballs are truly international, making them a perfect fit for sharing with friends or neighbors on World Kindness Day. Depending upon where you're from, they're known by lots of different names. Here in America, they are Southern pecan balls, pecan melt-aways, snow drops, snowballs, or just simply butterballs. Around the world, they are polvoróns (Mexican wedding cookies), Russian tea cakes, Viennese sugar balls, or Danish smør bullar.

No matter their name, everyone agrees on the basic recipe for these powdery white, melt-in-your-mouth short-bread cookies—always with butter, powdered sugar, flour, and very finely chopped nuts, whether pecans, almonds, or walnuts—and also on the shape—rolled into round balls that bake up with a slightly flat bottom due to their contact with the baking sheet. Their simplicity is indeed perfection!

1¼ cups [150 g] raw pecans, walnuts, or hazelnuts

2 cups plus 3 Tbsp [310 g] all-purpose flour

1 cup [220 g] unsalted butter, room temperature

1 tsp fine sea salt

1⅔ cups [190 g] powdered sugar

1 tsp vanilla extract

1. Preheat the oven to 325°F [165°C].

2. Toast the nuts on a baking sheet for 10 to 12 minutes, or until fragrant and deeply colored; start checking them after 8 minutes. Do not under-toast; if that happens, the flavor of the cookies will be more mild than intended. Allow the nuts to cool completely to room temperature. Once cooled, pulse the nuts with the flour in a food processor until the nuts are finely ground, then set aside.

3. Increase the oven temperature to 375°F [190°C]. Line two baking sheets with parchment paper.

4. In a medium mixing bowl, cream together the butter, salt, and ⅔ cup [75 g] of the powdered sugar with a wooden spoon. If using a stand mixer, use the paddle attachment and mix on medium speed. Add the vanilla extract and mix until smooth. Add the flour and nut mixture to the creamed butter mixture and stir until incorporated.

5. Using a ⅓ oz scoop (#100), portion out the dough, form it into balls using your hands, and place them 1 in [2.5 cm] apart on the prepared lined baking sheets. If you don't have a scoop, you can use a small spoon; dough balls should be the size of a large marble. Bake for 12 minutes, until the cookies are light brown.

6. Allow the cookies to cool completely on the baking sheets. Place the cooled cookies, a few at a time, into a resealable plastic bag with the remaining 1 cup [115 g] of powdered sugar. Seal the top of the bag and gently shake until the cookies are coated. Remove the cookies from the bag and gently shake off any excess powdered sugar. Store in an airtight container for up to 1 week or in the freezer for up to 3 months. Thaw frozen cookies at room temperature before enjoying.

PUMPKIN CHEESECAKE

makes one large cheesecake

Our Pumpkin Cheesecake has become a Thanksgiving favorite in our community. It's familiar enough to comfortably tuck its way onto the holiday table without raising any eyebrows from family members staunchly committed to classic dishes, while being just different enough to encourage even the fullest members of your crew to find a little more space for dessert.

We make the crust with a spicy ginger molasses cookie (also known as our Ginger Jump-Up cookies) and enhance the rich and creamy pumpkin filling with warm autumn spices and fresh farm cheese from our neighbor, Zingerman's Creamery. You can follow the recipe for making your own cookies, or use 1 lb [455 g] of store-bought ginger snap cookies.

MOLASSES GINGER COOKIE CRUST

¾ cup [150 g] muscovado brown sugar, packed

½ cup [110 g] unsalted butter, room temperature

⅓ cup [110 g] molasses

1 large egg, room temperature

2 cups plus 3 Tbsp [310 g] all-purpose flour

1 tsp baking soda

1 tsp ground cinnamon

1 tsp ground ginger

¼ tsp ground cloves

½ cup [75 g] chopped crystallized ginger

6 Tbsp plus 2 tsp [95 g] unsalted butter, melted

PUMPKIN CHEESECAKE FILLING

1½ cups [360 g] cream cheese, room temperature

1½ cups [360 g] farm cheese, room temperature (or the same amount of cream cheese)

1⅓ cups [265 g] granulated sugar

1 Tbsp all-purpose flour

2 tsp ground cinnamon

1 tsp ground cloves

1 tsp ground ginger

3 large eggs, room temperature

1 egg yolk, room temperature

2 tsp vanilla extract

1¼ cups [300 g] canned pumpkin purée

¾ cup [175 g] heavy cream, room temperature

cont'd

Thanksgiving is arguably the holiday with the most specific American food traditions that transcend each of our families' cultural foodways. It is in this way the most American holiday. The consistency of our menus is notable, as is the adherence to tradition in a culture known to prioritize uniqueness and innovation. Roasted turkey, bread stuffing, sweet potatoes—perhaps with marshmallows—and green beans in some form are classic dishes on most Thanksgiving tables. There are often dinner rolls and special breads, and pie is the dessert of choice.

The most basic roots of the holiday are as a harvest celebration before winter sets in. The origination story and the relationship depicted between the Pilgrims and Indigenous peoples is now being reconsidered as something to celebrate. For many Americans, the weekend is disconnected from its beginnings. Instead, it marks the kick-off of the holiday season for many Americans—Thanksgiving, Christmas, and New Year's—and has turned into an important time to gather our far-flung families, resulting in it being the busiest travel day of the year in the country. For some of us, the day is elevated above the food and football by taking some time to express gratitude for people and events of the past year, and some of us spend a portion of our day serving the less fortunate in our communities.

At the bakery, the few days before Thanksgiving are our busiest baking days of the year. Our pastry ovens are full of pumpkin, apple, and pecan pies. The bread bakers have the single biggest day of the year, the Tuesday before Thanksgiving. The physical effort on that day to make the thousands of loaves of nourishing breads and buttery brioche rolls is truly Herculean. Although our work is daunting and occupies our minds for weeks ahead, we are grateful to play a flavorful part in so many of the Thanksgiving meals in our community.

make the molasses ginger cookie crust

1. Preheat the oven to 350°F [180°C]. Line a baking sheet with parchment paper.

2. In a large mixing bowl, cream the brown sugar, room-temperature butter, and molasses with a wooden spoon until well blended. If using a stand mixer, use the paddle attachment and beat on medium speed. Add the egg and mix until the mixture is light and creamy.

3. In a medium bowl, whisk together the flour, baking soda, cinnamon, ground ginger, and cloves until evenly combined. Add the dry ingredients and the crystallized ginger to the creamed butter mixture and mix until completely incorporated. If using a stand mixer, mix on low speed.

4. Weigh out 1 lb [455 g] of dough (3½ cups) onto the prepared baking sheet and press the dough out to ½ in [12 mm] thick . Bake for 35 minutes, or until uniformly firm. Cool completely on the baking sheet (it will crisp once cooled), then break into large pieces.

5. In a food processor, add the baked pieces (or store-bought ginger snaps) and grind into fine crumbs. If you are doing this by hand, place the pieces in a resealable plastic bag and gently hit with a rolling pin or frying pan. In a small bowl, mix together the crumbs and melted butter until fully combined.

6. Coat the bottom and sides of a 9 in [23 cm] spring-form pan with nonstick cooking spray. Press the mixture into the pan so that the crust is compact and an even thickness across the bottom and 1 in [2.5 cm] up the sides of the pan.

7. Carefully wrap the outside of the springform pan with aluminum foil and place it in a larger pan with at least 3 in [8 cm] sides. This will be the water bath in which it bakes, and the foil prevents water from leaking into the cheesecake.

make the pumpkin cheesecake filling

1. In a large mixing bowl, beat the cream cheese with a wooden spoon until smooth. If using a stand mixer, use the paddle attachment and beat on medium speed.

2. If using farm cheese, smooth the curds by processing it in a food processor first. Add the farm cheese to the cream cheese and beat the two together until smooth.

3. In a medium mixing bowl, whisk together the sugar, flour, cinnamon, cloves, and ginger until evenly combined. Add the dry ingredients to the cheese mixture and stir with a wooden spoon until evenly mixed. If using a stand mixer, use the paddle attachment on low speed. Scrape down the sides of the bowl well with a bowl scraper or spatula.

4. Add the eggs and the egg yolk one at a time, mixing each one until incorporated before adding the next, and scraping the bowl periodically. Add the vanilla extract and stir to combine. Add the pumpkin and mix in completely. If using a stand mixer, use the paddle attachment on medium speed. Add the heavy cream and stir until the batter is completely smooth. Scrape the bowl well and transfer the batter to the springform pan with the prepared crust.

bake the cheesecake

1. Transfer the springform pan and the larger pan to the oven and slowly add boiling water to the larger pan until it reaches halfway up the outside of the springform pan.

2. Turn the oven temperature down to 250°F [120°C] and bake for 2 to 2½ hours, or until the top surface is set and the cheesecake moves like gelatin when jiggled, not like waves. The cheesecake is completely baked when a tester inserted in the center comes out moist, but is not coated in batter, and the internal temperature registers 175°F [80°C] on an instant-read thermometer.

3. Turn the oven off and allow the cheesecake to rest for 20 minutes in the oven, still in the water bath. Remove the pan from the oven and run a warm, dry, offset spatula around the edge of the cheesecake; this will help prevent cracks as the cheesecake cools. Cool for 20 minutes at room temperature, then transfer to the refrigerator, uncovered, to cool completely; this will help prevent condensation. Once cool, cover the top with plastic wrap.

4. When the cheesecake is fully cooled, it may be carefully removed from the springform pan. To remove the cheesecake from the pan, first remove the sides of the springform pan. Next, use a knife or offset spatula to loosen the cheesecake from the bottom of the pan. Using a wide spatula, transfer the cheesecake to a serving plate or platter. Serve chilled. The cheesecake can be stored, wrapped in plastic, in the refrigerator for up to 5 days or freezer for several months. Thaw frozen cheesecake in the refrigerator before enjoying.

TIP!

The extra dough from the crust can be baked as cookies. Portion the dough using a ¾ oz [22 g] portioner, or shape it by hand into balls, using about 1½ Tbsp of dough for each. Place onto a baking sheet lined with parchment paper, leaving space for the cookies to spread. With the palm of your hand, press each cookie down into a thick disk. Top each cookie generously with demerara sugar. Bake the cookies for 12 to 14 minutes, or until the edges are firm and the centers are not visibly wet. Or, portion the cookies, but wait to bake them later. Disks of cookie dough can be stored in an airtight container in the refrigerator for 1 week or in the freezer for up to 3 months. If baking frozen disks, you'll need to add a couple of minutes to the baking time.

CHOCOLATE CHESS PIE

makes one single-crust pie

We think this pie is a perfect addition to Friendsgiving, and will no doubt be particularly appreciated by all of the chocolate lovers at your gathering. The filling has a texture similar to that of a flourless chocolate cake and it's paired perfectly with an all-butter crust. We enjoy it served with whipped cream or ice cream.

PIE DOUGH

1¼ cups plus ½ Tbsp [180 g] all-purpose flour

½ tsp fine sea salt

½ cup [110 g] unsalted butter, cold

2½ Tbsp water, cold

CHOCOLATE CHESS FILLING

¾ cup [170 g] unsalted butter

¼ cup plus 1 Tbsp [55 g] unsweetened chocolate, chopped

1½ cups [300 g] granulated sugar

4 large eggs, room temperature

1 egg yolk, room temperature

1½ tsp vanilla extract

½ tsp fine sea salt

FRIENDSGIVING

Friendsgiving is the name given to a gathering with friends, held on a day near Thanksgiving. It's a very new American tradition. According to *Merriam-Webster's Dictionary*, it first appeared in writing in 2007 and has grown in popularity ever since.

Unlike Thanksgiving menus, which have a tendency to accumulate non-negotiable family-favorite dishes, Friendsgiving offers more leeway. Not only is it likely to be a fun, relaxed gathering with friends, it's also a good time to take a dish for a test drive to see if it could pass muster at the Thanksgiving main event.

make the pie dough

1. In a large mixing bowl, mix together the flour and salt with a fork.

2. Cut the cold butter into ¼ in [6 mm] cubes and add three-quarters of the cubes to the bowl. Cut the butter into the flour mixture using a pastry blender, two knives, or your hands. Cut or work the butter into the flour until the mixture looks like coarse cornmeal. If using your hands, break the pieces of butter up in your fingers and rub the butter and flour together. Pick the mixture up between your hands and rub your palms together as if they're cold. This will break down the butter and rub it all over the flour.

The flour will take on a creamy yellow color during this step. When you pick the mixture up in your hand, it should be possible to squeeze it into a mass that will hold together. When you see the color change and the mixture holds together when squeezed, you know that you've worked the butter in enough. Work quickly so that the butter doesn't become warm. The goal of this step is to cover the flour with fat so that the gluten strands are not able to develop.

3. Add the remaining butter and cut it into the mixture as before. These butter pieces should be left in pea-size chunks to create flakiness in the final pie crust—when they melt during baking, they create steam, which separates layers of the coated flour, making flakes of crust.

4. Create a well in the center of the flour mixture and add the cold water, using a fork to blend it in. The flour mixture will still be crumbly in the bowl, but it should look moist. If it still looks dry, add up to an additional 1 Tbsp [15 g] of cold water, until the mixture looks moistened but still crumbly.

cont'd

If the butter has been rubbed into the dough adequately in step 2, the amount of water specified should be enough. More water is usually necessary only when the butter has not been adequately distributed. It's not desirable to add more water, because it tends to make a tougher crust.

5. Turn the mixture out onto a clean, unfloured work surface, form into a mound, and push out sections of dough across the work surface with the heel of your hand. We call this "schmearing." Push each section of dough once, not twice. Make sure to schmear enough so that the dough loses its dry, crumbly appearance. At the end of the schmearing, all of the pie dough will be pushed out flat on the work surface.

6. Fold the dough back onto itself with a bench scraper. Gather it into a ball, pressing it firmly so it holds together, then shape it into a disk, and wrap with plastic wrap. Chill the dough in the refrigerator for at least 1 hour before rolling it out.

roll out the pie dough

1. Remove the chilled dough from the refrigerator. While the dough is still in the plastic wrap, firmly but gently tap on it with a rolling pin until it is flexible but still cold. Lightly flour the work surface. Place the unwrapped disk of dough on the work surface and lightly dust the top of the disk with flour.

2. Using a rolling pin, start rolling the dough from the center to the edge, away from you. Do not use too much pressure, or the dough will crack. If this happens, brush away any excess flour near the cracking area and press the dough back together.

3. Stop and give the dough a one-eighth turn. This rotation will prevent the dough from sticking to the work surface and will help make a perfect circle.

4. Reflour the work surface and the top of the dough to prevent the dough from sticking. Continue to roll the dough until it's about ⅛ in [4 mm] thick and the circle is about 1 in [2.5 cm] wider than the top diameter of the 9 in [23 cm] pie plate you will be using. Flour is your friend in this process. Use it liberally to avoid sticking.

5. When the rolled-out pie dough has reached the correct size, use a pastry brush to brush away any extra flour from the top of the dough. Turn the dough over and brush off any extra flour from the bottom. One way to do this is to roll the dough up on your rolling pin and then unwind it with the bottom surface now facing up.

6. Using a rolling pin, gently roll the dough loosely around the pin. Position the edge of the dough over the edge of the pie plate and unroll the dough. Gently ease the dough down into the pie plate, making sure not to stretch the dough. Trim the dough to ½ in [12 mm] from the edge of the pie plate, rolling the excess dough underneath (like rolling a sleeping bag, not just folding it under) to make a thicker edge. Finish the edge with your choice of decorative crimping. Pie dough can be stored wrapped in disk form or fully formed as a pie shell in the refrigerator for up to 5 days.

partially blind-bake the pie crust

1. Preheat the oven to 375°F [190°C].

2. Using a fork, dock the pie shell all over the bottom and sides (see page 242). Place the pie shell in the refrigerator or freezer and chill for at least 20 minutes before baking.

3. Remove the chilled pie shell from the refrigerator or freezer and line the chilled crust with parchment paper, pressing it snugly against the bottom and sides. Fill the lined pie shell with dried beans, rice, or pie weights, to hold down the parchment paper. It will take 3 to 4 cups of whatever weights you choose. (If using dried beans or rice, they cannot be used for any other purpose, and should be reserved exclusively for use as pie weights.)

4. Bake the crust for 25 minutes, or until the edge begins to color. Remove the parchment paper with the beans or pie weights and bake for an additional 5 minutes. At this point, the crust is considered partially blind-baked. Allow the pie crust to cool slightly while you make the filling.

make the filling and bake the pie

1. Lower the oven temperature to 350°F [180°C]. Line a baking sheet with parchment paper.

2. In a double boiler or heatproof bowl set over a saucepan of simmering water, melt the butter and unsweetened chocolate, stirring frequently. Set aside to cool slightly.

3. In a medium mixing bowl, whisk the sugar, eggs, egg yolk, vanilla extract, and salt until smooth and well combined. Add the chocolate mixture to the egg mixture and whisk until fully combined.

4. Pour the filling into the cooled, partially blind-baked pie crust. Place the filled pie on the baking sheet and bake for 45 to 50 minutes, or until the center is just set and the filling jiggles a bit, like a gelatin dessert.

5. Let cool to room temperature before serving. Store at room temperature for up to 2 days, then lightly covered in the refrigerator for up to 5 days.

NO.4
WINTER

WINTER IS JAM-PACKED WITH HOLIDAYS TO CELEBRATE and many baking traditions to accompany them. The special days range from some of the world's most celebrated—Christmas, New Year's Day, and Valentine's Day—to the all-American special day, the Super Bowl. We've placed Hanukkah, the Jewish Festival of Lights, in this chapter since it usually happens sometime during the month of December. February is Black History Month; March has St. Patrick's Day; and Fat Tuesday (Mardi Gras), celebrated uniquely by groups of different national heritage, falls sometime in February or March. One of our specialties at Zingerman's Bakehouse is Hungarian baking, and we also feature our full Hungarian repertoire during this season. Winter has become three months of multicultural celebration for us!

It's also a season that can benefit from the distraction of not-so-serious events, especially here in Michigan where we endure a long winter. "Snow Day," a day when school is canceled due to winter weather, is a joyful tradition, for kids at least, and we've provided a couple of baking projects to occupy everyone while cozying up inside with this unexpected free time. Pi Day has officially become a thing. On March 14, people are now enjoying the excuse to indulge in pie eating. We've got you covered there as well with both a sweet and a savory pie. Have an all-pie meal!

Winter is the reason I became a baker. I grew up on Cape Breton Island in Nova Scotia, Canada; our winters extended well past the official dates on the calendar, giving us lots of time to perfect our winter activities. While some people embraced winter sports, I embraced winter baking. We not-so-infrequently had entire snow weeks off from school and I headed to the kitchen. My mother always had it well stocked with the non-perishable ingredients—chocolate, nuts, dried fruit, spices—most commonly used in winter baking. After a couple of hours of measuring, mixing, and baking, we all won with something tasty to enjoy.

For me, the answer to winter weather is still to turn on the oven and enjoy making something nourishing and deeply flavored to share with friends and family. With this chapter, which includes twenty-five recipes of varying difficulty, it can become your winter activity as well!

—*Amy Emberling*

DURUM OLIVE OIL CAKE

makes one small bundt cake

Although you might think that butter-laden cakes would be the richest cakes around, this cake will have you rethinking that idea. This is a super moist cake, so it's still soft and luscious days after you bake it. (No promises that it'll last all eight nights of Hanukkah though—ours normally disappears long before that!) This cake gets a boost of citrus flavor from orange juice, lemon zest, and orange liqueur (just use more orange juice if you'd rather skip the booze) and nuttiness from toasted almonds and durum flour (substitute an equal amount of all-purpose flour if you'd rather). We chose durum flour because it is commonly grown in regions also known for their olive oil.

⅓ cup [50 g] whole raw almonds	½ cup [130 g] whole milk, room temperature
1 cup [140 g] whole durum or all-purpose flour, plus more for dusting	1 large egg, room temperature
	2 Tbsp orange juice
½ tsp baking soda	1 Tbsp fresh lemon zest
½ tsp baking powder	1 Tbsp orange liqueur, like Cointreau
½ tsp fine sea salt	
1 cup [200 g] granulated sugar	⅔ cup [130 g] extra-virgin olive oil

1. Preheat the oven to 350°F [180°C]. Generously coat a 6-cup [1.4 L] Bundt pan (see Tip) with nonstick cooking spray, then coat the pan with flour and tap out any excess.

2. Toast the almonds on a baking sheet for 8 to 12 minutes, or until fragrant and golden brown. Allow to cool completely, then finely chop and set aside.

3. In a medium bowl, whisk together the flour, baking soda, baking powder, and salt.

4. In another medium bowl, whisk together the sugar, milk, egg, orange juice, lemon zest, and orange liqueur. Gradually whisk the dry ingredients into the wet ingredients, mixing until just combined. Stir in the olive oil and mix until well combined (it needs to completely emulsify), then fold in the chopped almonds.

5. Pour the batter into the prepared pan and bake for 40 minutes, or until a tester or toothpick inserted into the center comes out clean and the surface bounces back to the touch.

6. Let the cake cool in the pan for 5 minutes, then transfer it to a wire rack to cool completely to room temperature.

7. Store the cake, covered, at room temperature for up to 1 week or freeze, well wrapped, for up to 3 months.

TIP!

If you don't have a 6-cup Bundt pan, this cake can also be baked in an 8½ by 4½ in [21.5 by 11 cm] loaf pan for 50 to 55 minutes.

HANUKKAH

Hanukkah, the Jewish Festival of Lights, is a relatively minor Jewish holiday but has many traditions associated with it that are enjoyed particularly by children. The ancient history it celebrates is the retaking of the temple in Jerusalem by the Jewish Maccabees and the lighting of the candles of the temple menorah. They burned for eight days even though there was only enough oil for one day. Now in Jewish households, the holiday is celebrated for eight days, and another candle is lit each night on the menorah to celebrate the miracle. In many households, children receive a gift each night, adding to the joy.

Foods eaten to celebrate the holiday usually feature oil in some way. Sufganiyot (filled donuts) and potato latkes are the most commonly enjoyed foods to mark the holiday. We've chosen to share our Durum Olive Oil Cake. It can be a nice dessert for a weeknight meal or a Hanukkah brunch. Many families celebrate Hanukkah by giving children Hanukkah gelt, chocolate coins covered in embossed gold and silver foil. We're not chocolatiers, so we wanted to come up with a slightly different way to participate in the holiday fun. The Chocolate Coins on page 175 are our baker's nod to the beloved chocolate gelt tradition, and we think they taste better than the run-of-the-mill chocolate coins that are available.

CHOCOLATE COINS

makes 32 to 34 cookies

We emboss our chocolate treats with a cookie stamp—the design makes them look like the designs on a coin. But if you don't have one, don't let that stop you from making these cookies! When chilling the dough, form it into a long log instead of a disk and then cut 1/2 in [12 mm] slices. If you still want that Hanukkah gelt look, you could wrap the cookies in foil after they're baked. These lend themselves to being flavored too; try orange or mint flavoring if you'd like some variety.

CHOCOLATE COOKIES

1 cup [140 g] all-purpose flour

½ cup [60 g] powdered sugar

¾ cup [60 g] Dutch-process cocoa powder (see Tip, page 176)

¼ tsp fine sea salt

½ cup [110 g] unsalted butter, cold

2 Tbsp whole milk, room temperature

1 tsp vanilla extract

GLAZE

¾ cup [90 g] powdered sugar

1 Tbsp water, warm

1½ tsp corn syrup

½ tsp vanilla extract

make the chocolate cookies

1. Preheat the oven to 350°F [180°C]. Line a baking sheet with parchment paper.

2. In a medium bowl, whisk together the flour, powdered sugar, cocoa powder, and salt.

3. Cut the cold butter into ¼ in [6 mm] cubes and add them to the flour mixture. Use a pastry blender or your hands to work the butter into smaller pieces. Then, using your hands, rub the mixture between your palms until there are no butter pieces left. Check by gently shaking the bowl; clumps will sift up to the top. (Please note that a clump isn't necessarily butter—the ingredients themselves will start to clump together after the butter is fully incorporated.)

4. Add the milk and vanilla extract and mix, first with a spatula or scraper and then with your hands, until the dough comes together. It will start out looking really dry, but it will come together! Knead the dough a few times in the bowl until well combined.

5. Place the dough on a piece of plastic wrap and shape it into a disk. Wrap and then chill the disk in the refrigerator for at least 20 minutes.

6. Remove the chilled dough from the refrigerator and portion out the dough using a 2-tsp scoop (#100) until you have 32 to 34 cookies. Roll each piece of dough between your hands into a ball and place the balls of dough at least 1 in [2.5 cm] apart onto the prepared baking sheet. Or if you're not using a cookie stamp, roll the dough into a log, about 1 in [2.5 cm] in diameter, chill, and then cut into ½ in [12 mm] slices.

7. Dip a cookie stamp in flour, tapping off the excess. Center the stamp over a ball of dough and press down firmly until it flattens; do not twist the stamp. The dough should be about ¼ in [6 mm] thick. Carefully remove the dough from the stamp. Reflour the stamp and repeat with the remaining dough balls.

cont'd

8. Bake the cookies for 11 to 13 minutes, until they look set. Move to glazing the cookies while they are still warm because the glaze spreads more evenly and they will look much nicer.

make the glaze

1. Using a sifter or fine-mesh sieve, sift the powdered sugar into a mixing bowl, then add the water, corn syrup, and vanilla extract. Mix with a fork until smooth; the mixture should have the consistency of runny honey but not be as liquid as maple syrup.

2. When the cookies are still warm (not hot), dip a pastry brush into the glaze and brush a generous amount over each cookie, getting it into all the crevices. Allow the cookies to cool completely and the glaze to fully harden before storing them in an airtight container. The dough can be made in advance and stored in the refrigerator, well wrapped, for up to 5 days or in the freezer for up to 6 months. Store baked cookies in an airtight container for 7 to 10 days or in the freezer for up to 6 months. Thaw frozen cookies at room temperature before enjoying.

TIP!

Cocoa powder is the dry solid remains of fermented, dried, and roasted cacao beans. The beans are cracked into nibs, which are then ground into a paste made of cocoa solids suspended in near-flavorless cocoa butter. Dutch-process cocoa powder is treated with alkali to neutralize acidity; it is darker and more mellow in flavor. At the bakery, we use both alkalized and non-alkalized cocoa in our recipes. For this recipe, we want the color and texture that Dutch-process cacao brings to the end result.

We find a little spice is nice throughout the winter months, but especially on the shortest day of the year. Our Gingerbread Coffee Cake is made with a bevy of ground spices, rich molasses (any brand you like, but not blackstrap), and crystallized ginger. It's marvelously flavorful.

GINGERBREAD COFFEE CAKE

makes one large bundt cake

Our sweet and spicy Gingerbread Coffee Cake was the recipe our guests were most disappointed not to find in our first cookbook, Zingerman's Bakehouse, *so we had to make sure to include it this time around. Our sister business, Zingerman's Mail Order, calls it "the hip, spicy uncle" of our coffee-cake family, which just might perfectly capture its broad appeal—it's a little sweet, a little quirky, and a most welcome holiday visitor (especially when paired with whipped cream or vanilla ice cream!).*

½ cup [110 g] demerara sugar for preparing the baking pan (optional)

2¾ cups [385 g] all-purpose flour

1⅛ tsp baking soda

¾ tsp fine sea salt

¾ tsp ground cinnamon

¾ tsp ground cloves

¾ tsp ground long pepper (about 3 peppers, optional; see Tip, page 179)

¾ tsp ground ginger

½ tsp ground dry mustard

1 cup plus 1 Tbsp [215 g] granulated sugar

½ cup [110 g] unsalted butter, room temperature

½ cup [100 g] canola oil

2 large eggs, room temperature

1 cup plus 2 Tbsp [360 g] molasses

½ cup [110 g] orange juice, room temperature

½ cup [110 g] brewed coffee, room temperature

¼ cup [45 g] crystallized ginger, chopped into ¼ in [6 mm] pieces

1. Preheat the oven to 325°F [165°C] and place a rack in the middle position of the oven. Thoroughly coat a 10-cup [2.4 L] Bundt pan with nonstick cooking spray, then coat the inside well with demerara sugar (if using). Pour out the excess sugar. If you don't have demerara sugar or prefer not to use it, coat the pan with flour after spraying it.

2. In a medium mixing bowl, whisk together the flour, baking soda, salt, ground spices, and mustard until combined. Set aside.

3. In another medium mixing bowl, stir together the sugar and butter with a wooden spoon. If using a stand mixer, use the paddle attachment and cream for 4 minutes on medium speed. It will be fairly dry. Drizzle in the oil and mix until light and smooth. Scrape down the sides and bottom of the bowl with a bowl scraper or spatula. Add the eggs one at a time, mixing on medium speed until well combined. Scrape the bowl well. Add the molasses and mix on medium speed until there are no streaks of color. Scrape the bowl well.

4. In a small bowl or measuring cup, combine the orange juice and coffee. On low speed, add one-third of the mixture to the batter and mix together well. Then, add one-third of the sifted dry ingredients and mix until well combined. Continue alternating the addition of wet and dry ingredients to the batter until everything is incorporated. Stir in the crystallized ginger and scrape the bowl well. Pour the batter into the prepared pan and smooth the top with an offset spatula.

cont'd

5. Bake for 65 minutes, or until a tester or toothpick inserted in the thickest part of the cake comes out clean and the top of the cake springs back when you press it gently with your fingers.

6. Cool for 15 minutes in the pan before carefully removing the cake from the pan onto a wire rack. Serve warm or at room temperature. Store the cake wrapped in plastic at room temperature for up to 1 week or freeze for up to 3 months.

TIP!

Long pepper looks like a tiny, bumpy cattail, but there's nothing small about its flavor profile. It's deep and complex, walking the line between peppery heat, warm earthiness, and floral sweetness. Look for it in spice shops, whether brick-and-mortar or online. We think it makes this cake a touch more special. If you can't find it, you'll still have a great dessert.

In the United States, Christmas has both religious and secular traditions, making it broadly celebrated in a variety of ways and to different degrees. Regardless of the many different ways of engaging with the holiday, special foods are a common element of many people's enjoyment of the season.

A beloved tradition for many is the opening of gifts very early on Christmas morning, followed by a special breakfast. To help celebrate that breakfast in a tasty but easy way, we've included a savory bread pudding that we've made at the bakery for years. Another commonly enjoyed tradition is the making of holiday cookies. We spend the entire month of December teaching cookie classes to excited students. It's become an annual tradition for many to make their cookies with us. Holiday cookies are commonly exchanged in all sorts of settings, from casual gatherings of friends to office parties and school events, to name a few.

MANDELPLÄTZCHEN

makes 36 bite-size cookies

Mandelplätzchen, little almond cookies, are simple-looking cookies of German origin, but they are deceptively delicious and easy to make. And, if you have almond lovers in your midst, as we discovered here in the Zingerman's community, they will adore them.

Once they made their holiday appearance, we found out from Ari Weinzweig, cofounder of Zingerman's, that his life partner, Tammie, was in love with these cookies. For her Christmas present, he asked Amy if he could get a holiday box of only mandelplätzchen. Well, of course, he could, came the enthusiastic reply, but not just one box with eighteen cookies; Ari thought that five or six dozen cookies would make Tammie oh so happy! (We suspect you'll find them easy to love too, so double the recipe if you'd like to pull off your own Ari-size presentation of cookies!)

¾ cup plus 1 Tbsp [225 g] almond paste

2 Tbsp granulated sugar

Pinch of fine sea salt

⅔ cup [70 g] almond flour

1 large egg white

⅛ tsp almond extract

1⅓ cups [125 g] sliced almonds, raw

1. Preheat the oven to 375°F [190°C]. Line a baking sheet with parchment paper.

2. Using a stand mixer with the paddle attachment, mix together the almond paste, sugar, and salt on medium speed. Add the almond flour, egg white, and almond extract to the bowl, mixing until well combined. Divide the dough into three equal portions.

3. Pour the sliced almonds onto a clean work surface. Roll each portion of dough in the almonds until it is an 18 in [46 cm] log. Rolling the dough in the almonds gives the cookies a distinctive garnish.

4. Cut each log into twelve equal pieces. Transfer the cookies to the prepared baking sheet, placing them at least 1 in [2.5 cm] apart. (They do not spread while they bake but need some space in order to color nicely.) Bake for 8 to 10 minutes or until the cookies are lightly browned.

5. Cool completely. Store in an airtight container at room temperature for up to 1 week or in the freezer for up to 3 months. Thaw frozen cookies at room temperature before enjoying.

BREAKFAST ITALIAN SAUSAGE AND PEPPER STRATA

serves 6 to 9

Strata, a savory bread pudding, shines on days like Christmas when you want a special breakfast but don't want to spend the morning tethered to the kitchen, potentially missing out on all of the fun. This recipe does require some advance prep the day before, but in the morning, just pop it into the oven to bake and get right back to peeking in the stockings—you're less than an hour away from an egg-cellent breakfast.

We make ours with sweet Italian sausage, roasted red peppers, and a mix of three cheeses, but a strata is an ideal canvas to play with—don't hesitate to make it your own by tweaking it to include your family's favorite flavors.

1 lb [455 g] ground sweet Italian sausage	3 large eggs
1½ cups [210 g] thinly sliced white onion	1½ cups [340 g] whole milk
Olive oil, for sautéing, if needed	⅓ cup [75 g] heavy cream
½ cup [110 g] thinly sliced roasted red peppers	1½ tsp dried oregano
½ cup [40 g] grated Cheddar cheese	½ tsp fine sea salt
½ cup [40 g] grated Provolone cheese	¼ tsp freshly ground black pepper
½ cup [40 g] grated Parmesan cheese	5 cups [230 g] large, torn chunks of artisan bread (sourdough and full-flavored crusty breads are optimal; feel free to use a variety)

TIP!

To make strata for a crowd, just double this recipe. Use a 9 by 13 in [23 by 33 cm] baking pan and increase the baking time to 1 hour, covered, and 10 minutes, uncovered.

the day before

1. In a large skillet over medium-high heat, cook the sausage, actively breaking it up to avoid clumping. Transfer into a medium mixing bowl. Add the onions to the skillet with the fat leftover from the sausage and sauté over medium-high heat for about 10 minutes, or until the onions are tender and start to take on a slightly caramelized color. Add olive oil to the skillet if needed. Transfer to the mixing bowl with the sausage. Add the peppers and toss to combine.

2. In a small mixing bowl, combine the three cheeses.

3. In another medium mixing bowl, whisk together the eggs, milk, cream, oregano, salt, and pepper until combined.

4. Coat an 8 in [20 cm] square baking pan with non-stick cooking spray. Neatly lay enough chunks of bread, probably about half, on the bottom of the pan until covered, with minimal holes showing through. Add half of the sausage mixture, spreading it evenly across the pan. Add half of the cheese, spreading it evenly across the pan. Repeat to create another layer of bread, sausage, and cheese.

5. Ladle the egg mixture over the strata. Lightly coat a piece of aluminum foil with cooking spray, then wrap the pan with the foil, sprayed side down, and refrigerate overnight.

in the morning

1. Preheat the oven to 400°F [200°C].

2. Bake the strata, covered, for 50 minutes, then remove the foil and bake for an additional 10 minutes to brown the cheese on top.

3. Cool on a wire rack for 10 minutes before serving. Refrigerate leftovers, covered, for up to 3 days and reheat to enjoy.

PFEFFERNÜSSE

makes about 24 cookies

For many in Germany, Denmark, the Netherlands, and here in America, the holidays just wouldn't be complete without pfeffernüsse. These festive spice cookies, dusted in powdered sugar, are traditionally made with an abundant blend of aromatic spices—ours feature anise and black pepper, which give them a really distinctive flavor, as well as cinnamon, nutmeg, and cloves.

Of sturdy stock, these cookies are made to last, and their spicy infusion only gets better with age. Historically, they've been a popular part of yuletide celebrations throughout the month of December. Since the mid-nineteenth century, these cookies were eaten from the Feast of St. Nicholas, celebrated in Germany and the Netherlands in early December, to Christmas at the month's end. Pfeffernüsse came to America in part with Mennonite Christian immigrants from the German- and Dutch-speaking parts of Central Europe, as early as the eighteenth century, and are now a holiday favorite here at the Bakehouse. So beloved are these cookies that we feature them regularly in our annual Fancy Schmancy holiday cookie box.

1. Preheat the oven to 350°F [180°C]. Line two baking sheets with parchment paper.

2. In a medium mixing bowl, cream together the brown sugar, butter, anise, baking soda, cream of tartar, cinnamon, nutmeg, pepper, cloves, and salt until well combined. Add the egg and beat until the mixture is light and creamy. It will go from a dark, separated appearance to a light, fluffy, caramel-colored mixture. Add the flour and mix until well combined.

3. Portion out the dough using a ½ oz scoop (#70) onto the prepared baking sheets, placing each cookie 2 in [5 cm] apart. If you don't have a scoop, portion out level 1 Tbsp balls of dough.

4. Bake for 10 minutes or until the cookies are slightly puffed and lightly browned. Cool completely on the baking sheets.

5. Place cooled cookies, a few at a time, into a plastic bag with the powdered sugar. Seal the top of the bag and gently shake until the cookies are coated. Remove the cookies from the bag and gently shake off any excess powdered sugar. Store in an airtight container at room temperature for up to 2 weeks or in the freezer for up to 2 months. Thaw frozen cookies at room temperature before enjoying.

1 cup [200 g] brown sugar, packed	¼ tsp finely ground black pepper
¼ cup [55 g] unsalted butter, room temperature	¼ tsp ground cloves
½ tsp ground anise	⅛ tsp fine sea salt
¼ tsp baking soda	1 large egg, room temperature
¼ tsp cream of tartar	1¼ cups [175 g] all-purpose flour
¼ tsp ground cinnamon	½ cup [60 g] powdered sugar
¼ tsp ground nutmeg	

NANAIMO BARS

makes 16 bar cookies

Nanaimo is a port city in Vancouver, British Columbia, Canada, and Nanaimo Bars are triple-layered, no-bake bar cookies named after, well, the city! Two ingredients in this recipe might be a bit more challenging to find. The custard powder is key to the bars' authentic flavor; look for it in the baking aisle of well-stocked grocery stores, or procure it online. The other ingredient, fresh coconut, is perishable, so it is often found frozen and puréed.

Nanaimo Bars are one of many, many cookies we've taught at BAKE!, our hands-on baking school, for our most popular class ever: Fancy Schmancy Holiday Cookies. We started the class in December 2009 and have been teaching it every holiday season since, adding more sessions along the way—now we teach the class one hundred times between Thanksgiving and Christmas.

BASE

¼ cup [25 g] walnuts, raw

1 cup [85 g] fresh coconut

½ cup [110 g] unsalted butter, room temperature

⅓ cup [25 g] cocoa powder

¼ cup [50 g] granulated sugar

1 large egg, room temperature

2¼ cups [225 g] graham cracker crumbs

CUSTARD CREAM

¼ cup [55 g] unsalted butter, room temperature

2 cups [230 g] powdered sugar

3 Tbsp [45 g] heavy cream

2 Tbsp custard powder (see headnote)

CHOCOLATE TOPPING

⅔ cup [115 g] semisweet chocolate

2 Tbsp unsalted butter

make the base

1. Preheat the oven to 350°F [180°C]. Toast the walnuts on a baking sheet for 8 to 10 minutes, or until fragrant and golden brown. Let cool, then chop them or grind them in a small food processor until they are very fine, like coarse cornmeal. If using a food processor, take care not to overdo it; if ground too much, they will turn into nut butter.

2. In a double boiler or heatproof mixing bowl set over a saucepan of simmering water, add the coconut, butter, cocoa powder, sugar, and egg and stir with a wooden spoon for 1 to 2 minutes, or until the mixture has thickened and completely emulsified; it will look like chocolate pudding. Stir in the graham cracker crumbs and ground walnuts.

3. Press the mixture into an ungreased 8 in [20 cm] square baking pan, packing it down firmly with a flat hand or the bottom of a drinking glass. Set aside.

make the custard cream

1. In a medium mixing bowl, cream the butter and half of the powdered sugar with a wooden spoon until combined. If using a stand mixer, use the paddle attachment and beat on medium speed. Add the heavy cream and custard powder, stirring until smooth. Once the mixture is smooth, add in the rest of the powdered sugar and mix until combined.

2. Spread the custard cream over the base layer with an offset spatula, swiping in one direction, trying not to lift the spatula up, to avoid pulling up the base into the custard cream layer.

make the chocolate topping

1. In a double boiler or heatproof mixing bowl set over a saucepan of simmering water, melt the chocolate and butter, stirring frequently. Let cool slightly.

2. Pour the chocolate topping over the top of the custard cream layer and use an offset spatula to spread it out evenly.

3. Refrigerate for about 10 minutes or just until the chocolate is set, which will make it easier to cut. Cut into sixteen 2 in [5 cm] bars and serve. Store in an airtight container, with parchment paper between layers of bars, at room temperature for 3 to 4 days or in the freezer, well wrapped, for up to 2 months. Thaw frozen bars at room temperature before enjoying.

This is a night to have fun and play! People choose many different ways to enjoy it, from game night at home to festive dinners in restaurants to wild nights on the town. For home gatherings, finger foods tend to be prepared. We're sharing two festive recipes to add to your assortment—a rich puff pastry appetizer (page 190) special enough for the special night and a festive cookie with some caffeine in it (facing) to help everyone stay up until midnight.

CHOCOLATE-DIPPED ESPRESSO STARS

makes 24 to 36 cookies

We first created Espresso Stars for our Fancy Schmancy Holiday Cookies class, at the suggestion of Nikki Lohmann, one of our BAKE! instructors. They proved to be such a hit that, for a time, they made it into our regular lineup at the Bakeshop, Zingerman's Coffee Company, and Zingerman's Roadhouse. They are perfect as a small treat with a warm drink or at the end of a meal.

We flavor these shortbread cookies with freshly ground coffee beans, making them a rather adult addition to the dessert lineup, both in terms of flavor and the little jolt of caffeine. We like the added help staying awake until the celebratory ball drops at midnight in New York City's Times Square on New Year's Day, but if you'd prefer less of a burst of energy, feel free to use decaf beans. (Just don't be tempted to swap in instant espresso powder, which is designed to dissolve; we want both the flavor and the texture from the freshly ground coffee to be front and center.) To make them look as festive as they taste, we partially dip them in chocolate and make the effort to find gold luster dust or gold leaf to garnish them.

½ cup [110 g] unsalted butter, room temperature	2 Tbsp espresso beans, finely ground
¼ cup [50 g] granulated sugar	1 cup [170 g] semisweet chocolate, chopped
½ tsp fine sea salt	
1 cup plus 1 Tbsp [150 g] all-purpose flour, plus more for dusting	Gold luster dust or edible gold leaf (optional)

1. Preheat the oven to 300°F [150°C]. Line a baking sheet with parchment paper.

2. In a medium mixing bowl, cream together the butter, sugar, and salt until the sugar is well mixed in. Add the flour and ground espresso beans and mix until the dough holds together. If necessary, use your hands to gently knead the dough together into a ball.

3. On a lightly floured surface, roll the dough out to ¼ in [6 mm] thick. Cut out cookies using a 1½ to 2 in [4 to 5 cm] star cutter. You can reroll scraps and cut out more stars, but take care not to overwork the dough. This cookie will be delicious in many different sizes and shapes, so use whatever shape cutter you prefer and what you're able to find. If you choose a much bigger cutter, roll out the dough a little thicker. If they are large and too thin, they will break easily.

4. Carefully place the cut cookies on the prepared baking sheet, evenly spaced about 1 in [2.5 cm] apart. Bake for 30 minutes. The tops should look dry and the cookies should be slightly browned. Cool on the baking sheets for 5 minutes, then transfer to a wire rack to cool completely to room temperature.

5. Melt the chocolate slowly in the microwave or over a double boiler until just melted. This is a bit of a shortcut. By very gently melting the chocolate, it's possible that it will maintain its nice shine and not need to be tempered. If you prefer to go through the tempering process, see page 80.

6. Dip one-third of each cookie into the melted chocolate, then place onto a baking sheet lined with parchment paper. If using gold leaf, use a couple of small pieces as garnish and apply them to the soft chocolate.

7. Let the cookies sit at room temperature until the chocolate hardens. If desired, lightly brush gold luster dust over the hardened chocolate. Store in an airtight container, with parchment paper between layers of cookies, at room temperature for up to 1 week or in the freezer for up to 2 months. Thaw frozen cookies at room temperature before enjoying. If thawing cookies with luster dust, do so gradually, moving them from the freezer to the refrigerator, and then to room temperature.

CREAMY CREMINI TURNOVERS

makes 10 turnovers

Whether your New Year's Eve fête involves a large gathering or a party of one on the couch, little appetizers like our mushroom turnovers are bound to make it feel special. And bonus: Assembled, unbaked turnovers freeze well, so you can be ready for a celebratory shindig anytime. (Want to make this recipe simpler? Buy pre-made puff pastry. It's okay. We won't tell.)

BLITZ PUFF PASTRY

1⅔ cups [230 g] all-purpose flour, plus more for dusting

1 tsp fine sea salt

1 cup [220 g] unsalted butter, cold, cut into ¼ in [6 mm] cubes

½ cup plus 1 Tbsp [130 g] water, ice cold

MUSHROOM FILLING

1 Tbsp olive oil

1 Tbsp unsalted butter

1⅔ cups [230 g] diced yellow onions (½ in [12 mm] pieces)

1 cup [100 g] thinly sliced leeks

7½ cups [450 g] sliced cremini mushrooms or mini portobello mushrooms (¼ in [6 mm] slices)

1½ tsp fine sea salt, plus more for seasoning

⅓ cup plus 1 Tbsp [95 g] sour cream

2 Tbsp chopped fresh dill

1 tsp freshly ground black pepper

Water, for brushing

EGG WASH

1 large egg

1 egg yolk

1 Tbsp water

make the blitz puff pastry

1. In a large mixing bowl, mix together the flour and salt with a fork. Add the butter and, using your hands, coat the butter pieces with flour, then begin flattening the butter pieces into large flat butter flakes.

2. Create a well in the center of the flour mixture and add the cold water. Mix with a fork until the dough begins to form a shaggy mass; it will still be a bit crumbly in the bowl, but shouldn't look wet. Turn the dough out onto a lightly floured work surface and, with your hands or a bench scraper, fold it over on itself until it begins to come together. Shape the dough into a 4 by 6 in [10 by 15 cm] rectangle, wrap it in plastic wrap, and refrigerate for 30 minutes.

3. Unwrap the chilled dough, reserving the plastic wrap. On a lightly floured surface, roll out the dough to a 10 by 25 in [25 by 63.5 cm] rectangle.

4. Fold #1: Fold the dough into a book fold, brushing away flour in between layers as you fold. (For visual guidance, reference the diagram on page 245.) Rewrap the dough in plastic and rest for 30 minutes in the refrigerator.

5. Fold #2: Fold the dough into a letter fold. (See diagram on page 245.) Rewrap the dough in plastic and rest for 30 minutes in the refrigerator.

6. Fold #3: Repeat fold #1.

7. Fold #4: Repeat fold #2. At this point, you can proceed with rolling out the dough, or the dough can remain wrapped in plastic in the refrigerator for 1 day or frozen for up to 2 months. While the blitz puff pastry is resting, proceed with making the filling.

cont'd

make the mushroom filling

1. In a large, deep skillet or sauté pan, heat the olive oil and butter over medium heat until the butter has melted. Add the onions and leeks to the pan and sauté until just soft, 10 to 15 minutes. Add the mushrooms and salt. Increase the heat to medium-high and cook until the mushrooms have softened, reduced in size, and released all of their liquid, about 20 minutes; at this stage, there will be no visible liquid in the pan. Remove the mushroom mixture from the heat and set it aside to cool.

2. In a medium mixing bowl, combine the sour cream with the dill, cooled mushroom mixture, pepper, and salt to taste.

assemble the turnovers

1. Preheat the oven to 425°F [220°C].

2. On a lightly floured work surface, roll out the dough into a 20 by 8 in [50 by 20 cm] rectangle and then cut it into ten 4 by 4 in [10 by 10 cm] squares. Using a 1 oz [30 g] scoop, place the mushroom filling at the center of each dough square. Brush the edges of each dough square lightly with water and fold half of the dough over on itself to create a triangle, pressing out any air bubbles as you go and pressing down on the edges with a fork to make sure the turnovers are sealed and the layers stick together.

3. In a small bowl, make the egg wash by whisking together the egg, egg yolk, and water until well combined. Brush each turnover with egg wash. Using a sharp paring knife, cut a couple of vents in the top of each turnover and bake for 20 to 22 minutes or until golden brown.

4. Let the turnovers cool slightly before serving. They are best eaten warm. Store baked turnovers in an airtight container in the refrigerator for up to 5 days; reheat them in a 350°F [180°C] oven for 10 to 15 minutes before enjoying. (Resist the temptation to reheat in the microwave, as it will ruin the flaky puff-pastry crust.) Store assembled, raw turnovers in the freezer, in an airtight container, for up to 3 months. When you are ready to bake the frozen raw turnovers, heat the oven to 400°F [200°C] and bake for 23 to 25 minutes.

CHEDDAR HERB SCONES

makes 12 large scones

These tender, flaky Cheddar herb scones are loaded with fresh rosemary and aged sharp Cheddar cheese. They're a flavorful, savory way to ring in the new year in a less-involved manner than eggs Benedict with Zinglish Muffins (page 67) . . . though they would also be delicious given the eggs Benedict treatment!

    Enjoy them on their own, use them for breakfast sandwiches with soft scrambled eggs and crispy bacon, or bake the bacon right into them (see Tip, page 195).

2½ cups [350 g] all-purpose flour, plus more for dusting	2½ cups [290 g] packed, grated sharp Cheddar cheese, cold
2 Tbsp minced fresh rosemary	2 large eggs, cold
1 Tbsp baking powder	½ cup plus 2 Tbsp [145 g] heavy cream, cold
1 tsp fine sea salt	
¾ cup [165 g] unsalted butter, cold, diced into ¼ in [6 mm] cubes	

NEW YEAR'S DAY

Today is a day for marking the end of the holiday season and the beginning of a new year. It's a day of fresh starts and perhaps the making of resolutions. For some, it's the day to watch football and take the Christmas tree down. For others, it's the day to enjoy a great brunch. If that's you, we've got two additions to your meal: scones that can stand on their own or be great additions to an egg dish, and festive cupcakes made with Champagne Swiss buttercream (page 200).

1. Preheat the oven to 400°F [200°C]. Line two baking sheets with parchment paper.

2. In a large mixing bowl, whisk together the flour, rosemary, baking powder, and salt. Add the butter and, working quickly, cut the butter into the flour mixture using a pastry blender. Cut until the mixture looks like coarse cornmeal with pea-size pieces of butter. If you do not have a pastry blender, you can use two butter knives or your hands. If using your hands, break the pieces of butter up in your fingers and then pick up some butter and flour and rub it together in the palms of your hands. Add 2 cups [230 g] of the Cheddar to the flour mixture and gently toss to combine. Make a well in the center of the mixture.

3. In a small bowl, beat together the eggs and cream with a fork, then pour the wet mixture into the well in the dry ingredients and mix with a fork until the ingredients are just moistened.

4. Gently knead the dough in the bowl 6 to 8 times, using your hand or a plastic bowl scraper. The goal is to evenly distribute the moisture from the eggs and cream and to bring the dough together. By the end of kneading, there should be no loose flour remaining in the bowl.

5. Turn the dough out of the bowl onto a lightly floured surface, divide it into two equal pieces, and gently shape them into round balls.

6. Lightly sprinkle the work surface, as well as the tops of the dough, with flour. Place the balls of dough on the flour and roll out the dough into two logs that are 2 in [5 cm] in diameter and 8 in [20 cm] in length.

cont'd

7. Using a bench scraper or a chef's knife, cut each log into six even pieces. The scones may be a little misshapen after this step; re-round them if necessary. Place the scones on the prepared baking sheets, at least 2 in [5 cm] apart.

8. Using your thumb, press down to make an impression in the top of each scone. Fill these with the remaining Cheddar cheese. Bake for 17 to 20 minutes, or until the cheese in the center is melted and the scones are golden brown. Don't be shy about letting them get a little brown; this will add a toasty flavor and will give an added texture to the scone.

9. Eat warm or at room temperature. Store in a paper or plastic bag at room temperature for up to 3 days or freeze for several months. Reheat in the oven to restore the texture.

TIP!

For a flavor variation, make Bacon Cheddar Scones by leaving out the rosemary, adding in 7 slices [55 g] of cooked, crumbled bacon and 3 finely chopped scallions, and reducing the Cheddar to 1 packed cup [115 g]. Leave everything else the same.

FRENCH KING CAKE

makes one large cake

Our Galette des Rois features buttery layers of puff pastry filled with almond frangipane and is traditionally decorated with curved spiral lines on top and scalloping on the edge, in a semblance of a king's crown.

This recipe has two main components; we recommend planning ahead. Make your puff pastry dough and the almond filling on the first day, and then assemble and bake your French King Cake on the second day.

BUTTER BLOCK FOR PUFF PASTRY

1 cup plus 2 Tbsp [250 g] unsalted butter, room temperature

½ cup [70 g] all-purpose flour

⅛ tsp fine sea salt

¾ tsp lemon juice

PUFF PASTRY DOUGH

⅓ cup plus 1 Tbsp [50 g] cake flour

2 Tbsp unsalted butter, room temperature

⅜ tsp fine sea salt

¾ cup plus 2 Tbsp [125 g] all-purpose flour, plus more for dusting

½ cup [115 g] water

ALMOND FILLING

½ cup [70 g] skin-on almonds (whole or sliced)

⅓ cup [115 g] almond paste

3 Tbsp granulated sugar

2 Tbsp unsalted butter, room temperature

1 egg yolk, room temperature

1½ tsp dark rum

¾ tsp vanilla extract

CAKE

1 whole almond

EGG WASH

1 large egg

1 egg yolk

1 Tbsp water

APRICOT GLAZE [OPTIONAL]

¼ cup [85 g] apricot preserves

1 Tbsp water

form the butter block for the puff pastry

1. In a medium mixing bowl, combine the butter, all-purpose flour, and salt. Beat with a wooden spoon until the butter and dry ingredients are well combined. If using a stand mixer, use the paddle attachment and mix on low speed just to soften, not cream.

2. Add the lemon juice and continue mixing until the juice is completely absorbed. Transfer to plastic wrap and, using a bench scraper or spatula, form into a 4 by 4 in [10 by 10 cm] square. Wrap and set aside while you mix the dough.

mix the puff pastry dough

1. In the same mixing bowl (minimize dishes!), combine the cake flour, butter, and salt. Mix until well combined. Add the all-purpose flour and continue to stir until the mixture is well blended.

2. If mixing by hand, create a well in the center and add the water. Stir with a wooden spoon until the dough forms a shaggy mass. If using a stand mixer with the paddle attachment, gradually add the water to the flour mixture to the same point. Scrape off the dough from the spoon or paddle and turn the dough out of the bowl onto a clean, unfloured work surface. Knead the dough for 1 to 2 minutes or until it is smooth, soft, and supple.

cont'd

EPIPHANY

For those who don't know, the Twelve Days of Christmas, the nearly two-week period between December 25 and January 6, is a prolonged celebration leading to the Feast of Epiphany and the start of the Carnival season. Observed by Orthodox, Catholic, and Anglican Christians, Epiphany, which falls on the twelfth day after Christmas, commemorates the biblical story of the magi, noble pilgrims from Persia, who followed a miraculous guiding star to Bethlehem. Bearing gifts of gold, frankincense, and myrrh, the magi paid homage to the infant Jesus as king of the Jews and the son of God on the twelfth night after his birth. King Cakes are served from Epiphany until Mardi Gras (Fat Tuesday), the day before the season of Lent begins.

January is usually a quiet month for us after all of the celebrating in November and December. One of our baking treats of the month is to make a stunningly beautiful, traditional French King cake, or galette des rois, as it's known in France.

3. Wrap the dough in plastic wrap lightly coated with a neutral oil or nonstick cooking spray, and chill the dough and the butter block in the refrigerator for at least 30 minutes.

make the puff pastry

1. Remove the chilled butter block from the refrigerator and, still in the plastic wrap, firmly but gently tap the butter block with a rolling pin, left to right; rotate the block 90 degrees; and repeat. Flip the butter block over and repeat the tapping until it is pliable but still chilled.

2. Remove the chilled dough from the refrigerator; remove the plastic wrap and place it on a well-floured work surface, flouring the top of the dough as well. (For visual guidance, see the book and letter fold diagrams on page 245.) Using a rolling pin, roll the dough into a 6 by 12 in [15 by 30.5 cm] rectangle.

3. Brush away any flour from the dough surface and place the chilled but pliable butter block on the lower half of the dough. Fold the top half of the dough over the butter, creating a dough-butter-dough sandwich. On a lightly floured work surface, begin gently tapping the surface of the dough from left to right, rotate 90 degrees, and repeat. Flip the dough over and repeat. Continue until the dough is pliable, adding flour to the dough and/or work surface as needed. Roll the dough out to a rectangle about 8 by 14 in [20 by 36 cm]. It should be about ¼ in [6 mm] thick. Keep your corners as square as possible. Brush off any excess flour and place the dough with the roughest side facing up. (This will help hide imperfections.)

4. Fold #1: Fold the dough into a book fold, brushing away flour in between layers as you fold. (See diagram on page 245.) Rewrap the dough in plastic and rest for 30 minutes in the refrigerator.

5. Fold #2: Repeat tapping and rolling out the dough to an 8 by 14 in [20 by 36 cm] rectangle. Fold the dough into a letter fold. (See diagram on page 245.)

6. Fold #3: Repeat tapping and rolling out the dough to an 8 by 14 in [20 by 36 cm] rectangle, then do another letter fold. Rewrap the dough in plastic wrap and rest for 30 minutes in the refrigerator.

7. Fold #4: Repeat tapping and rolling out the dough to an 8 by 14 in [20 by 36 cm] rectangle, then do another letter fold. Rewrap the dough in plastic wrap and rest for 30 minutes in the refrigerator.

8. Fold #5: Repeat tapping and rolling out the dough to an 8 by 14 in [20 by 36 cm] rectangle, then do another letter fold. Rewrap the dough in plastic wrap and rest the dough for at least 1 hour in the refrigerator. It is preferable to rest the dough overnight before shaping. The dough can also be frozen for up to 2 months.

make the almond filling

1. Preheat the oven to 350°F [180°C]. Toast the almonds on a baking sheet until light golden brown. Sliced almonds will take 4 to 6 minutes; whole almonds will take 12 to 15 minutes. Let cool and then grind to a coarse consistency in the food processor.

2. In a medium mixing bowl, mix the almond paste and the sugar with a wooden spoon until combined and the sugar has been absorbed. If using a stand mixer with the paddle attachment, mix on medium speed. Add the butter and egg yolk and mix until smooth (about 30 seconds on medium in a stand mixer). Scrape down the sides of the bowl. Add the ground almonds, rum, and vanilla extract and mix until combined (about 30 seconds on medium speed in a stand mixer). Scrape down the sides of the bowl. The mixture should be creamy and will firm up when chilled.

3. Refrigerate until needed. This makes enough almond filling for two king cakes; extra filling can be stored in an airtight container in the refrigerator for 4 days or frozen for up to 2 months, or you can make a very indulgent cake and use it all! No one will complain and it won't interfere with the proper baking.

assemble the cake

1. Preheat the oven to 350°F [180°C]. Bring your almond filling to room temperature if it is cold. A few seconds in the microwave will do the trick. Line a baking sheet with parchment paper.

2. On a lightly floured work surface, roll the puff pastry dough to a 10 by 20 in [25 by 50 cm] rectangle. Brush away any excess flour. Lightly press the top of a 9 in [23 cm] tart pan onto one side of the dough rectangle to make an impression. Do not cut into the dough, and make sure your impression is far enough to one side that you'll be able to fold the rest of the dough over top of it. This will be a guide for where to place your filling.

3. Transfer the dough rectangle to the prepared baking sheet, aiming to have your tart pan impression circle at the center of the paper. It's okay that the other side of the dough will go past the paper and be on the work surface.

4. Spread the almond filling in the circle to within ½ to 1 in [12 mm to 2.5 cm] of the edge of the impression. Press the whole almond anywhere in the almond filling, avoiding the center 2 in [5 cm] of the circle.

5. In a small bowl, make the egg wash by whisking together the egg, egg yolk, and water until well combined. Brush the egg wash on the empty edge of the impression so the top and bottom pieces of dough can stick together. Fold the dough over to cover the almond filling, maintaining the border all around the almond filling (do not fold the dough right to the edge of the filling). Use the tart pan to cut through both layers of dough, like a giant cookie cutter. Brush only the top with egg wash, avoiding the sides of the dough. (Egg wash on the sides of the dough will seal the edges and it won't rise properly.)

6. Cut out a small round circle of dough, about 1 in [2.5 cm] in diameter, in the center of the top. This can be done with an appropriately sized cutter or freehand with a sharp paring knife. Using a paring knife, decorate the top with curved spiral lines starting from the center to the outer edge. There is no preferred number of lines; feel free to decorate it as you would like.

7. Bake for 45 minutes, or until nicely browned.

8. While the king cake is baking, make the apricot glaze, if using, by mixing the apricot preserves with the water; strain it through a fine-mesh sieve if there are pieces of fruit in the preserves. When the cake is done baking, immediately brush the glaze on the top to give it a pretty shine.

9. Allow the king cake to cool before serving. This is best enjoyed the day of baking, but it's pretty darn good the second day as well.

CHAMPAGNE AND STRAWBERRY-STUFFED CUPCAKES

makes 12 cupcakes

We make these cupcakes only two days a year at the Bakehouse—for New Year's Eve and New Year's Day—and every year we get feedback from guests who treated themselves to one or two and wished they'd had more. Now you can!

    Somewhat akin to a posh spin on strawberry shortcake, they're made with light and airy vanilla chiffon cake, stuffed with fresh strawberries and strawberry preserves, and iced with Champagne Swiss buttercream. Use leftover Champagne from last night's festivities, or pop open a new bottle for New Year's Day mimosas; you'll need only a small amount for the frosting. If you prefer raspberries over strawberries, they'd be a great substitute and in the winter may have better flavor.

    Making these cupcakes is a three-step process that can be done over several days. By separating the steps, a large project becomes a very manageable one.

CHIFFON CUPCAKES

½ cup [100 g] granulated sugar

½ cup [60 g] cake flour

¾ tsp baking powder

⅛ tsp fine sea salt

2 large egg yolks, room temperature

2 Tbsp vegetable oil

2 Tbsp water

½ tsp vanilla extract

2 large egg whites, room temperature

¼ tsp cream of tartar

CHAMPAGNE SWISS BUTTERCREAM

3 egg whites

¾ cup [150 g] granulated sugar

⅛ tsp fine sea salt

1 cup [220 g] unsalted butter, room temperature

½ tsp vanilla extract

6 Tbsp [85 g] Champagne or sparkling wine, room temperature

STRAWBERRY FILLING

½ cup [80 g] finely chopped fresh strawberries

1 Tbsp strawberry preserves, room temperature

make the chiffon cupcakes

1. Preheat the oven to 350°F [180°C]. Line the cups of a standard 12-cup muffin pan with cupcake liners. If you prefer not to use liners, coat the cups with nonstick cooking spray. Set aside.

2. In a medium mixing bowl, whisk together ¼ cup [50 g] of the granulated sugar, the cake flour, baking powder, and salt until well blended.

3. In a separate medium mixing bowl, whisk together the egg yolks, oil, water, and vanilla extract until well blended. Add the wet ingredients to the dry ingredients and whisk until the mixture is completely combined and smooth.

4. Using a stand mixer with the whisk attachment, whip the egg whites and cream of tartar on medium-high speed until the whites start to form soft peaks (see page 244). While still whipping at medium speed, gradually add the remaining ¼ cup [50 g] of sugar in a slow and steady stream to the egg whites. Increase the speed to high and whip until the sugar is incorporated and the egg whites form stiff peaks.

5. Gently fold one-quarter of the egg whites into the cake batter to lighten the mixture. Add another one-quarter of the egg whites and fold to combine, then fold in the remaining half of the whites until just combined. Divide the batter equally among 12 muffin cups, filling each cup about two-thirds full.

6. Bake the cupcakes for 15 to 18 minutes. The cupcakes are done when they spring back when lightly pressed in the center and an inserted tester or toothpick comes out clean.

7. Let the cupcakes cool in the pan for 5 minutes, then transfer to a wire rack to cool completely to room temperature.

cont'd

make the champagne swiss buttercream

1. In a medium heatproof mixing bowl, combine the egg whites, sugar, and salt, stirring with a wooden spoon to combine. Place the bowl over a double boiler or saucepan with gently simmering water and heat the mixture, stirring every couple of minutes, until the sugar is completely dissolved and the temperature registers 180°F [82°C] on an instant-read thermometer.

2. Transfer the egg white mixture to the bowl of a stand mixer. Using the whisk attachment, whip on high speed until it has doubled in volume, become thick and shiny, and cooled to room temperature. Lower the mixer speed to medium and gradually add the soft, room-temperature butter, one small piece at a time, mixing until all of it has been incorporated. The butter should be the same temperature as the egg white mixture to aid successful incorporation.

3. Add the vanilla extract and whip on medium speed to incorporate. Then add the Champagne slowly, 2 Tbsp at a time, whipping to incorporate. Each addition of Champagne will take a while to combine with the buttercream, and if you're using a newly opened bottle, it will foam up each time; that's okay, just be patient.

4. Use immediately or place in an airtight container and chill in the refrigerator for up to 1 week or freeze for up to 3 months. For tips on how to refresh the buttercream after it's been chilled or frozen, see page 242.

make the strawberry filling

1. Once the cupcakes are cool and you are ready to assemble, make the filling by mixing together the strawberries and preserves. Don't make the filling in advance; as it sits, moisture is drawn from the berries and the mixture becomes liquidy.

assemble the cupcakes

1. Using a small paring knife, cut a small cylinder out of the center of each cupcake that is approximately ½ by 1 in [12 mm by 2.5 cm]. Do not cut all the way to the bottom of the cupcake. Fill the empty space of each cupcake with strawberry filling.

2. To frost the cooled cupcakes, dollop frosting (eyeball 2 Tbsp or so) on top of each cupcake with an offset spatula or butter knife, then spread to smooth the frosting and cover the cupcake. We like to frost our cupcakes generously, with a nearly equal amount of frosting to cupcake; if your frosting preferences are more reserved, you'll have plenty of buttercream leftover for another batch.

3. Alternatively, place the frosting into a large piping bag fitted with a ½ in [12 mm] circle tip. Depending on the size of your piping bag, you may only want to use half of the frosting at a time. Pipe a swirl of frosting on top of the cupcake. These cupcakes, once assembled, keep well in the refrigerator, in an airtight container, for up to 3 days. Let them come to room temperature before serving.

CHICAGO-STYLE DEEP-DISH PIZZA

makes one small pizza; serves 4

These are days worthy of making some indulgent food that takes up a little of that newly found free time. What's better to make on a snow day than another favorite of American kids, pizza? Enjoy a super tasty pizza project with our recipe for Chicago-Style Deep-Dish Pizza. Since it's a snow day, we realize that you may not have the exact ingredients called for in this recipe. Yeast is a must, but after that, experiment with what you have on hand. Embrace the unexpected on this unexpected holiday.

You can add any vegetables that you'd like, as well as use them entirely in place of the sausage. It's best to cook them first so that they don't release too much water into your pizza. We suggest sautéing or oven-roasting them. We like red peppers (roasted are delicious), mushrooms, onions, and even oven-roasted zucchini and summer squash.

PIZZA SAUCE

One 16 oz [455 g] can crushed tomatoes

2 cloves garlic, finely minced

1½ tsp dried basil

½ tsp dried oregano

½ tsp fine sea salt

¼ tsp freshly ground black pepper

PIZZA DOUGH

1½ cups plus 1 Tbsp [220 g] all-purpose flour, plus more for dusting

½ cup plus 1½ Tbsp [140 g] water, room temperature

¼ cup [35 g] cornmeal

2 Tbsp olive oil

2 tsp granulated sugar

1 tsp fine sea salt

¾ tsp instant yeast

PIZZA TOPPINGS

2¼ cups [220 g] shredded mozzarella

4 oz [115 g] ground Italian sausage, raw

2 tsp olive oil, for drizzling

Grated Parmesan cheese, for garnish

make the pizza sauce

1. In a medium bowl, combine all of the sauce ingredients and stir together. Set aside.

make the pizza dough

1. In a medium mixing bowl, add all of the dough ingredients. Combine thoroughly with a wooden spoon or fork until the dough becomes a shaggy mass.

2. Turn the dough out of the bowl onto your lightly floured work surface and knead the dough for 6 to 8 minutes until the dough is smooth and elastic. Use the windowpane test to assess when the dough is ready. (See page 244 for more information.)

3. Coat a large bowl or plastic container with nonstick cooking spray or brush lightly with oil. Place the dough in the container and cover with plastic wrap or a tea towel. Ferment the dough at room temperature for 1½ hours. (If you prefer not to use the dough right away, see Tip, page 205.)

cont'd

Ah, snow days! They are one of the uniquely glorious days of childhood for American kids living in wintery areas. Nothing might be sweeter than receiving that call or text (or, depending on your generation, hearing on the radio or reading the scroll on the TV screen) that announces, "Schools are closed today!" In other words, an unexpected free play day! We can almost hear little kids whooping for joy and jumping up and down, while teens are rolling over in bed and pulling up their covers so that they can indulge in several more hours of deep adolescent sleep. We still love even the memory of our snow days.

4. Preheat the oven to 400°F [200°C]. Turn out the dough onto a lightly floured work surface.

5. Gently form your dough into a flat disk by gathering up the edges to the center with your fingers, pinching lightly so the dough sticks together. Press down lightly with your palm to flatten it. Do not put a lot of tension into the disk at this point. Place it onto a lightly floured surface and cover with plastic. Let rest for 15 minutes.

6. Take your dough and lightly pat it into a 9 in [23 cm] circle. Be as gentle and patient as possible with the dough to avoid developing the gluten and causing it to become tough.

7. Place the dough in a 9 by 2 in [23 by 5 cm] round cake pan or an 8 in [20 cm] cast-iron skillet, and use your hands to ease the dough up the sides 1½ to 2 in [4 to 5 cm]. Push out any air pockets if necessary.

top and bake

1. Sprinkle the mozzarella cheese evenly on top of the dough. Press it firmly together to remove any gaps. It should be about ½ in [12 mm] thick. Spread the sausage evenly on top of the cheese. Pour half of the prepared pizza sauce evenly on top of the fillings; reserve the rest for another use.

2. Drizzle the olive oil along the top edges of the crust around the sides of the pan. This helps the dough brown and makes it easier to remove the pizza from the pan after baking.

3. Bake for 35 to 40 minutes, turning the pizza halfway through for even baking, or until the crust is golden brown and pulls away from the sides of the pan. If you included sausage, use an instant-read thermometer to check the internal temperature of the pizza to assess doneness. The sausage is cooked when the internal temperature of the pizza is 155°F [70°C].

4. Sprinkle the top of the pizza with grated Parmesan cheese and cool for 5 minutes before removing from the pan with a spatula.

5. Cool for 10 minutes to allow the cheese and the sauce to set before cutting and serving. If you don't eat all of your pizza, place what's remaining in a storage container and refrigerate. It's best reheated in a moderate oven. If you can't wait, microwave it for a quick snack.

TIP!

You'll use about half of the sauce recipe for one pizza. If you'd rather not have extra, feel free to halve the recipe—we just like to be prepared for our next pizza-making adventure. The additional sauce may be stored in an airtight container in the refrigerator for up to 10 days or frozen for up to 3 months.

Don't want to use your dough right away? Go straight from the mixing stage to your refrigerator for up to 24 hours. The dough will slowly ferment in the fridge until you're ready to shape it in the pan.

HOT COCOA CRISPY RICE TREATS

makes one pan

There's nothing like hot cocoa on a snow day, and these crispy rice treats conjure up that exact flavor! They're delicious as is, but because sometimes more is more—especially with kids—we've also included optional mix-ins, just like you might use to top your mug of hot chocolate. Choose one or a multitude of mix-ins! Truth be told, we don't actually make these at the bakery but we have been known to indulge. Nothing like crispy rice treats to bring back the joy of childhood.

5 Tbsp [70 g] unsalted butter	OPTIONAL MIX-INS
One 16 oz [455 g] bag large marshmallows	Semisweet chocolate chunks, chopped
½ tsp vanilla extract	Mini marshmallows
½ cup [100 g] finely chopped semisweet chocolate	Candy cane pieces (maybe leftover from Christmas)
6 cups [200 g] crispy rice cereal	Chocolate-covered nuts
	Chocolate-covered raisins
	Sprinkles

1. Coat a 9 by 13 in [23 by 33 cm] pan evenly with non-stick cooking spray.

2. In a medium saucepan over medium heat, melt the butter. Lower the heat to low, add the marshmallows, and stir until completely melted.

3. Remove the saucepan from the heat. Stir in the vanilla extract, followed by the semisweet chocolate, stirring until melted. Add the rice cereal and stir until evenly coated. Let cool for a couple of minutes. If using mix-ins, add them now and stir to evenly distribute. (Aim for around ½ cup or so of one or a combination of multiple mix-ins.)

4. Scoop the mixture into the prepared pan and press to spread it out to fill the pan and gently compact the treats. Cut into fifteen bars—or as many as you'd like! Store at room temperature in an airtight container for up to 2 days.

BLACK
HISTORY
MONTH

One of America's greatest merits is its rich diversity. It feels more important than ever to celebrate our differences and honor the unique ways in which different groups of people can effect change and bring about a more just and inclusive culture. Throughout history, the Black community has made incredible contributions to all areas of life in America. We've had many conversations about how to honor Black History Month at the bakery, from featuring Black bakers to sharing traditional recipes, to using African ingredients that are now widely used in American cooking. For this book, we decided to feature our most requested soup recipe from the last twenty-five years, our West African—inspired peanut stew. The peanut is possibly the most widely used and adored food brought to America by enslaved people of West Africa.

Interestingly, peanuts are not actually native to Africa. They were brought by Portuguese explorers from South America to the West African coast in the early 1500s. Since they were similar to the African plant, the Bambara groundnut, they were substituted for the native nut in traditional dishes. Because peanuts were easier to grow, they eventually replaced the Bambara groundnut in soups and stews and became an important part of traditional West African cooking. They then followed the route of the African diaspora.

The famous African American botanist and scientist George Washington Carver studied peanuts in the early 1900s and promoted their use. He created a publication called *How to Grow the Peanut and 105 Ways of Preparing It for Human Consumption.* He would be pleased to know that today, peanuts are still a favorite American snack and recipe ingredient.

WEST AFRICAN PEANUT STEW

serves 6 to 8 as a main dish

This was one of our original soups and a customer favorite for many years. The Bakehouse and BAKE!, our hands-on baking school, are now peanut-free, so we no longer sell it in our shop or teach it, but it's still a flavorful favorite that we like to make at home. It's a rich and complex soup that we recommend serving with a cooling side salad of crisp vegetables. A fitting dessert to round it out would be chilled tropical fruits like mango, kiwi, and pineapple.

2 Tbsp canola oil	1½ tsp ground garam masala
1⅓ cups [150 g] diced celery	1 medium sweet potato [475 g], peeled and diced
1¼ cups [170 g] diced yellow onion	5 cups [1.2 L] vegetable stock (store-bought or see recipe on page 150)
1 cup [140 g] diced carrots	
Fine sea salt and freshly ground black pepper	1¼ cups [295 g] smooth peanut butter (natural, no salt added)
1 Tbsp minced ginger	2 Tbsp muscovado sugar
One 14½ oz [415 g] can diced tomatoes	1 tsp Marash pepper flakes

1. In a large stockpot, heat the oil over medium heat until shimmering, then add the celery, onion, carrots, and a generous sprinkle of salt and pepper, and sauté until the onions are translucent and soft, about 10 minutes. Add the ginger and sauté for an additional 5 minutes.

2. Add the tomatoes and garam masala and cook for 5 minutes more. Add the sweet potato and stock, bring to a boil over medium-high heat, then lower the heat to a simmer and continue cooking until the potatoes are cooked through, about 20 minutes. Add the peanut butter, sugar, and Marash pepper and purée the soup with an immersion blender until smooth. Season to taste with additional salt and pepper.

3. Warm to serving temperature and serve. Refrigerate for up to 1 week or freeze in an airtight container for up to 3 months.

JEWISH RYE BREAD

makes 2 loaves

This recipe takes some planning—start two days before you want to serve it. The first two days will be to get your rye sour starter going and the third day requires 5 hours to make the bread and cool it before serving.

Seem like a lot of preplanning? Know that nothing about it is hard, other than it not being instantaneous. The inconvenient aspects of many recipes are the steps that take a food from good to great. The rye sour is an example of this, as is using "old"—rye bread from the previous day's bake that we slice and soak in water and then add to the dough. It adds a layer of texture, moisture, and color to the bread. It's also a tradition for Jewish bakers to take something from yesterday and put it in today's recipes, representing the continuity and interconnectedness of life. Flavor takes time, and we think it's worth it.

RYE SOUR (DAY 1)

1 cup [110 g] medium rye flour

¾ cup [175 g] water, room temperature

⅛ tsp instant yeast

½ cup [70 g] coarsely chopped onion

1½ tsp caraway seeds

RYE SOUR (DAY 2)

¾ cup [175 g] water, room temperature

1 cup [125 g] medium rye flour

THE OLD

½ cup minus 1 Tbsp [105 g] water

¼ cup [95 g] day-old bread, preferably rye, torn into pieces

RYE BREAD

¾ cup [175 g] water

1½ tsp instant yeast

½ tsp ground caraway

3½ cups plus 1 Tbsp [500 g] all-purpose flour, plus more for dusting

1 Tbsp [20 g] fine sea salt

Cornmeal, for dusting

day 1: make the rye sour

1. In a medium bowl, mix the rye flour, water, and yeast. Stir until the mixture is completely smooth. Tie the onion and caraway seeds together tightly in cheesecloth (like a homemade tea bag), then sink the whole package completely into the flour mixture.

2. Cover the bowl tightly with plastic wrap and put it in a nice warm spot (70 to 75°F [21 to 24°C]) overnight.

day 2: feed the rye sour

1. Remove the onion/caraway bag and scrape the sour off the bag and back into the bowl. Add the water and rye flour to the sour and mix until smooth. Cover the sour with plastic wrap and let it sit for 3 to 4 hours more, until it is visibly fermented and frothy.

2. The rye sour can now be used in your rye bread recipe, with plenty left over to put in the fridge until the next feeding (see Maintaining Your Rye Sour, page 212). Store it in a tightly sealed container.

prepare the old

1. In a small bowl, combine the water and bread and let sit for 15 minutes.

cont'd

The Big Game deserves big flavor, and this is exactly what you'll get with our classic Jewish Rye Bread. Whether you use it for sandwiches or for slathering with Liptauer Cheese Spread (page 213), it will be a sensational addition to your game-day spread.

make the rye bread

1. In a large, wide mixing bowl, combine 2¼ cups [420 g] prepared rye sour, the water, ¼ cup [95 g] prepared old, the yeast, and ground caraway. Stir with a wooden spoon until well blended. Add half of the flour and stir until the mixture looks like thick pancake batter. Add the salt and remaining flour and mix with a wooden spoon until the dough starts to form a shaggy mass.

2. Scrape the dough out of the bowl onto a clean, unfloured work surface and knead for 6 to 8 minutes, until it forms a smooth ball. Rye flour tends to be sticky, but don't be alarmed if that's the case, and resist the temptation to add flour. Use a bench scraper to clean the work surface and keep gently kneading—the dough will come together.

3. Lightly oil the mixing bowl and place the dough in the bowl. Cover with plastic wrap and ferment it at room temperature for 1 hour. The dough will increase in size by about 50 percent.

4. After 1 hour, uncover the dough and turn it out onto a lightly floured work surface. Divide the dough into two equal pieces. Pre-shape the dough pieces into loose and round shapes, cover with plastic wrap, and let rest for 30 minutes.

5. Shape the rested rounds into football-shaped loaves approximately 12 in [30.5 cm] long. To do so, gently pat the dough into a circle approximately 8 in [20 cm] in diameter. Fold the top edge to the center of the dough, gently pressing the edge into the dough; repeat for a second time, folding the dough to meet the bottom edge. Seal the edges by pressing down with the base of your hand. With the seam side down, place both hands on top of the dough; with your palms cupping the dough towards the tips, rock it back and forth into a tapered football shape. Place on a clean, unfloured work surface coated with cornmeal and cover with plastic wrap.

6. Ferment the loaves for 40 minutes to 1 hour while the oven is preheating.

7. Preheat the oven with a baking stone, and a cast-iron skillet on the bottom rack, to 450°F [230°C] for 45 minutes before baking (see page 244). Use the touch test (see page 244) to see if the dough is ready.

8. Uncover the loaves and spray heavily with water. Place the loaves on a wooden or metal peel dusted with cornmeal. With a lame or sharp knife, score the tops of the loaves with five uniform slices perpendicular to the length of the loaf (see page 243).

9. Slide the loaves onto the hot baking stone. Bake for 8 minutes with steam (see page 244), uncover, then bake for an additional 32 to 35 minutes, or until the desired color has been achieved. To check for doneness, take the loaf's internal temperature with an instant-read thermometer; 190°F [88°C] is thoroughly baked. If you don't have an instant-read thermometer, pick up the loaf and tap the bottom; if it sounds hollow, it is done.

10. Remove from the oven, place on a wire rack, and spray heavily with water. Allow the loaves to cool completely at room temperature before cutting into them to serve. Store in a paper bag right on your countertop.

maintaining your rye sour

1. Once a week, add ¾ cup [175 g] of water and 1 cup [125 g] of medium rye flour to 1 cup [205 g] of rye sour, and mix until smooth. Cover with plastic wrap and let ferment at room temperature for 3 to 4 hours, until it is nice and frothy and full of fermentation bubbles. Use the sour to make more rye bread, or put it back into the refrigerator, where it will be OK for another week. Feed the sour at least once per week and you will be able to use it indefinitely.

LIPTAUER CHEESE SPREAD

makes 1¼ cups [295 g]

We're always looking for full-flavored, easy-to-eat foods for game-day gatherings. This cheese spread often starts as a curiosity and then becomes a favorite. All of our recipes were tested by both Bakehouse staffers and home cooks. One of our favorite responses from a tester was, "I can typically guess how a recipe will taste by reading the recipe but not this! All the flavors melded together nicely, in such a way that no one ingredient was overpowering. It's a simple recipe but the outcome is greater than the sum of its parts." We can't agree more!

This tastes great with Bavarian Soft Pretzels (page 147), Jewish Rye Bread (page 211), and vegetables. Adapted from Zingerman's Creamery.

2 Tbsp capers (in salt is best, if available)	1½ tsp Hungarian sweet paprika
½ tsp caraway seeds	¾ tsp freshly ground black pepper
1 garlic clove	¼ tsp coarse sea salt
2 anchovy fillets in olive oil	1 cup [230 g] cream cheese

1. Thirty minutes before you prepare the recipe, soak the capers in water. When you're ready to start, rinse them thoroughly.

2. In a small frying pan over medium heat, toast the caraway seeds. Put them into the warm pan and swirl or stir until they are lightly colored and fragrant. Transfer to a bowl or onto a plate to cool.

3. Mince the garlic and the anchovies together to make a paste with a mortar and pestle, food processor, or knife. Add the paprika, pepper, toasted caraway seeds, and salt, stirring until well combined. Toss in the capers and mix until well coated.

4. In a medium bowl, mix the cream cheese with a wooden spoon to soften. Add the spice mixture a little at a time, mixing until well combined after each addition. Check the seasoning and adjust to taste.

5. Store refrigerated in an airtight container for up to 5 days.

OMG CHOCOLATE CUPCAKES

makes 12 cupcakes

Our OMG Chocolate Cupcakes have been such a big hit that we've never stopped making them: They're now a Bakehouse standard. Make one for your valentine! Making these cupcakes is a three-step process that can be done over several days. By separating the steps, a large project becomes a very manageable one.

CHOCOLATE CUPCAKES

¾ cup [105 g] all-purpose flour

⅓ cup plus 2 Tbsp [35 g] unsweetened cocoa powder (45 to 60% cocoa)

½ tsp sea salt

⅓ tsp baking powder

⅓ tsp baking soda

¾ cup plus 3 Tbsp [195 g] granulated sugar

¾ cup plus 1 Tbsp [180 g] unsalted butter, room temperature

2 large eggs

1 tsp vanilla extract

⅓ cup [80 g] buttermilk

CHOCOLATE SWISS BUTTERCREAM

1 cup plus 3 Tbsp [220 g] semisweet chocolate (56% cacao), chopped

1 cup [200 g] granulated sugar

4 large egg whites

½ tsp sea salt

1⅓ cups [295 g] unsalted butter, room temperature

½ tsp vanilla extract

CHOCOLATE GANACHE

2¾ cups [460 g] semisweet chocolate

4 Tbsp [55 g] unsalted butter

2 cups [460 g] heavy cream

Chocolate chips, for garnish

We wanted to create a dessert for Valentine's Day that was completely indulgent and over the top, just like the intense feelings of new love. The OMG Chocolate Cupcake is just that—a rich chocolate cupcake stuffed with chocolate ganache, topped with a large dollop of creamy chocolate buttercream that is then dipped in melted ganache.

make the chocolate cupcakes

1. Preheat the oven to 350°F [180°C]. Line the cups of a standard 12-cup muffin pan with cupcake liners. If you prefer not to use liners, coat the cups with nonstick cooking spray. Set aside.

2. In a medium mixing bowl, using a sifter or fine-mesh sieve, sift together the flour, cocoa powder, salt, baking powder, and baking soda. Whisk together until well blended and set aside.

3. Using a stand mixer with the paddle attachment, cream the sugar and butter together on medium speed until light and well blended. Scrape down the sides of the bowl as needed to make sure the butter is fully incorporated. Add the eggs one at a time, beating to incorporate each egg completely before adding the next one. Add the vanilla extract and mix until combined. Take care not to add too much air to the mixture.

4. With the mixer on low speed, alternate adding the dry ingredients and the buttermilk to the creamed butter mixture, one-third at a time, mixing well after each addition. Start with one-third of the dry, mix well, add one-third of the buttermilk, and repeat two more times with the remaining ingredients. Scrape down the sides of the bowl well throughout.

5. Divide the batter among 12 muffin cups. Fill each paper cup two-thirds full. Portion out any remaining batter among the 12 cups.

6. Bake the cupcakes for 15 to 18 minutes. The cupcakes are done when they spring back when lightly pressed in the center and an inserted tester or toothpick comes out clean. Let them cool in the pan for 5 minutes, then transfer them to a wire rack to cool completely to room temperature.

make the chocolate swiss buttercream

1. Melt the chocolate in a small bowl over a double boiler, or very carefully in the microwave (20-second intervals and stirring frequently), and let it cool to room temperature.

cont'd

2. In a medium heatproof mixing bowl, add the sugar, egg whites, and salt and stir to combine. Place the bowl over a pan of simmering water and heat the mixture until the sugar is completely dissolved and the temperature registers 180°F [82°C] on an instant-read thermometer.

3. Transfer the egg white mixture to the bowl of a stand mixer. Using the whisk attachment, whip the mixture on high speed until it doubles in volume, becomes thick and shiny, and has cooled to room temperature.

4. When the egg white mixture is at room temperature, turn the mixer on medium speed and add the soft butter, 1 Tbsp at a time, until it's all incorporated. The butter should be approximately the same temperature as the egg mixture to ensure easy incorporation and a smooth texture.

5. Add the vanilla extract and the melted chocolate and mix to incorporate. Beat on high speed for 1 minute to ensure that everything is combined, then scrape down the sides of the bowl and mix briefly to make sure the buttercream is homogenous. Use immediately or place in an airtight container and refrigerate for up to 1 week or freeze for up to 3 months. For tips on how to refresh the buttercream after it is chilled, see page 242.

make the chocolate ganache

1. Place the chocolate pieces and the butter in a medium heatproof mixing bowl.

2. In a saucepan over medium heat, heat the heavy cream until the edges just start to simmer.

3. Pour the hot heavy cream over the chocolate and butter and let sit for 30 seconds so the chocolate can melt. Stir the ingredients until they are smooth and shiny. Refrigerate a third of the ganache and leave the remainder at room temperature; it will be used to dip the cupcakes.

4. Every 10 minutes, stir the refrigerated ganache until it is the consistency of peanut butter.

5. When the ganache is thick but still pliable, place it in a pastry bag without a piping tip. When ready to use, cut off the tip of the bag so that the ganache can be piped.

assemble the cupcakes

1. Using a small paring knife, cut a small cylinder out of the center of each cooled cupcake that is approximately ½ by 1 in [12 mm by 2.5 cm]. Do not cut all the way to the bottom of the cupcake. Fill the empty space in each cupcake with the ganache in the prepared pastry bag.

2. To frost the filled cupcakes, place the buttercream in a large pastry or piping bag fitted with a ½ in [12 mm] star tip. Depending on the size of your piping bag, you may want to use only half of the buttercream at a time. Pipe a swirl of chocolate buttercream on top of each cupcake. The swirl should circle the cupcake twice and be cone-shaped when done. Make sure the buttercream doesn't extend beyond the edge of the cupcake. We like to frost our cupcakes generously, with a nearly equal amount of frosting to cupcake; if your frosting preferences are more reserved, you'll have plenty of buttercream leftover for another batch.

3. Place the cupcakes in the refrigerator for 1 hour so the buttercream can firm up completely. It must be completely firm before dipping in the melted ganache.

4. When ready to dip, gently melt the remaining ganache in a double boiler until it is fluid, but *not* hot. It must be barely warm or it will melt the buttercream as you dip the cupcakes. The maximum temperature for the ganache is 120°F [50°C]. Place the liquid ganache in a bowl deep enough to dip the cupcakes, free and clear, without smashing the top.

5. One by one, hold the cupcakes by the bottom and dip them in the ganache, up to the end of the frosting, where the cupcake starts. Let the ganache drip for a moment, then turn them over and place on a wire rack to cool. Immediately place a chocolate chip at the top of the buttercream cone before the ganache sets.

6. Let the ganache set for 1 hour at room temperature or in the fridge and then serve. Leftovers can be held at room temperature or frozen. The cupcakes can be refrigerated in an airtight container for up to 1 week. Let them come to room temperature before serving. The buttercream and the ganache can also be made ahead of time and refrigerated or frozen.

MARDI GRAS

In New Orleans, Carnival celebrations and King Cake go hand in hand. Starting in early January around Epiphany and kicking off the Carnival season, bakeries throughout the city churn out, around the clock, countless King Cakes for Carnival revelers right up through Mardi Gras, or Fat Tuesday. A local delicacy since the 1870s, the New Orleans—style King Cake is traditionally a rolled or braided oval of yeasted sweet dough spiced with cinnamon sugar that is baked up and then smothered with white icing, followed by lavish dustings of multicolored sanding sugar that salute the city's official colors of Mardi Gras: green for faith, purple for justice, and gold (or yellow) for power.

NEW ORLEANS KING CAKE

makes one oval cake

Get ready for a Mardi Gras celebration with this festive, colorful King Cake. While the French King Cake we make for Epiphany (page 196) also joins the Fat Tuesday fun to close out the Carnival season, this New Orleans style of King Cake is probably the more recognized version here in the United States. If you'd like, add a small trinket to the cake after it's baked, like a plastic baby or an uncooked bean; tradition has it that you'll have good fortune if you find it in your slice.

SPONGE

1 cup plus 3 Tbsp [170 g] all-purpose flour

½ cup [115 g] whole milk, room temperature

1 tsp instant yeast

SWEET DOUGH

½ cup [110 g] unsalted butter, room temperature

¼ cup [50 g] granulated sugar

1½ tsp fine sea salt

1 large egg, room temperature

1 egg yolk, room temperature

1 cup plus 3 Tbsp [170 g] all-purpose flour, plus more for dusting

FILLING

¼ cup plus 2 Tbsp [80 g] brown sugar, packed

2 Tbsp ground cinnamon

FINISHING

2 cups [220 g] powdered sugar

2 to 3 Tbsp water, warm

½ Tbsp corn syrup

1 tsp lemon zest or almond extract (optional, if you'd like a little more flavor in your glaze)

Small plastic baby or uncooked bean (optional)

¼ cup [60 g] green sanding sugar

¼ cup [60 g] gold or yellow sanding sugar

¼ cup [60 g] purple sanding sugar

make the sponge

1. In a medium mixing bowl, combine the flour, milk, and yeast, stirring to incorporate the ingredients as much as possible. Scrape the mixture out onto a clean, unfloured work surface and knead for a minute or two, or until the sponge is firm and smooth. Place the sponge in a medium mixing bowl coated in vegetable oil. Cover with plastic wrap and ferment for 1 hour in a warm spot in your kitchen. When ready, the sponge will hold a fingerprint and be almost double in size.

make the sweet dough

1. After 1 hour, in another medium mixing bowl, cream the butter, granulated sugar, and salt with a wooden spoon until light and creamy. If using a stand mixer, use the paddle attachment and mix on medium speed. Add the egg and yolk one at a time, mixing just long enough to blend them in completely each time. Tear up the sponge into small pieces and add them to the egg mixture in the bowl, then add all the flour and mix until completely combined.

cont'd

2. Turn dough out onto a clean, unfloured work surface and knead for 6 to 8 minutes. For the first few minutes, press and schmear the dough across the surface to help break down the sponge pieces. Once you no longer see streaks of white sponge, start using a lighter touch and knead, scraping up the dough from the table often with a bench scraper, until the dough is tacky but not sticky. (Tacky dough will adhere to your hand or finger, but it will release without leaving much of a trace. Sticky dough will leave a residue on your hand.) The dough will become smoother and stronger as you knead it. If doing this by hand, we like to say, "trust the process." It will seem like it may not work, but it will; just keep kneading and don't add flour. If using a stand mixer, use the paddle attachment and mix on medium-low speed. Look for the same visual cues. Wrap the dough in plastic wrap and chill in the refrigerator overnight (or at least 4 hours if you're in a rush for cake).

fill and shape the cake

1. On a lightly floured surface, roll out the dough into a 10 by 24 in [25 by 60 cm] rectangle. Brush away any excess flour.

2. In a small bowl, whisk together the brown sugar and cinnamon, then sprinkle the mixture over almost the entire surface of the dough, leaving bare a 1 in [2.5 cm] strip on the long sides of the rectangle and a ½ in [12 mm] strip on each of the shorter ends.

3. Starting with the long edge closest to you, begin rolling the dough into a tight cylinder away from you, keeping the roll even all the way across and avoiding the "snake that ate a bowling ball" look. Once the dough is rolled, pinch the seam together.

4. Line a baking sheet with parchment paper and transfer the rolled cylinder to it, seam side down, and connect the ends, pinching them together and shaping it into an oval ring.

5. Cover the ring with plastic wrap and let proof for 1½ to 2 hours at room temperature, or until the dough ring passes the touch test: Gently press the pad of a fingertip into the dough and remove it; the indentation should slowly come back most, but not all, of the way.

6. While the ring is proofing, preheat the oven to 375°F [190°C] at least 20 minutes prior to baking. Once proofed, remove the plastic wrap and bake the ring for 25 to 30 minutes, or until nicely browned and the internal temperature in the center registers 190°F [90°C] on an instant-read thermometer. Allow the cake to cool to room temperature before glazing.

make the glaze and finish the cake

1. In a medium mixing bowl, sift the powdered sugar. Add 1 Tbsp of the warm water and the corn syrup and stir to combine. Gradually add additional water, 1 tsp at a time, until the glaze is very thick and just barely pourable.

2. Press the plastic baby or uncooked bean, if using, into the bottom of the cake before glazing.

3. For the least mess when glazing, place the cake on a wire rack set over a baking sheet. Pour the glaze over the top of the cake, letting it fall over the sides on its own. If necessary, use an offset spatula to help it just begin to pour over the sides.

4. Immediately apply green, gold, and purple sugar to the icing before it sets in alternating stripes around the cake. In total, you will create twelve stripes, four of each color. Choose a color and gently shake it to make a 2 in [5 cm] stripe from the top of the round to the bottom of the round. Then do it in the opposite direction, making a cross. Repeat this with the two other colors, going around the cake.

5. Serve at room temperature. Store the glazed cake in an airtight container at room temperature for up to 3 days. If you know you want to freeze the cake, don't glaze it. Wrap the baked and cooled cake in plastic wrap and freeze for up to 2 months. When ready to serve, thaw the frozen cake at room temperature, then glaze and top it with the sanding sugars.

GABOR'S HUNGARIAN BEAN SOUP

serves 6 to 8 as a main dish

This Hungarian-inspired soup is one of our most popular, hands-down; we've been making it once a week since at least 2010. While we rotate our soups out with the seasons and the interests of our Bakeshop guests, Gabor's (as we refer to it) has rarely come off the shop's soup menu.

From a cook's perspective, this soup has a few points of interest. First, we make it with a pork stock, which we haven't come across much in our culinary adventures. Then comes the use of lard. In Hungary, lard is the fat of choice and is used much more often than butter in cooking, though you can use butter or vegetable oil if you'd rather. You'll also notice that the paprika, Hungarian for pepper and Hungary's signature spice since the eighteenth century, is added to the vegetables and fat. Paprika is best incorporated into a recipe by adding it directly to the fat rather than into the liquid as you might add other flavorings.

This is a filling dish and is perfect served with a green salad and some light crusty bread, like our Rustic Italian Baguettes (page 130).

make the ham hock stock

1. In a large stockpot, add all of the ingredients for the stock. Bring the mixture to a boil over medium-high heat, then lower the heat to medium-low and simmer for 3 hours. Remove the ham hock from the pot and set aside. Strain the stock through a fine-mesh sieve and reserve 5 cups [1.2 L] for the soup. Any extra stock can be refrigerated for 1 week or frozen for 3 months for later use.

make the soup

1. In a large stockpot over medium heat, melt 1½ Tbsp of the lard. Add the bacon and cook until crispy. Lower the heat to medium-low and add the onion, carrot, and ½ Tbsp of the salt and sauté until tender, not browned. Add the paprika and cook for 2 minutes, stirring occasionally.

2. Add the ham hock stock, three cans of beans with their liquid, and three cans of beans, rinsed and drained, to the pot and bring the soup to a strong simmer.

3. Meanwhile, make a roux. In a medium saucepan over low heat, melt the remaining 7 Tbsp [90 g] of lard, then add the flour and stir with a wooden spoon until well combined and the flour has absorbed all the lard. Continue to cook the roux over low heat for 3 to 4 minutes, stirring constantly and taking care not to let it color. This essentially cooks the flour.

4. Stir the roux into the simmering soup. Once all of the roux is added, continue to simmer the soup for 10 minutes until thickened and any remaining raw flour flavor has cooked out.

5. While the soup is simmering, pick the meat off the ham hock and chop it into ½ in [12 mm] pieces. Add to the soup and simmer for another 5 minutes. Remove from the heat and add the sour cream and parsley. Stir until evenly combined. Season to taste with the remaining ½ Tbsp of salt and serve. Refrigerate in an airtight container for up to 1 week.

HAM HOCK STOCK	SOUP
14 cups [3.4 L] water	8½ Tbsp [110 g] lard or vegetable oil
One 1½ lb [680 g] smoked ham hock	6 or 7 slices [180 g] bacon, diced
1 medium onion, roughly chopped	1½ cups [230 g] small diced yellow onion
1 medium carrot, roughly chopped	1¼ cups [180 g] small diced carrot
1 celery rib, roughly chopped	1 Tbsp fine sea salt
3 to 5 peppercorns	1 Tbsp plus 1 tsp sweet paprika
1 bay leaf	Six 15 oz [425 g] cans butter beans (jumbo preferred)
1 Tbsp fine sea salt	⅔ cup [90 g] all-purpose flour
	¾ cup [180 g] sour cream
	¼ cup [15 g] chopped parsley

HUNGARIAN MONTH

In 2010, we started studying the cuisine of Hungary. We've now developed a large repertoire of Hungarian sweets, soups, and savory items. To make our winters tastier, we've declared March Hungarian month and we bake our entire repertoire. The two most popular items we make are Dobos Torta (page 223) and Gabor's Hungarian Bean Soup (facing). Make your own Hungarian celebration with these two recipes. For other Hungarian recipes, check out our other cookbook, *Zingerman's Bakehouse*.

DOBOS TORTA

makes 1 five-layer torte

This torte is a five-layered, light vanilla sponge cake filled and iced with chocolate espresso buttercream and garnished on top with a distinctive layer of crispy golden caramel. The famous dessert evokes the elegance of Budapest's late nineteenth-century coffeehouse culture and the pastry traditions of Hungary, a country touted as "the land of ten million pastry lovers," by George Lang, the Hungarian-born American restaurateur.

In 1884, József C. Dobos (pronounced *doh-bosh*), an influential and enterprising pastry chef and culinary entrepreneur, sought to capitalize on Hungarians' love for elegant cakes and created his iconic Dobos Torta. The torte's chocolate buttercream, which Dobos had discovered while traveling in France, was new to Hungarian pastry-making. Also novel was the flat, shiny, crisp caramel top. Both these innovations allowed for a significantly extended shelf life, keeping the torte fresh for longer during a time when refrigeration was rare. What's more, the hard caramel top made the torte durable enough to travel, prompting Dobos to begin touring with the cake, personally introducing it in all the great European capital cities, and then shipping it in specially designed wooden boxes to pastry-loving customers all over Europe and beyond. The torte may very well have been the first mail-order cake!

Today, most Dobos Tortas are round, but in many of the older recipes from Dobos's day, it was actually rectangular, so we chose to make ours rectangular as well.

CAKE LAYERS

7 large eggs, room temperature, separated

¼ tsp fine sea salt

¾ cup [150 g] granulated sugar

⅔ cup [90 g] pastry flour

CHOCOLATE ESPRESSO BUTTERCREAM

1 cup [180 g] bittersweet chocolate (60 to 65%)

1⅓ cups [290 g] unsalted butter, room temperature

1 large egg, room temperature

3 Tbsp instant espresso powder

1 Tbsp water, hot

1⅓ cups [160 g] powdered sugar, sifted

½ tsp vanilla extract

CARAMEL GLAZE

1½ cups [340 g] water

1 Tbsp corn syrup

3⅓ cups plus 1 Tbsp [680 g] granulated sugar

make the cake layers

1. Preheat the oven to 350°F [180°C]. Line two half baking sheets (13 by 18 in [33 by 46 cm]) with parchment paper and spray the parchment and sides of the baking sheets generously with nonstick cooking spray.

2. Using a stand mixer with the whisk attachment, mix the egg whites and salt on medium speed until the egg whites are frothy, then increase the speed to high and whip until they form stiff peaks (see page 244).

3. Gradually add the egg yolks, one at time, mixing on medium-high speed until the batter is a homogeneous yellow color. Lower the speed and gradually add the sugar in a steady stream. Remove the bowl from the machine.

4. Use a hand sifter or fine-mesh sieve to sift the flour into the bowl in four additions. After each addition, gently fold in the flour using a spatula. Check for pockets of flour and mix thoroughly if you discover them.

5. Divide the batter evenly between the prepared baking sheets, spreading it with a spatula or an offset spatula. It will be quite thin; this is to be expected.

6. Bake for 10 to 12 minutes, or until the top springs back when touched. If you have room in your oven, you can bake both sheets at the same time. If one sheet needs to wait a few minutes while the first one bakes, that will work too! Let each cake layer cool to room temperature in the baking sheet.

7. Lightly coat a large piece of parchment paper with nonstick cooking spray. To remove each cake layer from the sheet, run a metal spatula around the side to loosen, then turn out the cake onto the prepared parchment paper.

cont'd

make the chocolate espresso buttercream

I. In a double boiler or heatproof bowl set over a saucepan of simmering water, melt the chocolate, stirring frequently. You can also melt the chocolate in a microwave, checking and stirring at 20-second intervals. Do not allow the chocolate to get very hot. Set aside to cool.

2. Using a stand mixer with a paddle attachment, add the butter to the bowl and mix on a medium speed until soft and smooth. Add the egg and mix well.

3. In a small bowl, dissolve the espresso powder in the hot water. Add the powdered sugar, vanilla extract, and dissolved espresso powder to the butter mixture and mix on low speed until all of the ingredients are fully incorporated.

4. Mix in the cooled melted chocolate until homogeneous. Refrigerate the buttercream if not using right away. For tips on how to refresh the buttercream after it's been chilled or frozen, see page 242.

make the caramel glaze and garnish

I. Divide each half sheet cake layer into four equal rectangles; each will be 5 by 7 in [12 by 17 cm].

2. In a medium saucepan, pour in the water. Add the corn syrup and carefully pour in the sugar, trying to keep it off the sides of the pan. Turn on the heat to medium-high. Do not stir the solution or adjust the heat; stirring the solution may cause it to crystallize.

3. Cook until the sugar is caramelized to a dark honey color, 25 to 30 minutes. Let sit until thickened like molasses, about 7 minutes.

4. Pour a layer of caramel over one 5 by 7 in [12 by 17 cm] cake rectangle, leaving ¼ in [6 mm] on the edge caramel-free. Let the caramel layer cool for 1 to 2 minutes, then spray or oil a sharp knife and trim off the cake edges free of caramel.

5. Cut the rectangle into eight triangles: First cut the entire rectangle in half horizontally, then cut it in half vertically. You will now have created four equal-size rectangles. Cut each of these in half into two right-angle triangles, for a total of eight.

assemble the cake

I. Place one cake rectangle on a quarter-sheet cake board (9 by 13 in [23 by 33 cm]) or a platter with similar dimensions. Using an offset spatula, spread about ⅓ cup [45 g] of the buttercream evenly on the bottom cake layer. Place the second layer of cake on top of the buttercream, pressing gently to adhere the layers together and to make the cake as level as possible. Continue until you have stacked five layers, finishing with buttercream. (Note that you'll have two cake layers left over—consider them a cook's treat!) Cover the sides of the cake with buttercream, which can be left smooth or formed into vertical or horizontal lines. Reserve some buttercream for the shell border.

2. Carefully place the caramel-glazed pieces on the top of the cake. Add the reserved buttercream to a pastry bag fitted with small star tip and pipe a small decorative border around the top layer to finish the cake. Use the border to fill in the space from the caramel garnishes to the edge of the cake and to cover the edges of the caramel glazed pieces.

3. Serve at room temperature. Store the cake in the refrigerator for up to 5 days, but bring it up to room temperature before serving. Note that it can take 2 to 3 hours for the cake to fully warm up.

BANANA CREAM PIE

makes one single-crust pie

At home, we like to celebrate Pi Day with something a little different, like our Banana Cream Pie, a beloved favorite of both staff and guests that makes an appearance a few times a year as what we call a "special bake." We make this pie with vanilla bean pastry cream, fresh bananas, vanilla bean whipped cream, and a scrumptious sugar cookie crust. We use our own sugar cookies, but if you'd like to streamline your pie-making experience, feel free to substitute store-bought sugar cookies or vanilla wafers instead.

SUGAR COOKIES (OPTIONAL, SEE HEADNOTE)

¼ cup [55 g] unsalted butter, room temperature

2 Tbsp granulated sugar

1 Tbsp whisked egg

⅛ tsp vanilla extract

⅔ cup [80 g] pastry flour, plus more for dusting

⅛ tsp fine sea salt

⅛ tsp lemon zest

⅛ tsp orange zest

SUGAR COOKIE CRUST

1 batch sugar cookies (from above) or 5 oz [140 g] store-bought sugar cookies or vanilla wafers

1 Tbsp plus 2 tsp granulated sugar

⅛ tsp fine sea salt

2 Tbsp plus 1 tsp unsalted butter, melted

PASTRY CREAM

½ cup [115 g] whole milk

2 Tbsp cornstarch

3 large egg yolks

½ cup [115 g] heavy cream

¼ cup plus 2 tsp [60 g] granulated sugar

Pinch fine sea salt

½ vanilla bean, scraped

½ tsp vanilla extract

2 Tbsp unsalted butter

WHIPPED CREAM

1 cup plus 1 Tbsp [245 g] heavy cream

½ vanilla bean, scraped

1 Tbsp plus 2 tsp [25 g] granulated sugar

5 to 6 [545 g] peeled fresh bananas

1 Tbsp lemon juice

make the sugar cookies

1. Preheat the oven to 325°F [165°C]. Line a baking sheet with parchment paper.

2. In a medium mixing bowl, cream the butter and sugar with a wooden spoon until well blended. If using a stand mixer, beat with the paddle attachment on medium speed. Add the whisked egg and vanilla extract and mix until light and creamy. Add the pastry flour and salt to the creamed mixture and mix until completely incorporated. Add the lemon and orange zests and mix until evenly distributed.

3. Scrape the dough out onto a lightly floured work surface and roll it out to ¼ in [6 mm] thickness, turning it as you go to prevent it from sticking. Transfer the rolled dough to the prepared baking sheet and bake for 15 to 20 minutes, or until golden brown.

4. Let cool completely on the baking sheet, then break into large pieces.

make the sugar cookie crust

1. Preheat oven to 325°F [165°C].

2. In a food processor, grind the baked cookie pieces into fine crumbs. In a small bowl, stir together the cookie crumbs, sugar, and salt. Add the melted butter and mix until well combined.

3. Place the cookie crumb mixture into a 9 in [23 cm] pie pan and shake it gently to even out the crumbs. Using your fingertips, press the mixture into the pan so that the crust is compact and an even thickness across the bottom and up the sides of the pan.

4. Place the pie pan on a baking sheet and bake for 20 minutes, or until golden brown. Set aside to cool completely.

cont'd

make the pastry cream

1. In a medium saucepan, whisk together the milk and cornstarch until the cornstarch has dissolved. Add the egg yolks and whisk until they are completely incorporated. Whisk in the heavy cream, sugar, and salt. Add the vanilla bean seeds to the mixture.

2. Cook the pastry cream over medium heat, stirring constantly with a rubber spatula, and bring to a light boil. Continue to cook for 1 minute, stirring constantly. The goal is to cook the cornstarch and thicken the pastry cream.

3. Remove the pastry cream from the heat and pour it into a clean, medium mixing bowl. Beat the pastry cream with a clean whisk until it cools slightly and becomes smooth and shiny. If using a stand mixer, use the whisk attachment and whip on medium speed for 4 minutes until it cools slightly. Add the vanilla extract and butter and whisk until smooth.

4. Place plastic wrap directly onto the surface of the pastry cream to prevent a skin from forming. Refrigerate until at least room temperature. It will keep in the refrigerator for 3 to 5 days if you would like to make it ahead.

make the whipped cream and assemble the pie

1. Add the heavy cream and vanilla bean seeds to the bowl of a stand mixer fitted with the whisk attachment and whip at the highest speed. While the mixer is running, slowly add the sugar, aiming for the side of the bowl. If whisking by hand, get ready for a serious arm workout and add the sugar in increments of teaspoons. Whip until you get firm peaks (see page 244), then set aside.

2. Slice the bananas diagonally, about ½ in [12 mm] thick. In a medium bowl, combine the banana slices and lemon juice.

3. Whisk the cooled pastry cream until it is smooth. Add it to the bananas and gently fold together.

4. Fill the cooled pie shell with the banana and pastry cream filling and level it with an offset spatula.

5. Top the filling with whipped cream, taking care to cover it completely; this will help keep the bananas from oxidizing. For a rustic look, add all of the whipped cream to the pie and use an offset spatula to spread and smooth it across the top. For a more decorative look, add the whipped cream to a pastry bag fitted with a star tip and pipe rosettes on the top of the pie starting from the outside and working toward the center. Store the pie in the refrigerator until ready to serve. This pie is best enjoyed the day it is assembled.

ZINGERMAN'S DELI CHICKEN POT PIES

makes 8 individual double-crust pies

For Pi Day, we like to do it up and eat pie for our main course too. Our friends at Zingerman's Delicatessen make it easy for us; in the winter months, they make six different flavors. They started making them as a way to keep their kitchen staff gainfully employed during a notoriously slow time of year for restaurants. Now, pot pie season is eagerly anticipated, and the original recipe, the one we're sharing here, is so popular that it's now available year-round. The recipe starts with already roasted chicken meat. Roast your own or make the recipe simpler and buy a rotisserie chicken. Either way, it will taste great. Be sure to use both white and dark meat for great flavor and a nice variation in texture.

PIE DOUGH

3¾ cups plus 2 Tbsp [545 g] all-purpose flour

1 tsp fine sea salt

1½ cups plus 2 Tbsp [360 g] unsalted butter, cold, diced into ¼ in [6 mm] pieces

½ cup plus 4 tsp [135 g] water, ice cold

FILLING

½ cup [110 g] unsalted butter, room temperature

2 cups [280 g] diced yellow onions (½ in [12 mm] pieces)

1 cup [140 g] diced carrots (½ in [12 mm] pieces)

1 cup [170 g] diced mushrooms (½ in [12 mm] pieces)

½ cup [70 g] diced celery (½ in [12 mm] pieces)

⅓ cup [50 g] diced red bell peppers (½ in [12 mm] pieces)

¼ cup [35 g] diced green bell peppers (½ in [12 mm] pieces)

1 tsp minced garlic

½ cup [70 g] all-purpose flour

2 cups [455 g] unsalted chicken stock, room temperature

½ cup [120 g] heavy cream, room temperature

3½ to 4 cups [450 to 500 g] roasted chicken, some shredded in 2 in [5 cm] strips and some cubed

2 cups [280 g] steamed and diced red-skinned potatoes (½ in [12 mm] pieces)

2 tsp fine sea salt

½ tsp freshly ground black pepper

1 Tbsp minced fresh Italian parsley

½ tsp fresh thyme leaves

EGG WASH

1 large egg

1 egg yolk

1 Tbsp water

make the pie dough

1. In a large mixing bowl, blend the flour and salt together with a fork. Add the butter and cut it into the flour mixture using a pastry blender, two knives, or your hands until the mixture looks like coarse cornmeal. If using your hands, break the butter pieces up between your fingers and rub the butter and flour together between your hands as if your hands are cold. This will break down the butter and rub it all over the flour. There should be no chunks of butter remaining.

2. Create a well in the center of the flour mixture and add the cold water, using a fork to blend it in until the mixture is moistened and there is no dry flour left in the bowl. Knead the mixture a few times in the bowl if necessary.

3. Gather the dough into a ball, pressing it firmly so it holds together. Wrap the dough in plastic wrap and let rest at room temperature for 1 hour.

make the filling

1. In a large stockpot or Dutch oven over medium heat, melt the butter. Add the onions, carrots, mushrooms, celery, bell peppers, and garlic. Stir occasionally and cook until the onions are translucent and the rest of the vegetables are softened, about 15 minutes, lowering the heat if necessary to avoid the vegetables taking on color.

2. Add the flour to the pot, then toss and stir the mixture until all the vegetables are well coated in the flour. Cook for 1 minute over medium-low heat.

3. Add the chicken stock and heavy cream to the vegetable mixture, stirring over medium heat until it has thickened and any raw flour flavor has cooked out, 2 to 3 minutes, then remove from the heat. Add the chicken, potatoes, salt, pepper, parsley, and thyme. Taste and adjust seasonings to taste and then set the filling aside to cool to room temperature.

cont'd

roll out the dough and fill the pies

1. Preheat the oven to 425°F [220°C] at least 20 minutes prior to baking.

2. Once the dough has rested for 1 hour, use a bench scraper or chef's knife to divide it into sixteen equal-size pieces to make eight mini double-crust pot pies.

3. Place each piece of dough on a lightly floured work surface and dust the top with flour. Using a rolling pin, roll out each piece of dough into a 6 in [15 cm] circle.

4. Line each of the 5 in [12 cm] pie plates with one circle of dough. Distribute the cooled filling evenly among the pies, then top with another piece of dough.

5. Seal the edges by lightly pressing both layers of dough together with your fingers against the top of the pie plate. Finish the edge with your choice of decorative crimping.

6. Make the egg wash by whisking together the egg, egg yolk, and water until well combined. Lightly brush the tops of the pot pies with the egg wash, then cut a vent or two in the top of each pot pie with a paring knife. Bake for 30 to 35 minutes, or until the crust is golden brown and the internal temperature registers 165°F [75°C] on an instant-read thermometer.

7. These are very make-ahead friendly—both the components and whole pies! Pie dough can be stored in the refrigerator for up to 5 days or frozen, well wrapped and preferably in an airtight container, for up to 3 months. The filling can be stored in an airtight container in the refrigerator for up to 5 days. Chill or freeze fully assembled (but not egg-washed) pot pies until firm, then wrap in plastic wrap before freezing or refrigerating. Unbaked pot pies can be refrigerated for up to 3 days or frozen for up to 2 months.

to bake refrigerated pot pies

1. Preheat the oven to 400°F [200°C] at least 20 minutes prior to baking.

2. Brush the egg wash on top of the pot pies, cut a vent or two in the top of each, and bake for 30 to 35 minutes, or until the crust is golden brown and the internal temperature is 165°F [75°C].

to bake frozen pot pies

1. Preheat the oven to 350°F [180°C] at least 20 minutes prior to baking.

2. Brush the egg wash on top of the pot pies, cut a vent or two in the top of each, and bake for 60 minutes, or until the crusts are golden brown and the internal temperature of each pot pie is 165°F [75°C].

ST. PATRICK'S DAY

St. Patrick's Day is the feast day honoring St. Patrick, one of Ireland's patron saints. It's a holiday tradition the Irish have been celebrating with religious services and feasting for over a thousand years. While St. Patrick's Day celebrations were at first largely religious, over time, patriotic Irish immigrants to America secularized the celebrations, and they became steeped in Irish cultural pride. American cities with large Irish immigrant populations, such as Boston, Philadelphia, and New York, were the first to stage elaborate, patriotic celebrations, with Boston beginning the American tradition of an annual St. Patrick's Day parade in 1737.

Today, St. Patrick's Day parades are held all across the United States, with the largest celebrations taking place in New York City and Boston. People celebrating from coast to coast, Irish and non-Irish alike, spend the day feasting and drinking when they are not cheering bagpipers, step dancers, and marching bands parading through city streets. The color green, a reverent nod to Ireland and Irish culture, permeates all the festivities here, from wearing green clothing adorned with the ubiquitous shamrock to feasting on traditional Irish food, such as corned beef, green cabbage, and bacon, to, of course, drinking beer that has even been dyed green.

St. Patrick's Day is a fun holiday for us that brightens the end of winter. By March in Michigan, we're ready for some festivities and new flavors after months of short days, gray skies, and cold weather.

BEEF AND GUINNESS STEW

serves 6 to 8 as a main dish

We bring out the Beef and Guinness Stew in the winter when we're all ready to eat something filling and deep in flavor. It's also just right for St. Patrick's Day celebrations too—with more Guinness for drinking, of course. The French improve it with red wine, and here, the Irish improve it with the rich, malty, sweet, and slightly bitter Guinness stout. All of these flavors come through in the final stew. Add the smoky flavor of the bacon and the distinctive taste of fresh rosemary to create a nourishing meal, enhanced all the more with a wedge of Irish Brown Soda Bread (page 234) slathered with Irish Kerrygold butter.

4 [110 g] thick-cut bacon slices	Fine sea salt and freshly ground black pepper
3 lb [1.4 kg] beef stew meat, cubed	2 cups [225 g] quartered cremini mushrooms
½ cup [70 g] all-purpose flour	2 cups [300 g] diced carrots
2 Tbsp canola oil, plus more as needed	2 cups [245 g] diced celery
2 Tbsp unsalted butter, plus more as needed	38 oz [1.2 L] Guinness stout
4 cups [575 g] diced yellow onion	4 cups [910 g] beef stock
	2 tsp minced fresh rosemary
	2 tsp dried thyme

1. In a large stockpot over medium heat, cook the bacon until crispy. Drain on a paper towel. Pour out the bacon fat and save for another use, then wipe out the pot. When the bacon is cool, chop it into small pieces, ¼ in [6 mm] or smaller.

2. In a medium bowl, toss the beef with the flour.

3. In the large stockpot, heat the oil and butter over medium heat until the butter has melted, then add the onion, and salt and pepper lightly. Cook until the onions have softened and lightly browned, about 12 minutes. Remove the onions from the pan.

4. Add more oil to the pan if it has been absorbed by the onions. Carefully add the beef in a single layer (working in batches if necessary), season with salt and pepper, and cook until browned, 3 to 5 minutes. Turn to brown any uncooked sides, and remove the beef from the pan. Repeat with any meat that did not fit in the initial layer. When all the beef has been seared, remove it from the pot and set aside.

5. If necessary, add more butter and oil to the stockpot. Add the mushrooms and sauté until cooked, about 10 minutes. Remove and set aside with the reserved meat and onions.

6. Add the carrots and celery to the stockpot, sprinkle with salt, and sauté, stirring occasionally, until the vegetables are soft, 10 to 15 minutes. Remove the vegetables and set aside with the mushrooms, meat, and onions.

7. Increase the heat to high and add the Guinness. Let it boil and use a wooden spoon to scrape the browned bits off the bottom of the pot. Let cook until the beer is reduced by one-third.

8. Return everything to the stockpot—bacon, onions, beef, mushrooms, carrots, and celery—and add the beef stock, rosemary, and thyme. Allow the soup to come to a boil, then lower the heat to medium-low and gently simmer the stew until the beef is fully cooked and very tender, 1½ to 2 hours. Stir occasionally.

9. Taste and season as needed with salt and pepper, then serve. Refrigerate for up to 1 week or freeze in an airtight container for up to 3 months.

IRISH BROWN SODA BREAD

makes one loaf

To celebrate Ireland's patron saint on the cusp of spring, we turn our efforts, for a few days in mid-March, to baking up our Irish Brown Soda Bread. Ours is a traditional brown soda bread using whole-meal wheat flour and oats that we import from Ireland. It creates a wheaty, flat, round, nubby-textured loaf best eaten in thin slices with rich butter or red fruit preserves or with a slice of Irish smoked salmon and a little dill. Since the actual Irish grains and flours are very difficult to find in the United States, we've adapted our recipe using easier-to-find ingredients that result in a loaf very similar in flavor and texture and true to the spirit of the traditional Irish version.

3 Tbsp oat flour or finely ground rolled oats	⅓ cup [35 g] rolled oats
1½ cups [240 g] steel-cut oats	1¼ tsp fine sea salt
⅔ cup [90 g] stone-ground whole-wheat flour	1 tsp baking soda
½ cup plus 2 Tbsp [100 g] all-purpose flour	1½ cups [350 g] buttermilk

1. Preheat the oven to 425°F [220°C] at least 20 minutes prior to baking if using a baking sheet and 1 hour before baking if using a baking stone, which should be placed in the oven as soon as you turn it on. We recommend using a stone; it helps to create a more authentic texture.

2. Place the oat flour on a baking sheet and toast in the preheated oven for 5 minutes.

3. In a large mixing bowl, combine all of the dry ingredients. Make a well in the center of the dry ingredients and add the buttermilk. Stir with a fork until no visible streaks of dry ingredients remain. Scrape down the sides of the bowl and gently knead the dough in the bowl until all the ingredients are well combined.

4. If using a baking sheet to bake the bread, line it with parchment paper. If using a baking stone, flip the baking sheet over and top it with a piece of parchment so that the bread and parchment will be easy to slide off onto the preheated stone in the oven.

5. Using wet hands, scoop the dough, which will be loose and sticky, out of the bowl and shape it into a mound in the center of the parchment paper lining the baking sheet. Flatten the mound evenly into a 7 in [17 cm] disk.

6. Using a wet bench scraper or a chef's knife, cut an X about ½ in [12 mm] deep into the flattened round from one side to the other, dividing the loaf into four quadrants, which symbolize the four counties of Ireland. In the middle of each quadrant, near the edge of the round, make a small slit to let the Irish fairies out. Don't worry if you didn't see fairies on the ingredient list!

7. If baking on a baking sheet, place the sheet on the center rack in the preheated oven. If baking on a stone, slide the bread and parchment paper from the underside of the baking sheet onto the preheated baking stone. Bake the loaf for 35 minutes or until golden brown and the internal temperature is 190°F [88°C].

8. Allow the bread to cool to room temperature either on the baking sheet or a wire rack before enjoying. Store the bread in an airtight container at room temperature for up to 3 days.

RESOURCES

INGREDIENTS

As is always the case with our food, what distinguishes our versions from someone else's is great execution and the best, most flavorful ingredients we can find. As we say at Zingerman's, "You really can taste the difference."

Here you'll find our recommendations for what products to use for this cookbook's most commonly used ingredients. Our basic advice is to use the most flavorful ingredients you can find to make these dishes special. Don't skimp on flavor!

All-purpose flour   As excited as we are about freshly milled whole-grain (FMWG) flours, our standard organic all-purpose wheat flour comes to us from Bay State Milling in Platteville, Colorado, a medium-size milling company in today's commercial milling world with an ethos similar to ours. We had a chance to visit Bay State Milling when we made the switch to this flour in 2018. Even though the flour is a blend of various wheats to achieve the consistency needed for bakeries like ours, it is made primarily from wheat grown on Ray Freeburg's farm in Pine Bluffs, Wyoming, a generations-old family farm that values and practices organic regenerative farming. All-purpose flours have a protein content between 10% and 12%, and ours has a mid-range protein content—about 11%, for the scientifically inclined bakers out there. That's a high-enough amount of protein for giving great structure to breads, but also a low-enough amount to still make for soft and tender pastries. Our all-purpose flour is available in our Bakeshop and from Zingerman's Mail

Order; it's a high-quality, all-purpose flour you can feel good about!

If you are buying all-purpose flour in your local markets, we suggest using organic flour that has never been bromated. Bromation is a chemical process used to age flour and it's not necessary.

Butter   Butter is more flavorful than shortening and margarine, and we're all about flavor. Start using butter in your baking and you'll never go back to another fat. (Unless it's lard in your pie crust, then we're on board!)

We use unsalted butter in all our recipes, whether it's for scones or soups. Salt in butter is unregulated, so depending on the brand you choose, it may be more or less salty. It's easiest to control the salt in a recipe by using unsalted butter and adding the amount of salt that is optimal for the recipe.

When a recipe calls for room-temperature butter, plan to leave it on your countertop for 2 to 3 hours, but longer is fine too. Don't worry about spoilage; butter can sit at room temperature for several days without any problems.

Our sweet cream butter comes to us from Wisconsin in 50 lb [22.5 kg] blocks. You probably don't need that much though, so we recommend looking for Plugra®, Lurpak®, Kerrygold®, or other brands labeled "European-Style"—they tend to have higher than the minimum required 80% butterfat.

Chocolate   Chocolate is basically made of cacao, cocoa butter, vanilla, sugar, and occasionally milk. The percentage of each of these elements in the chocolate is one of the basic differentiators of one chocolate from another. On chocolate packages these days, producers note the percentage of cacao on the label. The rest of the

ingredients in the chocolate make up the remaining percentage. For each recipe, we indicate the percentage of cacao we think would be best.

Chocolates also have particular flavors, depending on the bean and region of origin and how it is processed. The flavors can range from fruity to earthy to coffee or nutty. Chocolates made of a single variety of beans from a particular region emphasize the difference in these flavors. Other chocolates are blends of beans chosen by the chocolatier to achieve a particular flavor profile. The most cautious choice would be to try a sample before you buy enough for the recipe to make sure you like its particular flavor profile.

When a recipe calls for chocolate to be melted, we recommend using bar chocolate, roughly chopped, rather than chocolate chips. Chocolate chips often contain additional ingredients and are designed to hold their shape. Bar chocolate will melt more easily, providing a smoother result (and will taste better too).

Coconut   We didn't quite realize until writing this cookbook (and trying to articulate which type of coconut we were talking about!) just how many types of coconut products there are. These are the different types we call for in our recipes.

Coconut compound: Found in our Summer Fling Coconut and Lime Coffee Cake (page 88), this is a flavorful blend of coconut pulp and coconut cream. It can be found online or at specialty baking shops (note that it's not the same thing as coconut butter or puréed coconut).

Desiccated coconut: This is ground (rather than shredded) coconut found in our Black and White Magic Brownies (page 47). Sometimes shredded coconut is confusingly labeled as desiccated coconut. Making sure your package has the word *fine* on it will ensure it's the very short, ground coconut that you're looking for.

Fresh coconut: Also found in our Black and White Magic Brownies (page 47), this is simply raw coconut meat. It's often found frozen, but it could also be fresh in the produce area of grocery stores. If you're having trouble finding it, check local Asian, Indian, or Latin American grocery stores. If all else fails, it can be found online, like most everything else these days.

Shredded coconut: This comes as both unsweetened or sweetened (the latter of which is sometimes labeled as fancy), and untoasted or toasted. Shredded coconut can also come in larger pieces and called flakes.

Demerara sugar　We also like to use demerara sugar, most often for garnishing baking goods, as its large crystals add a nice textural contrast. Demerara sugar is less processed than regular granulated sugar, so some molasses is left in the sugar crystals. If you can't find demerara sugar, look for turbinado sugar, also called sugar in the raw.

Durum flour　Want to try whole durum flour? Look for it in the baking aisle. Some specialty flour brands may be selling it. It is definitely available by mail from several small specialty millers. Our go-to is Janie's Mill. Check them out for many interesting grains.

Eggs　We call for large eggs in these recipes, as they are the most common size, but large and extra-large can be used interchangeably for good results. If you only have smaller eggs, you'll need to use a little more, so go by

weight—one large egg (without the shell) weighs 1¾ oz [50 g].

Freshly milled whole-grain (FMWG) flours　Since acquiring our first stone mill, back in 2018 (we now have two!), we've been delving more deeply than ever into the world of grains—locally grown, heritage and ancient wheat varieties, freshly milled, as well as non-wheat varieties. We are passionate about stone milling our own whole-grain flours and investing in our regional grain economy by supporting others with the same goal. We feature these freshly milled flours in our newly developed naturally leavened breads and porridges, and we've also added them to some of our classic bread and pastry mainstays. You'll find some FMWG flours featured within these pages. Many of them are available online. We also give alternatives of more readily available flours.

We use many different flours other than just standard organic all-purpose these days. If you'd like to elevate your pie baking, try using a flour that contains more (or all!) of the grain's kernel. For our pies, we use Frederick's Pastry Flour from Janie's Mill in Illinois. It has more flavor and nutrition and still creates a tender pie crust. Janie's sells to home buyers, so check them out or look for a mill close to you that may be doing a similar style of milling.

Glycerin　Glycerin is used in baking to stop sugar crystallization and to maintain moisture. In fondant making, it helps keep the fondant malleable. It is readily available in stores with cake-decorating supplies and online.

Harissa　Don't confuse harissa (a spicy paste) with harira (the

Moroccan soup). Not familiar with harissa? It's the condiment of choice in Morocco, Tunisia, and Algeria—the North African equivalent of ketchup or hot sauce. It's a spicy paste made from hot chile peppers, garlic, olive oil, and a combination of spices, commonly caraway, cumin, and coriander, and it sometimes includes tomatoes. Harissa is sold in jars and is now often available in local grocery stores and in Middle Eastern markets, and is definitely available online.

Key lime juice　Key limes, also known as Mexican limes, have a distinctive tart and acidic flavor and a strong appealing aroma, which make them particularly appropriate for sweet desserts. The more common lime sold in the United States is the Persian lime. It can be substituted but your dish will not have the same distinctive flavor. Key limes are sometimes available fresh. The yellow ones are the ripe ones. Choose these because they do not ripen after they are picked. They are grown in Mexico all year round and in Florida from June to September. The most common form of their juice is found in shelf-stable bottles in specialty food stores and online. We think using this juice is worth the small effort to find it.

Lye　Food-grade lye (also known as sodium hydroxide or caustic soda) can be found at hardware stores, stores that carry homebrewing supplies, and craft stores (it's also used in soap making). Just make sure what you buy is labeled food grade. And, of course, if you can't find it locally, you can order it online.

Marash pepper flakes　Marash pepper flakes, from Turkey, are deep red in color and irregular in shape. They give a distinctive earthy flavor with a touch of heat. They can often be found online from specialty retailers and sometimes in specialty food stores. If you can't find them, equally interesting and slightly different Aleppo or Urfa pepper flakes are good substitutes. If all else fails, substitute an equal amount of standard red pepper flakes, available in most American grocery stores.

Milk (and cream!)   Fat equals flavor! Just as we use butter because it's more flavorful than shortening and margarine, you'll notice that our recipes call for full-fat dairy products like heavy cream and whole milk. At the risk of sounding like a broken record, full-fat dairy provides more flavor, and you really can taste the difference! Besides flavor, we want to know the source of our dairy, and to ensure the animals are being well treated and are not receiving hormones and unnecessary levels of antibiotics.

Muscovado sugar   Muscovado is cane sugar that is refined less than white sugar, leaving much of the molasses in the end product and much more flavor. Organic brown sugar is not the same as muscovado. Typical American brown sugar is actually cane syrup refined to white sugar, with molasses removed as a byproduct of the process, and then some molasses is added back. (This explains the availability of light brown sugar and dark brown sugar.) If you can't get muscovado brown sugar, use dark brown sugar.

Nuts   Nuts are used in many of our recipes. It's important to buy nuts that have been handled properly and taste fresh. Since they have lots of oil in them, nuts can go rancid relatively quickly. For the best chance of finding

good nuts, go to a market that does a brisk business. We suggest buying from bulk bins because you can taste them prior to your purchase. The best way to store nuts for any length of time is in an airtight container in your freezer.

Produce   This likely goes without saying (we're going to say it anyway), but we always recommend buying produce when it's in season—that's when it's going to taste its best. As with other ingredients, use full-flavored produce. It doesn't need to look beautiful but it should taste great.

Sea salt   In the bakery, we use finely ground sea salt for everything from breads and baked goods to savory items. Using sea salt allows us to avoid the off flavors of iodized salt and to benefit from its more complex flavors. That said, if you don't have sea salt but you're ready to bake in every other way, use iodized salt. Please note: Different types of salt have different levels of saltiness. Due to disparate sizes and shapes of granules, other types of salt aren't always a direct substitution for finely ground sea salt. For small amounts (like 1 tsp or less), fine sea salt and table salt can be used interchangeably; for larger amounts, follow this guide:

1 Tbsp table salt = 1¼ Tbsp fine sea salt = 1½ Tbsp Morton Kosher Salt or fleur de sel = 2 Tbsp Diamond Crystal Kosher Salt or Maldon Sea Salt

Spices   Spices, like practically all foods, come in a full range of quality. For the best spices possible, finding a specialty grocer or spice store in your area could give you the most flavorful choices. Another good option is to purchase spices online, from vendors like Épices de Cru, a long-time Zingerman's

partner, at Spicetrekkers.com. The next best choice is to use recently purchased spices. Spices lose their aroma and flavor over time, so newly purchased spices will be much better than the jar that's been open in your cupboard for a year. If you open up your jar of ground cinnamon and it doesn't smell like much, it's time for a new one.

Stock (and broth)   We love making our own, but we also understand that sometimes it's more convenient to pick up premade stock. Flavors can vary widely by brand, so our suggestion is similar to the standard for cooking with wine—just as it's best to cook with wine that you'd enjoy drinking, it's also best to cook with a stock that you enjoy the flavor of on its own. Different stocks can also have strikingly different levels of salt, so when using premade ones, it's especially important to add the prescribed salt to the soup to taste.

Vanilla (bean/extract/powder/ paste)   Use the real stuff. Real vanilla extract is exponentially more flavorful than the artificial version and will make a significant flavor difference in your baked goods. There are many good brands on the market— just make sure the label says that it's 100 percent real.

Whole-wheat einkorn flour   We've been enjoying using ancient grains, and einkorn is the most ancient. It's more flavorful but also lower in protein content, making it challenging to create bread as we've come to know it. However, it's excellent in pastries.

Yeast   Our recipes are written for instant dry yeast. This yeast is created by a process that allows the yeast to be mixed with cool or room-temperature water and does not need to be proofed first. It is very convenient.

If you prefer to use fresh yeast, we recommend multiplying the weight of dry yeast in the recipe by 3 to get an equivalent amount.

EQUIPMENT

We want baking to be as approachable to as many people as possible! To do this, we try to choose the simplest equipment that will allow for success. We even encourage you to use your hands! They're great tools. If you come to BAKE!, our hands-on baking school, you'll see that it is relatively humble in appearance and we often use just a metal bowl, a fork, a wooden spoon, and a plastic scraper (spatula). That said, sometimes a specialized tool can help you make the recipe and get the best results most effectively. Here's a list of the common tools most of these recipes require.

Baking sheet　Just a basic plain rimmed baking sheet, or sheet tray, that fits into your oven will do. Having a few would make it easier to make large quantities so that you can bake two trays at a time and have two more ready to go into the oven when the first batch is out. Nonstick is not a bad idea if you want to skip the parchment paper.

Bench scraper or dough knife　This is a very helpful and inexpensive tool used by professional bakers. It's a rectangular implement with a metal blade and a wooden or plastic handle. It cuts dough easily and is also handy for cleaning work surfaces and transferring chopped ingredients from the cutting board to wherever they need to go.

Cooling rack　A cooling rack (also known simply as a wire rack) is used to allow air to circulate freely to cool freshly baked items and to prevent them from getting soggy from condensation. A tight grid is typically the best format for a cooling rack, to prevent thin cookies from breaking or falling through.

Couche　This canvas cloth is often used when baking baguettes, like our Rustic Italian Baguettes (page 130), to help give them their crackly crusts. As the baguettes rise, the cloth helps them keep their shape and keeps the surface of the dough dry, allowing it to form a thin skin. If you don't have one, use parchment paper instead. The baguettes might have a less-uniform shape, but they'll still taste delicious.

Digital scale　While this isn't a requirement, it's recommended. Highly recommended. (Honestly, we kind of wish we could make it a requirement.) We do all of our baking and cooking by weight, and encourage home cooks to do the same, as it allows for much greater consistency. The level of variation in both volume measurement tools and in how individuals measure ingredients is why you'll always get the most accurate result when baking and cooking by weight! It also can streamline the baking process; instead of needing to use (and then wash) multiple measuring cups, you can often simply set your bowl on the scale and keep measuring ingredients into the same bowl, using the tare button to zero the scale after each one.

Digital scales are readily available at many cooking equipment stores and online. Look for a simple one in your price range and make sure it weighs in a variety of measures, including grams.

Double boiler　Several recipes in this book call for the melting of chocolate using a double boiler. You can make your own by using a heatproof bowl that fits over the top of a pot. Fill the pot about one-third full of water and bring to a boil. Once boiling, lower the heat to medium, bring the water to a simmer, and place the bowl with the chocolate on top. Make sure the bottom of the bowl is not touching the water. Stir your chocolate until melted and smooth. Avoid overheating and continue to scrape the sides to avoid burning.

Knife or food processor　A number of our recipes call for chopped or ground nuts. A sharp chef's knife or a food processor will do this best.

Ice cream scoops or portioners Using these is one of those little baker's tricks. They allow us to make all of our cookies exactly the same size, which makes it easier to bake them accurately and have them look more perfect when they are displayed. They're available online and in some cookware stores. They aren't totally necessary though! You can use your hands and eyes and a spoon and still get the cookies pretty close to the same size. They'll taste just as good too.

Instant-read thermometer This is exactly what it sounds like—a thermometer that reads temperature instantly! Displays are often digital, though analog ones can be found as well, and prices vary widely. You don't have to spend a lot for accuracy though, so for a relatively small investment, this can help make sure your dishes are fully cooked.

Lame　A French word meaning blade, this sharp tool is used to score bread before baking.

Oven and oven thermometer
The temperatures for these recipes are intended for a conventional home oven. If you have a convection oven, just decrease the temperatures by 25°F. Always preheat the oven to the recipe's specified temperature at least 20 minutes prior to baking.

When preheating your oven to a set temperature, don't trust the oven dial as an accurate gauge! Instead, check the oven temperature with a free-standing oven thermometer set in the middle of the oven, where all the baking takes place. This will ensure that the oven temperature is accurate and remains consistent throughout the baking time.

As a general rule, you can safely assume that the oven rack should be at the center of the oven, unless otherwise specified. Of course, this isn't always possible—say when baking two sheets of cookies.

Parchment paper　One of our favorite baking tools is also the simplest. Cover your baking sheet with it and slide it off, baked goods and all, after baking. No sticking and no cleaning necessary for your next round of baking. If you're concerned about waste, feel free to use a relatively clean piece of parchment paper multiple times, and look for types that are recyclable as well.

Pastry bag and tips　Sometimes using a pastry bag allows for neater portioning and making particular shapes. We suggest buying disposable ones.

Pastry cutter　A pastry cutter or pastry blender will help you cut butter into flour for flaky scones, biscuits, and pie dough. They make the task go a little quicker, but they aren't essential; your hands will work just fine if you don't have one.

Peel　This is a convenient tool that aids in transferring bread and pizza in and out of the oven when using a baking stone. Peels are readily available in housewares stores and online.

Sifter or fine-mesh sieve　We use a sifter to simultaneously sieve and aerate flour and other dry ingredients used in cookie baking. A simple fine-mesh sieve can be employed for the same task, with the same result.

Spatula or plastic scraper
The instructions in these recipes will often direct you to scrape down the sides of the mixing bowl to make sure that all of the precious ingredients are incorporated into your batter or dough. Typical kitchen spatulas will do the trick. Professional bakers also like something we call plastic scrapers or plastic cards. They have a rounded side that makes it easy to scrape a bowl and a flat side that's handy for scraping flour off of your work area.

Springform pan　A springform pan is a deep, round pan with two pieces: a flat bottom with a channel around the edge and a circular band that fits in the channel and latches to secure the two together. We use them for cheesecakes and our Blueberry Buckle (page 75).

Tart pan　A tart pan is a shallow pan with two pieces: the edge, which is often fluted, and a flat bottom that lifts up for easy removal.

Whisk　A whisk is good for blending dry ingredients together before adding them to batter or dough. It's also useful for beating eggs and blending wet ingredients together as well as incorporating air into a mixture, in a process known as whisking or whipping.

Wide-mouth bowl　We like to make many recipes without a mixer. Why? Because a mixer is rarely 100 percent necessary, especially if your butter is at room temperature, so why bother? If you're going to go the old-fashioned way, we highly recommend mixing in a wide-mouthed metal bowl (but any material will do just fine) with a simple wooden spoon. The wide-mouthed bowl makes it much easier to stir effectively and scrape down the sides while mixing to ensure a homogeneous batter or dough.

Wooden spoon　We love wooden spoons for mixing. They're strong enough that they help us bakers put the force we need into activities like creaming. They last forever, they are readily available, and they're cheap. Amy and her husband still have a spoon they bought when they moved into their first apartment in 1988!

TECHNIQUES & DIAGRAMS

Shaping pretzels, kneading dough, and decorating cakes aren't always common home activities. To help, we've included this section on techniques. It's important to refer to this section as you're making the recipes for a thorough understanding of how to proceed.

Bulk fermentation   After the dough has been mixed and has completed its prescribed proofing or bulk fermentation time, it is ready to be divided. Most of the recipes call for being divided into two pieces. While a family member won't reject a loaf if it isn't exactly the same weight as the other, the loaves will bake most similarly if they are the same size. If you have a digital scale (which we strongly recommend, see page 239), you can be precise in dividing the dough as called for.

After the dough has been divided, it's time to gently round the piece of dough (if making a round loaf) or gently shape it into a loaf if the final shape is to be a loaf or a batard (see Shaping, page 244, for more information). The purpose of this step is to gently release some of the CO_2 that has been produced and to get those little microorganisms in the dough back in contact with their food.

After this pre-shaping step, we generally allow the dough to relax for a while (usually 20 to 30 minutes) before manipulating the dough into its final shape. The more the dough is allowed to relax, the easier it will be to get it into its final shape. The tighter the piece of dough initially is, the longer the resting period required. Listen to the dough; it will tell you when it needs more time to relax. If it's loose in your hands, then it has likely relaxed a bit too long. You can use it, but results won't be optimal.

Buttercream   If you made your buttercream and refrigerated or froze it, there are several ways to prepare it for icing the cake. You can leave it at room temperature overnight to warm up; it will likely be soft at that point and will easily whip up using the paddle attachment on a stand mixer. If you are using it straight from the refrigerator, break it up into the bowl of a stand mixer and use the paddle attachment to soften it. Initially, the buttercream will break up and look curdled. Do not freak out! Keep beating it and it will warm up and come back together to the beautiful silky consistency it was when you first made it. If you have a butane torch, you can gently warm the side of the mixing bowl as it's beating. This will quicken the process; just be careful not to melt your buttercream.

Flavor Variations   Vanilla Swiss buttercream is an excellent base for other flavors. Here are a few options we really like. For 1 lb [455 g] of buttercream, add the following and whip until completely incorporated. (The vanilla Swiss buttercream recipe for the Buttermilk Celebration Cake (page 60) makes 3 lb [1.4 kg], the one for Cosmic Cakes makes 2 lb [910 g]).

Banana: ¼ cup [60 g] puréed banana
Chocolate Mint: 3 oz [85 g] melted and cooled semisweet chocolate and 1 tsp mint extract, blended to completely combine. The buttercream might curdle slightly, so continue to beat until it becomes smooth again.
Coffee: 6 Tbsp [45 g] instant coffee, with enough water to make it a paste
Nuts: ¾ cup [115 g] toasted, ground hazelnuts; or ¾ cup [115 g] toasted, ground almonds and 1 tsp almond extract
Peanut Butter: 1 cup [260 g] smooth peanut butter
Preserves: ⅓ cup [105 g] of any fruit flavor
Salted Caramel: 1 tsp fine sea salt and ⅓ cup [100 g] dulce de leche
Strawberry: ⅓ cup [90 g] strawberry purée

Cream   Nope, we didn't mess up and put an ingredient in the wrong spot, this *cream* is a verb! It's the act of working two or more ingredients (most often butter and sugar) into a creamy paste. The creaming method is a technique used in baking to incorporate air into a batter to provide a natural rise. In the creaming method, a fat (normally butter) is beaten together with granulated sugar. The process creates pockets of air that are trapped in the butter around each sugar granule. When using this method, the fat should be at room temperature. Not creaming enough will result in a dense baked good, even if a chemical leavener is being used. Sometimes we can cream too much and the result will be overspreading of your batter or dough, so take caution.

Dock   When you're instructed to dock a dough, this simply means to prick it all over with a fork. This action allows steam (water found in the butter) to escape and keeps the pie dough from bubbling up during blind baking.

Folding   Folding is a step we sometimes include in our yeasted dough recipes, like in our Hot Cross Buns (page 51). We may recommend it intermittently during the bulk fermentation stage. Folding is necessary for high-hydration doughs (high proportion of water relative to dry ingredients) as well as lightly mixed doughs. The process of folding helps build structure in the dough by organizing and aligning the gluten network. It's an amazing little step that has an enormously positive impact on the strength of the dough.

Simple fold: Turn the dough out onto a lightly floured surface. For very wet doughs, make certain to have enough flour on the work surface to keep the dough from sticking, but avoid using too much flour. Gently form the dough into a rectangle. Take one short side and fold it to the middle of the dough. Take the other short side and fold it to the far edge of the other side. You now have a neat packet. Now take the opposite sides and repeat. One side goes to the middle and the other side goes all the way over. Usually, at this point, the dough is returned to its fermentation container and continues to bulk ferment.

Book fold (see diagram on page 245): Shape the dough into a vertically oriented rectangle. Fold the dough in half, from top to bottom. Unfold the dough. Fold the top and bottom edges to the center, starting by folding the top of the dough down to the middle mark you just created with the initial fold, then folding the bottom of the dough up to the middle. Now fold it in half, from top to bottom.

Envelope or letter fold (see diagram on page 245): Shape the dough into a vertically oriented rectangle. From top to bottom, fold the dough as you would a letter, bringing one-third of the dough down toward the bottom, and then pulling the remaining portion of the dough up over the top. Recipes will sometimes ask you to then repeat those folds horizontally.

Folding can also refer to a method for mixing something light and airy (like whipped egg whites) into something denser (like a batter). Folding is gently combining. So rather than vigorously stirring around a bowl, you're gently scooping under (let's say the cupcake batter already in the bowl), and up and over (let's say the whipped egg whites that you just added into the bowl), continuing until the two things are combined (in this case, until no more streaks of egg whites are visible, but hopefully delicately enough that you didn't lose all of the airiness you worked so hard to beat into your egg whites!).

Kneading   Wash your hands. Unless specifically instructed, turn your dough onto a clean, unfloured work surface that is at or slightly below waist height. You should place your mass of dough 3 to 4 in [7.5 to 10 cm] from the edge of the work surface closest to you. Hold a plastic scraper in one hand and with the heel of the other hand, press firmly into the mass of dough and stretch it several inches in front of you. With your bare hand or the plastic scraper, fold the dough farthest from you back toward you over the top of the dough. Rotate the mass 90 degrees and repeat. This stretching and folding technique is what will help align the gluten network in your dough. Find a gentle rhythm to press the dough out in front of you, fold it over, rotate, and repeat. If the dough is sticky, use the plastic scraper to clean the dough from the work surface as well as off your hand.

Don't add any additional flour to the work surface. Some doughs are intended to be sticky, and if you can embrace the stickiness, you will be rewarded with an open crumb and a delicious loaf of bread.

One hint for sticky doughs is to move your dough 6 in [15 cm] to the right or left to a "drier" work surface every couple of minutes, then continue to knead the dough. If it begins to stick to the work surface again, move back in the other direction. Each recipe will instruct you to knead for somewhere between 6 and 9 minutes to develop the dough properly. After several minutes of kneading, your dough should begin to hold together in a consolidated mass. That said, it may very well continue to stick to the work surface and your hand.

Mixing by hand   We've called for a stand or electric mixer throughout, but many doughs, fillings, and batters can be beaten by hand with a wooden spoon and some elbow grease.

Scoring   Scoring the bread before baking is done for two purposes—one functional and the other aesthetic.

As bread bakes, it expands. By scoring the bread, we create more surface area for the bread to expand into. If the bread is not scored, it is possible that it may expand unevenly and cause tearing or sections of dough to pop out. The scoring allows a more controlled and even expansion of the dough. If your bread is young (not as proofed as it should be) but you're baking it anyway, we suggest that the scores be deeper than normal to allow for more oven jump. If the bread is more proofed than optimal, make the scores delicate, as the bread may not have much energy left to fill them out. If your bread is very over-proofed, there is no need to score it, and actually, scoring it may cause it to lose any remaining gas and therefore completely ruin it.

Many patterns can be made to decorate your loaves. Choose one that you find appealing.

To score the bread, take a lame (or razor blade or sharp knife) and cut through the top surface of the dough as directed in the recipe. In general, the blade should be held at an angle of about 30 degrees relative to the top surface of the loaf.

Shaping   Place your portion of dough onto a lightly floured work surface. Gently manipulate the portion into a rectangular shape, with the longer section facing side to side. Pat the dough gently. With the fingers of both hands, lift about 2 in [5 cm] of the dough farthest away from you, press it gently down into the rest of the dough, then push it gently away from you. Don't let your piece of dough grow longer. Repeat this process a second time. Spin your piece of dough 180 degrees and repeat. At this point, you should have a nice log-shaped piece of dough with a seam running the length of the dough. Flip it over and place it seam side down. Cover it with plastic wrap and allow it to relax for the prescribed amount of time.

After your pre-shaped loaf or round has rested for the prescribed amount of time, it's time to give it its final shaping.

For a round, first, uncover the dough. Pick it up and tap the top surface gently onto a lightly floured work surface. Then follow the same instructions that you used for pre-shaping to get the final shape—no difference.

For a loaf shape, first uncover the dough. Pick up the pre-shaped loaf and gently tap it onto a lightly floured work surface. Press it out gently with the flat of your palms. As you shape your loaf, you will want to keep your piece of dough from elongating too much. It helps to arrange your two hands such that your opposing thumb tips are parallel and touching and your opposing index and middle fingers are touching. This creates a triangle between those fingers and helps contain your loaf from elongating too much during shaping.

Steaming   We often use steam in our oven when we bake bread to keep the exterior of the bread supple as it has its oven jump and expands.

Without steam, the crust of the bread may start to form before the crumb has expanded to its full capacity. The result will be a tighter crumb than is optimal.

Place your baking stone on a middle or lower rack at least 2 in [5 cm] from the front of the oven. Preheat your oven and baking stone for at least 45 minutes prior to baking. Place a cast-iron skillet on the bottom rack of the oven so that it is ½ in [12 mm] from the oven door. Have a large stainless steel bowl or aluminum baking pan ready that is taller and larger than your loaves.

When you're ready to bake, have several ice cubes at hand. Holding the peel in one hand, open the oven door, carefully place the ice cubes in the cast-iron skillet, and slide the loaves onto the baking stone. Carefully place the stainless steel bowl or aluminum pan over the loaves, making certain that the edge of the bowl extends over the edge of the baking stone, allowing it to capture and contain the steam produced by the ice cubes evaporating. Close the oven door and set a timer for 15 minutes less than the lowest prescribed baking time. Remove the bowl or aluminum pan at this time.

Touch test   This is how you assess the readiness of yeasted items for baking. Delicately uncover whatever it is you're baking. First use your eyes—are they larger? Then gently touch the dough with the pad of a fingertip. If you press your finger gently into your loaf and then lift it off, and the indentation immediately pushes back out, the dough requires more time before it's ready to be baked. Give it another 15 minutes and check again. The loaf is ready when the indentation of your finger pushes back very slowly and doesn't completely fill up the indentation. If you wait too long, your finger will leave an indentation that will just

remain an indentation. There's nothing you can do at this point other than bake it right away; it's over-proofed. If the recipe calls for the loaf to be scored prior to baking, score it very lightly if it is over-proofed.

Windowpane test   For doughs that won't be "folded," this is a method to check whether you have kneaded your dough sufficiently. After kneading for the recommended time, cut a 1 by 2 in [2.5 by 5 cm] section of your dough. Press it gently between both thumbs and index fingers and carefully and gently stretch it slowly in each direction. When the dough has been mixed sufficiently and the gluten matrix has been developed, one can take that small portion of dough and stretch it into such a thin layer of dough that you could imagine reading a paper through it, hence the name. If the piece of dough rips dramatically or quickly while you are carefully and gently stretching it, this indicates a need for more kneading. At this point, we suggest kneading another minute or two and then trying the windowpane test again.

Whipping eggs   Recipes will sometimes instruct you to whip egg whites until you get "soft peaks," "firm peaks," or "stiff peaks." To check what point you're at, stop your mixer, detach the whisk attachment, dip it in the whipped egg whites, and then pull the whisk straight up out of the whipped egg whites.

Soft peaks: The egg whites are just starting to hold a shape, but the peak is soft and melts back down into itself.
Firm peaks: The egg whites now hold a peak, but the tip of the peak folds over onto itself.
Stiff peaks: The peaks stand tall and proud!

book fold

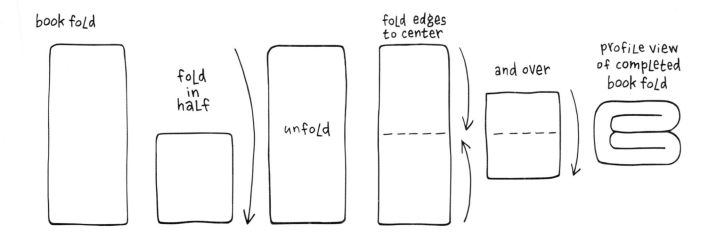

fold in half

unfold

fold edges to center

and over

profile view of completed book fold

letter fold

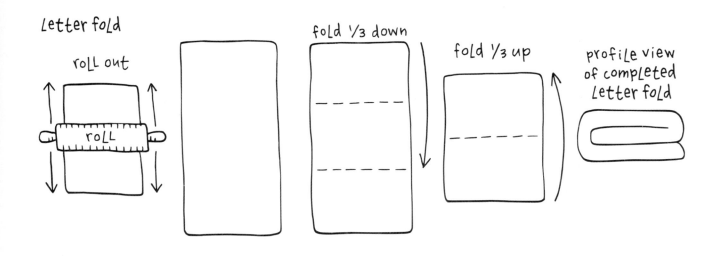

roll out

roll

fold 1/3 down

fold 1/3 up

profile view of completed letter fold

pretzel twisting

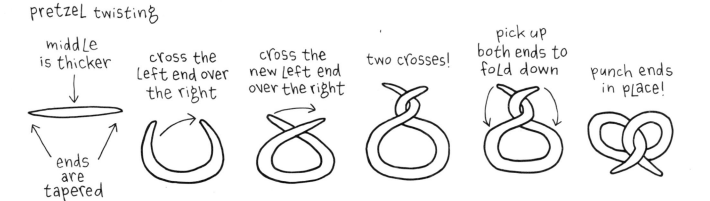

middle is thicker

ends are tapered

cross the left end over the right

cross the new left end over the right

two crosses!

pick up both ends to fold down

punch ends in place!

APPRECIATIONS

We end all of our meetings with the chance for attendees to express their appreciation for peers, work done, help, support, the weather . . . really it could be for anything. Creating this book was a multi-year project for us, and we have many people we'd like to recognize.

To our customers. Without you, we have no purpose. Thank you for your ongoing support, your words of encouragement, and your thoughtful feedback that helps us improve. We hope you find the recipes you've been waiting for.

To all of our Bakehouse teammates who make it happen every day. Your persistence, dedication to detail, and interest in learning and getting better is inspiring.

To the BAKE! school instructors, past and present, who did some of the heavy lifting in getting the recipes to their first drafts based on our much larger Bakehouse recipes with very different instructions.

To our Bakehouse recipe testers, all three dozen of you. It was fun and helpful to have so many of us working on the recipes to make them accurate and clear. Your skilled contributions made a big difference.

To our home recipe testers. Your questions, challenges, and suggestions were invaluable. Your enthusiasm to participate in this with us was energizing! Many thanks.

Sarah B.! What a pleasure to work with you again. Your expert editorial contributions made such a difference.

Mike McGovern, thank you for your academic perspective on people, culture, food, and holidays. Your framing brings greater meaning to our work.

Lizzie Vaughan, thank you for your expertise puzzle-piecing all our recipes and photos together.

E. E. Berger and Mollie Hayward, thank you for spending a week with us making our food look fantastically fun and delicious. We'll think of you every time we look at the book.

INDEX

bagel flavors

Zing 1610 (plain), Cinnamon Raisin, Garlic, Sea Salt, Sesame, Poppy, Enough Already (garlic bagel with sea salt, sesame , & poppy seeds)

$1.65 each

bostoc

buttery brioche, brushed wi
syrup, topped with almon
sprinkled with toaste